THE COMPLETE IDIOT'S GUIDE® TO

Starting and Running a Coffee Bar

by Susan Gilbert, W. Eric Martin, and Linda Formichelli

ALPHA

A member of Penguin Group (USA) Inc.

ALPHA BOOKS

Published by Penguin Group (USA) Inc.

Penguin Group (USA) Inc., 375 Hudson Street, New York, New York 10014, USA • Penguin Group (Canada), 90 Eglinton Avenue East, Suite 700, Toronto, Ontario M4P 2Y3, Canada (a division of Pearson Penguin Canada Inc.) • Penguin Books Ltd., 80 Strand, London WC2R 0RL, England • Penguin Ireland, 25 St. Stephen's Green, Dublin 2, Ireland (a division of Penguin Books Ltd.) • Penguin Group (Australia), 250 Camberwell Road, Camberwell, Victoria 3124, Australia (a division of Pearson Australia Group Pty. Ltd.) • Penguin Books India Pvt. Ltd., 11 Community Centre, Panchsheel Park, New Delhi—110 017, India • Penguin Group (NZ), 67 Apollo Drive, Rosedale, North Shore, Auckland 1311, New Zealand (a division of Pearson New Zealand Ltd.) • Penguin Books (South Africa) (Pty.) Ltd., 24 Sturdee Avenue, Rosebank, Johannesburg 2196, South Africa • Penguin Books Ltd., Registered Offices: 80 Strand, London WC2R 0RL, England

Copyright © 2005 by Linda Formichelli

International Standard Book Number: 978-1-59257-406-3
Library of Congress Catalog Card Number: 2005928081

18   17   16   20   19   18   17   16   15   14

Interpretation of the printing code: The rightmost number of the first series of numbers is the year of the book's printing; the rightmost number of the second series of numbers is the number of the book's printing. For example, a printing code of 05-1 shows that the first printing occurred in 2005.

Printed in the United States of America

Publisher: *Marie Butler-Knight*

Senior Managing Editor: *Jennifer Bowles*

Acquisitions Editor: *Tom Stevens*

Senior Development Editor: *Phil Kitchel*

Production Editor: *Janette Lynn*

Copy Editor: *Emily Bell*

Cartoonist: *Shannon Wheeler*

Cover/Book Designer: *Trina Wurst*

Indexer: *Tonya Heard*

Layout: *Angela Calvert*

Proofreading: *Donna Martin*

Contents at a Glance

Appendixes

Contents

Part 4:   Eat, Drink, and Be Merry: Choosing Which Products To Sell   125

12   Complete Coffee Compendium   127

13   Beans with a Boost   143

Foreword

Coffee, the fruit from which dreams can be made, adds much more to our daily lives than beverage bliss. The ripened cherries fill us with a taste for life, a heightened sensitivity for flavors and aromas that are a joy to cultivate. As café and home come ever closer to being synonymous as the principal residence for independent thought and ideas, the historical narrative of coffee is alive and well.

Fuel for the intellect, *stimulant* for the sage, coffee brings forth warmth and comfort. Often personified as the worker's *companion*, its singular status as the *universal cup*, so different from its culinary cousins tea and cocoa, invites all and excludes none! Readily accessible in cost and manner, this *rebel's drink* has found its place at the center of society's table. But where did this begin? And when was this table set? In other words, how was the popularity of coffee established? Why is today's coffee culture pouring into every street corner café? And most importantly, how do we participate, to express and preserve the many coffee traditions that traverse the globe? Where to begin the discovery?

My journey into coffee began in 1993 amidst the dusty shelves of a university library. It was there that I stumbled upon an amazing work, published in the 1930s—over 800 pages documenting coffee's amazing legacy. Of particular interest was the international scope of the work: cultural ties of ritual and presentation that bring us all together over a warm cup of "java."

It was a real surprise! A taste trek began as I explored the stories of exotic lands producing, protecting, and eventually exporting the magical beans. At the root of the modern specialty-coffee "tree" was American ingenuity: creating multiple locations for fast, consistent delivery of product and experience. This entrepreneurial expression may differ on the surface, but what seemed new was in fact old. At the core of the coffee experience, there has always been a need for a place, a quality product, and a service: a coffee bar!

The excitement of creating a niche brand—Ryan Bros. Coffee—with my two brothers, Carmine and Tom, was indescribable. Soon our parents moved west to join, and the blueprint for our family business was set: to "micro-roast" quality coffees from exotic lands, thus delivering a unique taste and a new philosophy: "Life is too short to be bitter."® Having lived overseas as kids, our appreciation for cultural exchange was set early. The relationships, the people, the traditions are all so interconnected and dependent upon one another. Having discovered the "why" behind the "how" of coffee, we, too, could partake in this exciting and rewarding business opportunity of perfect cup and company.

And you can, too! Perhaps coffee is the seed of your fruitful dream. But, as with any journey, you need a guide—that source of energy and inspiration that helps us step out and take a chance, to try what others say we can't do, to take action and realize our entrepreneurial potential and, finally, our dreams!

The success of *The Complete Idiot's Guide to Starting and Running a Coffee Bar* is that it is your personal, first-hand introduction to getting started. Its format is easy to read and its function is well-targeted at avoiding start-up pitfalls. Each phase of the start-up, from personal introspection to accomplishing actual business expectations, is clearly defined so that you are sure-footed on your journey. From what to serve to how to serve it, you and your employees are given a script so that everyone is on the same page!

So make use of this guide and take that all-important first step of realizing what it takes to get started. The world of specialty coffee is very competitive, and it takes a well-informed and directed effort to succeed. Once started, continue searching for the innovative while immersing yourself in the rich tradition that is coffee. Enjoy the many benefits this bubbling brew offers, and discover the passion for people and product it takes to succeed.

Harry Ryan is the Master Roaster and owner of Ryan Bros. Coffee, a family-operated San Diego roastery operating since 1994, providing unique coffee blends, cocoas, teas, and equipment to the wholesale and retail trades, and offering consulting services including the *Science and Art of Brewing, Espresso Basics and Beyond,* and *Menu Muscle for the Coffee Gourmet,* all at www.ryanbroscoffee.com.

Introduction

Forget computers, bubblegum pop, and Hollywood movies—what really fuels the American economy is coffee. After petroleum, coffee is the second-most-traded commodity in the world.

Aside from its obvious economical value, however, coffee fuels the economy in a much more meaningful way—namely, getting people out of bed in the morning and pushing them to work. Every day at dawn, timers click on coffee pots and a new batch of beans begins to brew. Cars line up outside coffee shop drive-thru's to get a fill-up for the driver. The green Starbucks siren pops up all over the place, an icon that might seem threatening if not for the hordes of people who rush to meet it.

If the media presented a true picture of the world, chain coffee shops would be in every town from coast to coast. But many people still rely on convenience stores and small restaurants for their coffee—establishments that typically brew a pot and then leave it sitting on the burner for an hour or two. This is the road to, if not madness, then at least coffee that's more to be tolerated than enjoyed.

This book is for those who want to man the pumps themselves, who want to provide their fellow citizens with a tasty brew made exactly how they want it. You've probably seen so-so businesses survive far longer than you imagined possible. Now's your chance to create a *better* business, one that treats its guests well *and* provides a good living for its owner. All you need to get started is determination and energy. Getting the first is up to you, but as for the second—would you like a refill?

How This Book Is Organized

To help you go from the daily grind to grinding daily, *The Complete Idiot's Guide to Starting and Running a Coffee Bar* is divided into six major sections:

Part 1, "Bean Business Basics," presents an inside look at running a coffee bar and explains what kind of person can hold this type of business together. Sitcoms make serving drinks look like a lot of fun—and sure, it can be—but that fun comes thanks to hard work and perseverance.

Part 2, "Getting Started," helps you lay the foundation of your coffee bar business, from writing a business plan and hiring expert help to building a brand identity and finding the perfect location. The same way that coffee can't last without its pot, your coffee business won't survive if you aren't building on solid ground.

Part 3, "Setting Up Shop," offers advice on how to dress your shop, both inside and out, to appeal to customers and provide them with the goods they want. You can't do it alone, though, so we also explain how to hire employees and train them to become the best baristas you can imagine.

Part 4, "Eat, Drink, and Be Merry: Choosing Which Products to Sell," covers the world of coffee beverages: hot and cold, plain and flavored, skinny and fat. Beyond coffee and espresso, though, you have a hundred other drinks to choose from—and then there's the food. We'll go over your choices and offer suggestions on what your customers should see when they walk through your door.

Part 5, "Day-to-Day Operations," looks past your opening day to view your shop in the weeks and months to come as you track inventory and sales, deal with difficult customers, keep your store spic-and-span, and dream about the day when you can open store number two.

Part 6, "Getting the Word Out," tells you how to throw word of your wonderful business to the world at large and make them pay attention, sometimes without you paying a dime. Publicity opportunities abound for the media-savvy coffee bar owner, and we'll explain how you can make the best of them.

The book concludes with a special appendix section that contains a complete glossary of coffee bar terms, an assortment of forms that you can copy or alter as needed, and a list of industry resources, suppliers, and associations.

Extras

Throughout the book, you'll find all sorts of useful information, words of warning, interesting quotes, unusual facts, and java jive in special sidebars that complement the main text. Specifically, keep an eye out for:

Beans of Wisdom
Smart advice that will make you a better business owner.

Instant Facts
Tidbits about the coffee industry that you can share with customers.

Coffee Quips
Funny, wise, and odd sayings about the drink that fuels the world.

Java-nitions
Definitions and explanations of common coffee industry terms, all of which can be found in the glossary at the end of the book.

Contents May Be Hot
There's more to be wary of in the coffee biz than a hot cuppa. We'll let you know what to keep an eye out for.

Acknowledgments

From Susan Gilbert: Special thanks to Eric and Linda for seeking me out to be a collaborative expert on this project and for their fun, humorous prose and style; to Harry Ryan for writing the foreword; and to all my mentors, family, and friends who have helped me grow to where I am today.

Trademarks

All terms mentioned in this book that are known to be or suspected of being trademarks or service marks have been appropriately capitalized. Alpha Books and Penguin Group (USA) Inc. cannot attest to the accuracy of this information. Use of a term in this book should not be regarded as affecting the validity of any trademark or service mark.

Part 1

Bean Business Basics

Coffee, java, joe—whatever you call it, you know you want to sell it! That's a good choice, because the coffee industry is booming. In Part 1, we'll talk about this growing section of the food service industry and help you discover whether the life of a coffee shop owner is for you.

You'll follow author Susan Gilbert, a longtime coffee shop owner herself, on a typical day at work from open to close. Not sure you're ready to take on this challenge? We'll explain how you can get the skills you need by landing a job at a coffee shop for some hands-on training.

Why Coffee?

In This Chapter

- ◆ Brewing yourself a nice glass of fruit
- ◆ A sign from heaven?
- ◆ Fuel for conversation
- ◆ Have beans, will travel
- ◆ Growth of an industry

Coffee is big business both in the United States and around the world, and when you look closely at how coffee is made and served, it's easy to see why.

In the morning, coffee provides the oomph that gets people going; at work, it's the social lubricant that brings people together over breaks and snacks; after dinner, it's the relaxant that caps off a fine meal; late-nights, it's the preferred pick-me-up for truckers and college students. In short, coffee is a little bit of everything to all people.

The universal appeal of coffee has made it the second-most-traded commodity in the world, after petroleum. Coffee sales comprise a multibillion dollar business, and coffee-related business opportunities continue to grow in the United States with new coffee shops opening in towns across the country each day.

But what do you really know about coffee? Let's take a closer look at the beans' background and see how this modest drink became the fuel that fires the modern economy.

What Is Coffee, Anyway?

When the smell of coffee hits you in the morning, you probably think of it as something essential to your environment, like oxygen or water. Some people can't start their day without orange juice; others need their coffee. You may not realize it, but coffee has a lot more in common with orange juice than just the water with which it's produced. Coffee is actually derived from a fruit; coffee beans are the seeds of the red and purple fruit on coffee trees.

In the wild, coffee trees can grow more than 35 feet tall, but since this makes it a tad difficult to pick beans, trees on plantations are kept between 6 and 15 feet. Coffee trees don't produce any fruit until they're 3 to 5 years old, but once they start, they produce fruit for up to 60 years.

> **Beans of Wisdom**
>
> The nitrogen, potassium, phosphorus, and other trace elements left behind by the brewing process turn used coffee grounds into an excellent plant fertilizer, especially when applied to rose bushes.

The white flowers on the coffee plant give way to red berries that resemble cherries during the growth process. The berry has a thin layer of flesh, and inside this pulp lay two seeds coated with a thin film that resembles parchment. These seeds, measuring only 8 to 11 millimeters long and taking 9 months to ripen, are the essence of coffee.

A Brief History of Coffee

So how did we get from the seeds to the brew anyway? Who ever thought of skinning a fruit to roast the seeds, grind them, and then steep the grounds in water? Seems kind of random, right? The true origin of coffee is lost in time, but many legends have evolved around the substance, all starting with the fruit from which coffee itself begins.

Well, If the Sheep Like It ...

The most well-known story of coffee's origin, dating anywhere from 600–800 C.E., involves a sheep (or goat) herder named Kaldi who noticed something strange with his flock after moving the animals to a new pasture in the Ethiopian region of Caffa.

After eating the red berries from a certain plant in this new field, Kaldi's sheep became very restless and excited, not even sleeping at night. Kaldi, curious about this development, tasted these berries himself and found that he was invigorated and more awake than usual.

A monk from a local monastery passed by and scolded Kaldi for "partaking of the devil's fruit." Kaldi managed to convince the monk that the berries had no ill effect, so the monk tested them himself, crushing the berries to powder and pouring hot water over the powder to make a drink.

Before long, word of this fabulous drink spread throughout the monastery and all the monks were using the berries to help them stay awake through their long hours of prayer. Word of the beans' power spread from monastery to monastery, and thus the legend of coffee was born, with devout Muslims believing that the plant was a gift to reward the faithful.

Nothing in Hand vs. Berries in the Bush

Another legend, dating from about the same time period, involves an Arabian who was banished to the desert with his followers to die of starvation. Desperate to survive, the man and his friends boiled the fruit from an unknown plant to make soup.

The broth provided enough sustenance to save the exiles, and residents of the closest town, Mocha, took the survival of the banished men to be a testament to their religious faith. To honor their successful trip out of the desert, the plant and the beverage made from it were both named "mocha."

Beans Break Out

While the identity of the person who took the first sip of coffee remains unknown, the coffee plant spread from Ethiopia to the Arabian Peninsula and Turkey as users discovered its wondrous properties.

As the coffee plant entered new lands, users found new ways to consume it. The Galla tribe in Ethiopia, for example, used the beans as a type of energy bar, wrapping them in animal fat to provide sustenance while raiding nearby areas. Others made wine from the pulp of the berries.

Turkey is believed to be the first country where coffee was roasted, brewed, and drunk, with the process starting sometime between 1000 and 1200 C.E. Turks often added spices like cinnamon, cloves, cardamom, and anise to the brew, which they called "qahwa," a word that literally means "that which prevents sleep."

Instant Facts

In the fifteenth century, Turkish law allowed a woman to divorce her husband if he failed to provide her with her daily quota of coffee.

In 1475, the world's first coffee shop, Kiv Han, opened in Constantinople. Within a few years, the city contained hundreds of coffee shops in which people listened to music, played chess, talked with travelers and storytellers, and (naturally) drank coffee. Coffee shops in Turkey came to be known as "Schools of the Wise" because patrons could learn much inside their doors.

Despite the wide acceptance of coffee, not everyone was pleased with the availability of the brew. In 1511, for example, Khair Beg, the governor of Mecca, banned coffee from the city because he feared its presence might fuel opposition to his rule. When the sultan heard of this decree, he ordered the governor be put to death.

Out of the Desert

The growth of coffee across the Arabian lands took many hundreds of years because traders jealously guarded their plants. Coffee beans couldn't be taken to other lands unless they had first been boiled in water or dried in the sun to kill any potential germ of growth within the seed.

Eventually, though, live seeds or cuttings from a plant made their way to non-Arabian lands, including India and Italy. Acceptance of the drink wasn't a foregone conclusion. Some Christians, unknowingly repeating the claims of earlier generations, dubbed coffee the devil's drink. To their surprise, Pope Clement VIII—instead of banning coffee—baptized it, claiming that the drink was so delicious that "it would be a pity to let the infidels have exclusive use of it."

Coffee came to Vienna, Austria, in 1683, after war ended between the city and invading Turks. A Polish army officer, Franz Georg Kolschitzky, who had previously served in Turkey, knew all about the drink. So when the Turkish army left behind stocks of coffee in their retreat, Kolschitzky claimed them for himself. He opened the first coffee house in Vienna, and his habit of filtering out the grounds and adding milk and sweetener established the tradition of Viennese coffee.

Coffee houses quickly sprang up in major cities across Europe, and these locations furthered the Turkish idea of gathering with your neighbors and seeing what everyone knows. In England, for instance, coffee houses earned the nickname "penny universities," because for the price of a penny, you could purchase a cup of coffee and learn incredible things from those around you.

The practice of tipping waiters and waitresses apparently started in English coffee houses. Customers who wanted good service and seating placed money in a tin labeled "To Insure Proper Service"; the first letters of each word in the phrase read "TIPS."

Instant Facts

I HAVE A COFFEE BAR!

In 1674, London saw the founding of The Women's Petition Against Coffee, which complained that husbands spent too much time enjoying themselves in coffee houses and not enough time at home. Part of their petition protested against "the grand inconveniences accruing to their sex from the excessive use of the drying and enfeebling liquor."

Coming to America

Coffee is believed to have been a part of American culture since Captain John Smith brought the plant across the ocean in 1607 while helping to found the Jamestown colony in Virginia.

Despite this early introduction, coffee remained an also-ran behind tea for the position of favorite hot drink. This finally changed in 1773 when Boston residents threw boxes of tea into the harbor to protest the taxes placed on the tea by King George. People switched from tea to coffee to show their patriotic support for the Boston Tea Party.

While the American colonists enjoyed drinking coffee, the growth of coffee as a business in the Americas resulted primarily from the efforts of a French naval officer, Gabriel Mathieu de Clieu. While in Paris on leave around 1720, de Clieu asked for clippings from the coffee tree in King Louis XIV's Royal Botanical Garden to bring back to the Caribbean island of Martinique, where de Clieu served.

De Clieu's request was turned down, but he raided the garden and stole a seedling from the greenhouse. The return trip to Martinique was harsh for both de Clieu and his prized possession: a jealous passenger stole a branch from the seedling; the ship was attacked and almost captured by pirates; and water grew scarce onboard, forcing de Clieu to use part of his own water ration to keep the plant alive.

Finally, though, de Clieu made it back to Martinique, where he planted the tree on his own estate and raised it under armed guard. By 1777, that one seedling had yielded an estimated 18 million trees.

Coffee came to Brazil in an equally fanciful way. As the Arabs had done centuries before, the French and Dutch traders did everything they could in the seventeenth and eighteenth centuries to protect their monopoly of the coffee market. Brazil's emperor thwarted these efforts thanks to one Lt. Col. Francisco de Melo Palheta.

In 1727, Palheta visited the colony of French Guiana to mediate a border dispute between the French and the Dutch. In addition to solving this crisis, Palheta started an affair with the governor's wife, who later presented him with live coffee seeds and cuttings from a plant as a farewell gift. These shoots are responsible for the enormous Brazilian plantations that enabled coffee to become an affordable drink for the general public.

By 1800, coffee had spread throughout the tropical belts of Asia and America to become one of the most important commercial crops in the world.

Instant Facts

Although espresso is widely considered an Italian treat, the first espresso machine was actually invented by a Frenchman in 1822. Louis Bernard Rabaut's creation forced hot water through the coffee grounds instead of merely having the water drip through.

The Booming Business of Coffee

As with many industries, the growth of coffee sales has resulted from a combination of smart business owners, lucky accidents, and chance.

Decaffeinated coffee, for instance, was invented in 1903 thanks to a ruined batch of coffee beans. German coffee importer Ludwig Roselius gave the beans to researchers and they perfected the caffeine-removal process and left the flavor largely intact. Roselius marketed the creation under the brand name "Sanka," a contraction of the phrase "sans [without] caffeine."

George Constant Washington, an English chemist, is responsible for the first mass-produced instant coffee. He got the idea while waiting for his wife to join him for coffee and watching a fine powder form on the spout of their silver coffee pot. After experimenting with different ways to create instant coffee, his finished product, Red E Coffee, hit the market in 1906.

In the 1920s, prohibition in the United States halted the (legal) sales of alcohol, and coffee sales boomed as a result. Market forces also led to the creation of freeze-dried coffee. In the late 1930s, Brazil was choking on a surplus of coffee and asked food manufacturer Nestle to create a product that could make use of the surplus. Nescafe was the result, which was first introduced in Switzerland.

Instant Facts _____

During World War II, American soldiers found Maxwell House instant coffee in their ration kits. As with cigarettes, the introduction of coffee to this market created a wealth of new users once they returned home.

Today, there are an estimated 15 different varieties of coffee trees worldwide, with one acre of growth providing 15,000 pounds of coffee beans. Even with production on such a massive scale, prices for coffee have still fluctuated wildly over the years. In 1989, for example, the coffee-growing nations of the world failed to reach a new agreement on exporting quotas; as a result, the market was flooded and coffee prices plunged. Within a decade, though, prices had shot up in response to wide-scale crop failures, most notably in Brazil.

Currently, the United States imports more than $4 billion of coffee each year. Are you ready to claim your piece of the pie? If so, then keep reading to find out what you need to know to succeed.

The Least You Need to Know

♦ Despite what commercials might suggest, coffee originated in Ethiopia, not Brazil or Columbia.

♦ From its earliest days, coffee was prized for its powers of wakefulness.

♦ Coffee houses have been known for hundreds of years to provide a meeting place for friends and strangers to become acquainted and share information.

♦ The desire for coffee throughout history has driven men to many daring and less-than-ethical feats, and their efforts created a world in which coffee is available anyplace at any time!

Chapter 2

Why You?

In This Chapter

- ◆ What you need to be a successful coffee shop owner
- ◆ Do you have what it takes?
- ◆ The pros and cons of going it alone
- ◆ How to get experience

Your dream: To tell your current employer to "take this job and shove it," sally forth on your own, and say good-bye to morning commutes, annoying co-workers, and getting up at 6 A.M.

Don't set fire to that bridge just yet—it takes a certain kind of personality, and heaping piles of commitment and motivation, to make it as a business owner. What's more, successful coffee shops often *open* by 6 A.M. to catch morning rush hour commuters, which means you'll need to get up even earlier than usual!

Do you have the chops? Read on to discover the personality of a successful business owner, the pros and cons of going solo, and how to get coffee shop experience if you've spent your entire life on the buying side of the counter.

Do You Have What It Takes?

You need more than a free-flying spirit and the ability to fill a cup without spills to make it on your own. Take the following quiz; if you answer "false" to any of these statements, think long and hard about whether you can make those statements "true" before you say good-bye to the comfort and regularity of the ol' nine-to-five.

You're a self-starter. True ❏ False ❏

Unless you're financed to the hilt, as a small business owner you usually start off doing every task in the business on your own, from marketing your business to sweeping the floors and everything in between. You need the motivation to rise early in the morning, phone people you don't want to talk to, and tackle even the most unpleasant jobs—without a boss threatening to dock your pay if you mess up.

You're a "people person." True ❏ False ❏

You'd think that if you were going solo, you'd be, well, solo. But in reality you'll be dealing with all sorts of people: accountants, lawyers, employees—not to mention (hopefully) hundreds upon hundreds of *customers*. Yikes!

Can you communicate and get along with a wide variety of people? Do you look forward to parties because you can meet new people, or do you hide in the closet and have someone tell you when it's over? Your personality will be a big selling point for many customers. The more of yourself you put into each transaction, the more likely they are to become repeat buyers.

You're good at making decisions. True ❏ False ❏

If you take a half-hour every morning deciding whether to wear the red shirt or the blue, you're in trouble. As a business owner, you'll be making decisions galore, from what color your business cards should be to how much to charge for an espresso.

In addition to decisions with long-term effects, you'll face a hundred daily situations that call for instant judgment, such as when a customer complains or a reporter on the phone asks for the health benefits of caffeine. (Think it won't happen to you? Check out Chapter 22 for the scoop on dealing with the press.)

You're a goal-setter. True ❏ False ❏

Goals keep you motivated and provide direction to your activities, both daily and over the course of a year. Sharing goals with employees helps them understand what you expect of them, in addition to making you more accountable for your actions. If you're not working toward these goals, why should they?

If you don't set goals—such as increasing flavored coffee sales by 30 percent or increasing
the number of transactions by 50 percent—
you leave your business floating on the
whims of the economy at large. When the
economy soars, your business will prosper;
when the economy tanks, your business will
soon follow.

Coffee Quips

"No matter how much
strong black coffee we drink,
almost any after-dinner speech
will counteract it."

—Kin Hubbard

If the last goal you set was a New Year's resolution—and you broke it—think about
how you can become a goal-setter (and meeter).

You have money in the bank. True ❑ False ❑

Few businesses are profitable when they first open. You spend a lot of money setting
up shop, and it takes time to gain a foothold in the community and build a regular
customer base.

This growth process is completely normal, and you need a stash of green stuff to pay
for groceries and rent until your business starts turning a profit. Most experts suggest
having at least six months' worth of living expenses in the bank before taking the leap.
You'll also probably need to live the frugal lifestyle while your business gets up to
speed. Can you cut costs and rein in your spending, or will you be continually whip-
ping out the credit card?

You're a problem-solver. True ❑ False ❑

When confronted with a problem, do you jump to the task, or do you avoid the issue
and cry to others for help? A business owner must be able to identify problems from
flagging sales to a choking customer, take aggressive action, and take responsibility
for the results of her actions.

Of course, jumping into action is only half of being a problem-solver. Your first solution may not tame the trouble after all, so you must be ready to re-evaluate the situation and try something new.

You're a great communicator. True ❑ False ❑

As a business owner, you need to communicate with customers, employees, suppliers,
and vendors on a daily basis—and by "communicate," we mean more than mere gum-
flapping.

You must express your needs and desires through both words and actions, while at the
same time listening to and understanding what the other person is saying. Do you

blame others for not grasping what you're trying to say, or do you search for new ways to present ideas so that everyone understands?

You can sell ice to the Eskimos. True ❏ False ❏

Your business will sell coffee, tea, other drinks, and pastries, but you, as an individual, must sell far more than the products on the menu. You must also sell a business plan to lenders, sell the concept for your business to the public, and sell yourself as an expert to the press.

You need to be able to communicate your sales message concisely without sounding like a huckster. When you have a political discussion, can you convince others to see things your way while avoiding arguments? Can you persuade the cashier at the local department store to make an exception for you when you return an item after the return date on the receipt? If so, you're a natural salesperson.

You're good at organization. True ❏ False ❏

Do you know where your 2003 tax documents are? If so, can you find a particular receipt in those documents within five minutes?

> **Beans of Wisdom**
>
> To learn how to get—and stay—organized, check out *The Complete Idiot's Guide to Organizing your Life* by Georgene Lockwood (Alpha Books, 2002).

This task might seem pointless, but as a small business owner, you need to track all sorts of papers and documents, as well as how much money you have coming in, whom you owe money to, how many pastries you sell on an average Saturday morning, and which employees can work when and for how long. Being able to create and keep up efficient filing and tracking systems is essential to your success as a businessperson.

You're a leader. True ❏ False ❏

If your business is successful (and we think it will be!), you'll probably want to hire employees. Can you inspire them to do everything from making correct change to cleaning toilets? Can you handle being the boss whom everyone else will want to tell to "take this job and shove it"?

Sometimes being a leader means making unpopular decisions—and sticking to them despite the fallout. At the same time, leading requires you to learn from your mistakes when a decision turns out to be a clinker. You might be great at leading—but that doesn't mean you're always right!

You have your family's support. True ❏ **False** ❏

Aside from you, the members of your family will be the ones most affected by your business. You'll probably be unavailable for long stretches of time as you work on developing the business, and you'll need privacy when you're creating a marketing plan or organizing a new menu. If your family isn't onboard with this new venture, you need to think of a way to bring them on—fast.

Being Your Own Boss: The Pros and Cons

Perhaps, after working your way through our quiz, you're still persuading family members that now is the time for a coffee bar in your town, or you're setting daily challenges for yourself to develop organizational skills.

While these obstacles might seem unsettling, you *can* look at them in a positive light: you care enough about following this path to change your ways and convince others to join you in your quest to open a coffee bar. You want to make this happen!

To make sure you know what you're getting into, we present here the ups and downs of owning a business. Use them to add to the mental picture you have of yourself as a business owner, and find out whether you're ready to take the plunge.

Do-It-Yourself Drawbacks

Some of these negatives are more serious than others, and only you can decide which ones might affect your decision to open your own business.

- **You have to be nice—to everyone.** If a customer rubs you the wrong way, you have to grit your teeth, smile, and play nice. Sure, you have to do the same as an employee, but your employer will usually shield you from customers who are truly abusive. As a business owner, though, *you're* the one who has to deal with jerky customers and live with the fallout that results from their dissatisfaction. When they demand to see the manager, that's *you!*

  Yes, you can rule the shop with an iron fist and throw out whiners, but that's hardly a long-term recipe for success, unless you've somehow developed a coffee blend that cures the blind and prevents malaria.

- **No locker room chitchat.** If you open a small or mobile coffee bar and hire no employees, you'll have no one to complain to about that customer from hell or to bounce ideas off of while developing a new marketing plan. Are you used to working by yourself, or does the thought of being all by your lonesome give you the shivers?

One alternative to talking to yourself is to find a business mentor, which we discuss in Chapter 4. While no substitute for the daily give-and-take of fellow employees, mentors can offer solid advice about running a business.

◆ **No company health insurance plan.** Employees often take health insurance for granted, but not small business owners. Finding an affordable health insurance plan for an individual—one that won't financially decapitate your business—can be painful. A local Chamber of Commerce can offer coverage, but the cost is likely to be far higher than anything you've paid as an employee.

◆ **Higher taxes.** Not only do you pay more for insurance, but Uncle Sam takes a larger chunk of your money as well. When you're an employee, your employer pays half of your Social Security taxes; when you go solo, you have to pony up the entire tax bill on your own.

In addition to paying more taxes, you don't have the luxury of an employer who's responsible for deducting taxes from your regular paycheck—you have to do the taxes yourself or hire an accountant.

◆ **Feast or famine lifestyle.** What's the solution to higher Social Security taxes? No paycheck at all, naturally, since 15 percent of nothing is nothing—take that, government gold diggers!

Contents May Be Hot

The biggest surprise for new business owners is often the sheer number of operational details they overlook in a nine-to-five job: Who empties the trash? Who empties the dumpster that holds the trash? Who changes the light bulbs? Who buys the light bulbs? Who answers sales calls? Now that you're in charge, responsibility for every detail, large or small, falls on you.

When you say good-bye to regular working hours, you also say good-bye to that steady biweekly paycheck. If your business doesn't make money, neither do you, and as with any business, the coffee trade will be crushingly busy during parts of the year and deadly slow during others. Like the fabled grasshopper, you must put aside money during the feast days to prepare for the inevitable famine.

◆ **No free equipment and supplies.** When you're an employee, all those sticky notes, paper clips, staples, and postage stamps are provided courtesy of your employer. When you're on your own, you have to schlep out to the office store yourself and cough up the dough to buy all those supplies—not to mention the fax machine, computer, and other pricey equipment.

Fortunately, you can deduct business supplies from your taxes—but that doesn't make it hurt any less when you have to shell out fifty dollars for a new ink cartridge for your printer.

The Benefits of Business

A black cloud of anxiety might have formed over your head while reading the previous list of liabilities associated with running your own business. But don't despair! For most people, the negatives of running a business are far outweighed by the benefits. If they weren't, why would so many people start businesses in the first place?

Read on to discover what you can look forward to once you're calling all the shots.

◆ **(Almost) unlimited income potential.** As an employee, you make what your employer gives you for as many hours as she schedules. As a business owner, you set your own hours and set your own prices. If you can charge $10 for an espresso in your market and stay open 16 hours per day, that's nobody's business but your own.

◆ **Your income lines your own pockets.** This ties in nicely with the previous perk. When you work for someone else, the fruits of your hard labor are delivered to your employers, who then pay you a fraction of that income. The health of the company is more important than the well-being of any individual worker, but that's probably small comfort to you.

Once you're the top banana, you decide how much of the profit is rolled over into future expansion and how much is added to your personal bankroll. You can't keep all the money the business brings in—employees want to get paid, and banks tend to be fussy about repaying loans, for example—but the distribution of funds is largely up to you.

◆ **You choose your hours.** As an employee, you work according to someone else's schedule. But when you work for yourself, your schedule is your own. Want to open your business from 8 until 2 so you can walk your kid to and from school? Go for it. Want to be open from 6 P.M. to midnight to cater to studying students? As long as you can keep paying the bills, feel free to set the bars where you wish. (For more on setting business hours, see Chapter 7.)

◆ **Going it alone is exciting.** Every day is a new learning experience as you figure out how to bring in more customers, price your offerings, and deal with your employees. What could be more exciting than the opportunity to create your own success?

◆ **You get the credit for your own success.** Speaking of success, the credit's all yours, baby. If your business succeeds, it's thanks to your hard work, commitment, and rugged good looks—and everyone else knows it. You're not slaving away in a cubicle while some corporate bigwig takes credit for your good deeds.

◆ **You choose your co-workers.** When you worked for an employer, you had to deal with them all—the show-off, the whiner, the one who was always a half hour late. Well, guess what? Now that you own your own business, you can choose employees who fit with your personality and with that of your business, and you don't have to take any guff from anyone. You're the boss!

◆ **Business supplies are deductible.** When you buy an ink cartridge, stamps, coffee beans, or anything else for your business, you can deduct the cost from your income for tax purposes. It can still be a pain to provide your own business supplies, but at the end of the year when you're slaving over your taxes, you'll be pleasantly surprised to find that you owe less than you thought because of those deductions! Talk to your accountant for more information, or check out books such as *The Complete Idiot's Guide to Tax Breaks and Deductions*, by Lita Epstein (Alpha Books, 2002).

Are You Experienced?

So you want to open a coffee bar, but your experience in the coffee trade is limited to making a fresh brew when that annoying co-worker drinks the dregs and leaves the pot empty. What's more, you've never run your own business, and you don't know a purchase order from a non-dairy creamer.

What can you do to rack up some experience? Get a job at a coffee bar! No, we haven't lost our minds. Rather than borrow lots of money from the bank and lose it because you don't know what you're doing, take the time to work for someone who does and learn the trade while earning start-up funds.

While working at a coffee bar, you'll learn how to:

- Deal with throngs of customers.

- Brew a great cup of java.

- Make specialty drinks such as espresso and chai.

- Take money and make change.

- Deal with other employees (while simultaneously watching how the employer works with her crew).

- Clean and maintain a coffee shop.

- Order and restock supplies.

- Open and close the shop.

- Multitask, multitask, multitask!

> **Beans of Wisdom**
>
> If you already have a job that you can't afford to leave just yet, work part-time in the evenings or on the weekends ... or even before work, since many coffee shops open long before the sun rises.

If you're a good worker and the owner comes to trust you, she may even let you try your hand at marketing, dealing with vendors, and other tasks that a business owner must know to succeed.

Learning the ins and outs of the coffee trade this way will also help you understand the job from an employee's point of view, which should make you a better, more sympathetic manager in the future. You'll know which tasks take a long time to master and which ones employees can handle without oversight.

"Help Wanted" Wanted

If bow ties were in style the last time you interviewed for a job, you may need a refresher course. Well, here it is—your very own class in snagging a job.

Though help-wanted ads are a good place to start, don't rely on them exclusively; apply shoe leather to asphalt and visit coffee bars in person. Even if you're only nabbing an application to fill out later, ditch the sweats and dress like a pro—you never know whom you'll run into. Maybe the owner will want to talk to you right then!

Fill out the application neatly, in ink, either at home or right in the shop. If the application asks for related experience, think about how your current or past jobs qualify you for the position you desire. If, for example, you were a customer service manager, you know how to deal with customers; if you worked the phone banks, you can communicate effectively; if you worked in fast food, well, you get the idea ….

To make an even better impression, turn in a resumé with your application. A resumé is a one- to two-page synopsis of your work experience, skills, and education laid out in an easy-to-read format. There are whole books on the subject of writing resumés, such as Susan Ireland's *Complete Idiot's Guide to the Perfect Resume* (Alpha Books, 2003), so turn to those titles for more advice.

(If the shop doesn't even have an application, a resumé is even better as it provides your contact information along with past experience—information the owner would otherwise never see.)

Grilled: The Interview

So the owner was impressed by your nicely completed application and your slick resumé, and would like to interview you. Congratulations! Your foot is in the door. Here are a few tips to get you through the interview with style:

◆ Arrive a few minutes early.

◆ Don't wear a suit if you're not applying for a management position, but do dress professionally.

◆ Think ahead about the questions the shop owner may ask—such as your greatest strengths and weaknesses, why you want to work there, and so on. Rehearse your answers in front of a mirror.

◆ Tell the owner up front that you want to gain experience so that you can open your own coffee bar.

> **Beans of Wisdom**
>
> Want honest feedback on your interviewing style? Recruit a friend or family member to grill you on your background and future plans. They know how you normally talk and react, so they can say whether you sound natural and confident or whether you need more practice time in the hot seat.

The owner might be taken aback at first by this confession, but she'll likely be flattered that you chose her shop to work in and be intrigued by the prospect of training you. Explain where and when you plan to open up shop, so she'll know you won't be with her for years, and so she can view you as an apprentice rather than a competitor. (This assumes, of course, that you don't plan to open a competing coffee bar right across the street!)

Getting a job when you're looking to fly solo may seem counterintuitive, but if you have no experience with the coffee industry, you should definitely consider the idea. Once you have a job in a coffee bar, keep your eyes and ears open and soak in as much information as you can—someday soon you'll be running your own shop!

The Least You Need to Know

- A successful business owner needs to be a problem-solver, a goal-setter, a people person, a leader, and a great communicator.

- Business owners aren't born, they're made; so don't put aside your dream just because you don't (yet) have all the skills you need.

- Running your own business has both pros and cons compared to working for someone else. Your comfort level with the benefits and drawbacks will let you know whether you're ready to be your own boss.

- If you lack business or coffee experience, consider working in a coffee bar to learn the ropes.

A Day in the Life: Susan Gilbert

In This Chapter

- ◆ What owning a coffee bar is *really* like
- ◆ How to be a master multitasker
- ◆ The ebb and flow of work
- ◆ How to earn the skills you need to succeed

So you've read the previous two chapters and decided that nothing could suit your personality and entrepreneurial skills better than owning and running a coffee bar. Or maybe you skipped right to this page to see what daily life will be like once you open a shop of your own. Or maybe the book fell open randomly to this page.

No matter—however you arrived at this point, we're glad to see you and eager to start your tour through a typical day as a coffee bar owner. Your tour guide, as might be expected, will be Susan Gilbert, owner-operator of a coffee bar in San Diego. Susan currently employs managers to run the shop for her, but when she first started out, she opened the shop, closed it, and did everything else in between.

Now that the sun has crept above the horizon and the morning dew has started to vanish, the tour can begin. Don't feel shy about stopping us and asking for more details, but we'll do the best we can to anticipate questions. Ready? Then let's go ....

The Workday Begins

We arrive at the shop at 8 A.M., one hour before we open for business, and prop open the back door to allow delivery people easy access.

Your hours of operation will depend, of course, on the customer base you serve. If you're located in a bedroom community, for example, you might open as early as 5 A.M. to service commuters before they head to work. For a coffee bar in a college town, your hours might change with the semesters. (For more on setting hours of operation, see Chapter 7.)

The Skills You Need: You wouldn't think that showing up for work takes any special skills, but it does—namely punctuality and the willpower to wake up every morning, rain or shine, and go to work. Some days you'll feel like pulling the blankets over your head and going back to sleep, but as the owner of a business, you don't have this luxury—unless you don't mind customers migrating to the competition, that is.

Where to Get Them: The importance of being punctual has probably been pounded into you with every job you've ever had or any class you've taken from kindergarten on. (If not, we envy you!) Business owners, however, must keep in mind that opening a shop late loses not only current sales, but future business as well, since customers will lose faith in late risers.

Coffee Quips

"If I asked for a cup of coffee, someone would search for the double meaning."

—Mae West

Exercise your willpower by not allowing yourself to make excuses and put off what needs to be done. When the trash needs emptying, empty it; when the lawn needs mowing, don't push it off to the weekend; and when the alarm clock rings, start moving immediately. Customers are counting on you for their morning java jolt!

Fixing Food and Concocting Coffee

Each day we begin anew, using the cold, unyielding equipment to provide warm treats and drinks. We retrieve the day's pastries from the pastry lock-box outside the shop (they were delivered earlier by the local pastry shop), turn on the espresso, coffee, and smoothie machines, and start brewing coffee. We track the brew times on a chart, so we'll know when to dump a batch and replace it with a fresh one. After all, nothing is worse than bitter, hours-old coffee!

We arrange fresh pastries in the display case (wrapping old ones for the day-old sale basket), brew coffee, prep the sandwich bar, fill the milk and half-and-half carafes, and brew more coffee. We place creamers, honey, sugar, and napkins in the coffee prep section.

A Thousand Details

While brewing yet more coffee, we have plenty of non–food-related tasks to do as well, such as unlocking the safe, counting the money in the till, stocking paper goods, replacing waxed paper in the pastry case that looks old, collapsing boxes, and compiling a to-do list of tasks for later in the day. If we don't get these tasks done before opening time, chances are we won't get to them at all.

We welcome the two employees who work the morning shift with us, and have them shake out the rubber mat in front of the door, pick up trash in the parking lot, and check that the windows are clean. As needed, we advise them what else needs to be done after they finish their tasks. In the few minutes before opening time, we'll take one more pass through the entire shop to make sure everything's in order. (Signs in the display case straight and not coated with icing? Tables lined up?)

Beans of Wisdom

When you've opened shop each day for the past 100 days or so, everything will become second-nature to you. You might not even need a to-do list by that point. When you first open, though, work from a written list of what to do when, to make sure you don't miss anything. You should even do a few practice runs before you officially open. Better to locate problems early rather than when customers are banging on the door!

The Skills You Need: A clear head in the mornings—there's a lot going on!—math skills, the know-how to make a good cup of java, and the patience to do the same tasks every morning without getting bored. You also need self-motivated employees who'll work without prodding. You have enough on your own plate without having to watch theirs as well.

Where to Get Them: We explain how to train and motivate employees in Chapter 11 and break down how to prepare the perfect pot and track brew times in Chapter 12. As for not getting bored, make a game of your tasks each morning:

how quickly can you do X? Can you do Y and Z at the same time and have everything come out right?

Open Sesame!

At 9 A.M., we flip over the "closed" sign, open the doors for business, and put the sidewalk signs outside. We greet the hordes of customers—okay, the two regulars who are always waiting—and start serving drinks. The first sales of the day!

As customers filter in, we take and fill orders and run the registers, chatting with customers the whole time. We clean as we go, wiping up drips and cleaning the foaming nozzle on the espresso machine; we wash dishes and replenish supplies so that we never run out of, say, coffee cups while 20 people are waiting impatiently for their drinks. Keeping ahead of the game when it comes to cleaning and restocking also makes clean-up easier at closing time.

As we approach lunch hour, we slice meats and cheeses, mix tuna and chicken salad, pull out bread and rolls, and chop vegetables. You might choose not to offer sandwiches and deli salads; in addition to the extra work, you also need extra permits to serve prepared food. Research your market, and see whether the extra work could be worth it!

The Skills You Need: Multitasking skills! You're serving customers, running the register, cleaning, and restocking all at once. The brain is juggling recipes, orders, names, and change, and you can't afford to drop anything. If you had more arms, you'd be doing even more.

Where to Get Them: If you've never worked in a coffee bar (or other food-service establishment) to learn what it's like in a real-life, non-*Friends* situation, we suggest getting some hands-on experience. (See Chapter 2 for information on how to find and get a job in a coffee shop.) You'll learn how to balance your time so that you can keep customers moving on one side of the counter while you clean and stock the other side.

> **Instant Facts**
>
> While we use the word "multitasking" to talk about people doing different jobs that require different skills, the term originally referred to a computer's ability to run more than one program at the same time.

Navigating the Waves of Customers

When we catch a break from taking orders, we travel around the seating area, clearing away empty cups that customers left behind and wiping down tables. It's fine to chat with customers while cleaning, but chatting can't be the only thing we do. Keep on the move while you clean, and customers will get the hint.

Speaking of understanding, we have to step in when a customer starts bearing into a barista over the lack of foam on her cappuccino. She distinctly asked for extra foam, and look—hardly any at all! Don't bother asking for the employee's side of the story right then. Apologize to the customer and make her a new drink. (We will talk with the employee later to find out his side of the story, but we should keep talk like this away from the customer's ears.)

Behind the Scenes

Customers see the obvious parts of our job, but they can't catch all the details we handle to keep the coffee bar running. We check the pastry case to see what's selling, then fax an order to the pastry shop for the next day's delivery. Along the same lines, we track stock levels on bottled drinks, breads, stirrers, lids, soap, trash bags—you name it, we track it, because the trash bag fairy is only a myth our parents told us as kids to keep us quiet.

Speaking of restocking, we have to receive deliveries in the back, count the cartons to match the totals listed on the invoice, and put everything away. As the lunch rush winds down, we wrap and store meats, clean cutting boards, refill napkin holders, empty trashcans, and restock refrigerators.

We use the register to print out sales readings each hour, so that we can track whether we've scheduled the proper number of employees for each hour of the day. As the hours pass, we also make new batches of coffee as needed to prepare for anticipated sales in the afternoon.

What, it's afternoon already? We need to take a break and make sure our employees take breaks as well. While federal labor law doesn't require that we give employees paid breaks, some states do, typically granting a paid ten-minute break for every four hours worked. We can tough out the day and skip these breaks if need be, but employees probably aren't as eager to work all day without stopping.

Beans of Wisdom

For details on which states require paid breaks and how long those breaks must be, consult your lawyer for the lowdown on local labor law or turn to the Department of Labor online: http://www.dol.gov/esa/programs/whd/state/rest.htm.

The Skills You Need: An ability to see into the future—by which we mean that you need to know how many pastries, cups, and other supplies to order each day. The numbers you come up with will depend on the day of the week, the time of year, the weather, special events in town, and the way the stars align.

You need to know and follow health department regulations for handling food, and you need to know how to assemble a darn good sandwich both safely and quickly (assuming, of course, that you serve sandwiches at your shop).

> ### Beans of Wisdom
>
> The Centers for Disease Control and Prevention (CDC) includes links to every state health department on its website (http://www. cdc.gov/other.htm), in addition to contact information for numerous other health and human welfare organizations.

Where to Get Them: Instead of signing up for psychic school, turn to Chapter 18 for advice on how to use sales records to estimate future needs. We'll also advise you on how to reduce shrinkage—both waste and theft—on a daily basis so that your inventory counts stay consistent.

We'll tally tips on preparing and storing food in Chapter 15. Check in with your local health department as well for handling procedures specific to your area.

Work of the Week

Depending on the day of the week and the phase of the moon, we have one or more special tasks to tackle. Maybe they're too time-consuming to do every day, or they only need doing once a week. Our list of special tasks includes cleaning the light fixtures, dusting the air vents, hosing out garbage cans, emptying the ice machine, and taking down all the coffee pots and French presses for sale and wiping down the shelves.

While our employees handle today's items, we'll create a work schedule for the next two weeks. Some employees can work only certain days and times—almost never the same days and times that they said when we hired them—and some have given us special requests for time off. There are also the needs of the shop itself to consider: when are sales fastest, which days do we receive the most deliveries. We filter all this info through our brains, and by the time we finish, the day is almost done.

The Skills You Need: Creating a schedule is an inexact science. Based on your sales records and other data, you might want to schedule only 2.5 employees for the morning rush—but half an employee doesn't work well because he's unbalanced and falls over a lot.

You also need to know your employees: who work well together, and who stands around all day flirting with other employees. Schmoozing is another required skill because sometimes you have no choice but to deny a request for time off and schedule an employee. Turn on the charm, and make her understand how much you need her!

Where to Get Them: We'll cover scheduling, along with everything else you need to know about hiring and firing employees, in Chapter 11.

As for how to sweet-talk employees into doing disagreeable once-a-week tasks—a topic we'll cover along with other cleaning clarifications in Chapter 20—you'll learn with experience what works best with different individuals: some are swayed by money, some by gratitude, and some by sympathy.

Closing Up Shop

A half-hour before closing, we switch into full-bore clean-up mode. Instead of, say, merely wiping up crumbs when we take a pastry out of the case, we empty the entire case and wipe down all the shelves and walls.

While we do this, we're still serving customers, making sure not to rush them despite our desire to focus on cleaning and getting out of here. Still, we dim the lights, flip over the "closed" sign, and pull in the signs from the sidewalk. They usually get the hint.

Time to Clean House

Once the store is empty and the doors locked, we break down the espresso machine and clean it; we refill the coffee grinder with fresh beans; we switch the smoothie machine to night mode and turn off the coffee machine. We wipe down all the counters and tables, put the chairs up on the tables, sweep and mop the floors, and take out the trash. We watch employees divide the tips and keep our hands to ourselves.

Most important of all, we deal with the money, counting the cash in the till and reconciling the total with the readout on the register tape. We enter sales for each type of item into our sales log so that we can use this sales history later for ordering, scheduling, and managing inventory. We complete the bank deposit slip and place the deposit in the safe and the empty till back in the register.

Don't Stop Thinking About Tomorrow

While we're minding the money, employees wrap leftover pastries and place them in the day-old basket, tossing items already there and recording them as waste. They sweep through the shop and refill everything that might run out before the end of the day tomorrow: the cinnamon and chocolate shakers at the coffee station; napkins, stirrers, and sugar packets; refrigerated drinks; bagged beans; the supply of pastry gloves by the food prep area.

Finally, we take one last look over the store, making sure everything is cleaned out, locked up, or turned off as needed. We lock the doors, drop the deposit off at the bank (with an employee, so that we have two pairs of eyes in case anything goes wrong with it), and say good-bye until tomorrow.

Beans of Wisdom

Perseverance and stamina also play a large role in the success of a coffee bar. After a hard day's labor, the owner (and her employees) must continue working to prepare for business the next day and years ahead. No grasshoppers need apply!

The Skills You Need: Math, math, math! You need to be able to quickly and accurately add the cash and credit slips, adjust the figures for voids, over-rings, and payouts, then compare your total against the register tape for discrepancies. You need to compute weekly and monthly sales figures as well to guide you in ordering supplies.

Where to Get Them: Chapter 18 has all you need to know about tracking sales, managing inventory, setting sales goals, and recording the numbers. You may be comfortable holding a wad of cash. After you finish this book, you'll be able to make it do all kinds of funky tricks.

As far as planning for the future goes, Chapter 21 discusses why and how to adjust your menu as you develop a sales history. We also cover how to prepare employees to serve as supervisors and how to scout for new locations should you feel ready to move on to bigger challenges. After all, the thoughtful ant is already planning for the future ….

The Least You Need to Know

- The coffee bar owner's day starts with cleaning, stocking, and prepping long before the first customer of the day.

- Slow times aren't break times, but merely opportunities to restock, clean, and prepare for the next rush.

- The owner of a coffee bar needs customer service skills, math skills, team-building skills, the ability to make great coffee and food, and the know-how to predict what you'll need and when you'll need it.

- The most important skill: the ability to multitask! The owner and employees must be able to serve customers, clean, restock, and run the register all at once.

Part 2

Getting Started

Ready … set … brew! Not so fast—before you pour your first cup, you'll need to do some prep work. In this part, you'll get the scoop on creating a business plan that will help you successfully start and run a coffee shop, not to mention impress potential lenders. You'll also learn how to hire professionals, such as an accountant and lawyer, to build a strong team.

Mall, city street, strip mall, office building—where you decide to set up shop can make or break your business. That's why we discuss the pros and cons of different locations.

What color is your parachute? Branding your coffee shop, from choosing your colors and logo to coming up with the perfect name, is essential for business success. We'll explain all you need to know to get started.

4

Building Your Business Plan

In This Chapter

- Doing market research
- Business plan basics
- Finagling financing
- Your advisory board and you
- Mentor methods

Stop! Before you lease a location, before you place any ads, before you brew your first cup, you need a plan—a business plan, that is. Writing the business plan will force you to confront such tough questions as "Why do I want to start a coffee business anyway?" and "How can I ensure that my business will succeed and dominate global markets for decades to come?"

Having a business plan is essential for two reasons. First, it gives you guidelines to keep your business on track and make sure that you're reaching your goals.

Second, and more importantly, unless you're fabulously wealthy and a real estate baron—and if you are, we should have lunch together sometime—you'll need to borrow money and rent property to open your business. With a business plan in hand, you can show lenders and landlords that you're serious about your plans and a trustworthy recipient of their generosity.

A Road Map for Success

This chapter, like most writing you encounter, follows a nice left-to-right, top-to-bottom pattern that makes it visually pleasing and easy to read.

Don't let that fool you! Writing a business plan is rarely that straightforward. As you answer questions in one section, you might have to reinvestigate sections that seemed settled only days before. You might want to cater to philosophers and practicing Buddhists, but if, while investigating potential competition, you run across the Drink and Think on the other side of town, you'll need to reconsider your target market.

Nailing the Who-What-Where-Why

What do you want from your business? How do you want to live and work? Whip out a pen and paper and answer the following questions to discover the first glimpses of how to structure your business plan—and your business.

◆ What are your personal goals? Do you want to be your own boss, make more money, have a flexible schedule, build a business to support your next of kin, meet and work with a wide assortment of people?

◆ Where do you want your business to be in six months, a year, five years from now? Do you want to stay small or extend your business into a major coffee chain? (Either a chain with many stores, or a chain that sells giant coffees—it's up to you!)

◆ Whom do you want to serve? Students, executives, families, vacationers?

◆ What services and products will you provide clients? Will you offer catering or delivery? Will you sell coffee-related gifts and accessories?

◆ How are you going to let customers know that you exist? (We'll have much more to say about advertising and promotion in Part 6.)

◆ Why will customers come to you? What makes you and your products better than the coffee shop down the street—or the coffee maker on their counter?

Don't dismiss spending time on these questions as unproductive navel-gazing. Sure, you could rent the first empty building you see, plug in a Mr. Coffee or two, and open for business—but that's hardly a recipe for success.

You'll have plenty of time for hard labor in the weeks and months ahead. First, though, you need to know how to direct that labor, what you hope to accomplish with this venture. Spend time on these questions and keep your answers handy as you read the rest of this chapter. You'll refer to them frequently!

Researching the Market

Want to play spy? C'mon, we know you do—and this is your chance to go undercover and dig up the dirt on the people who will become your customers—and the people who will steal those customers away from you if you let them.

You'll need to know the demographics of the area you're thinking of starting your business in, from the average age of its residents to their genders and average income. This will let you know whether there are enough potential customers in a chosen area to support your business.

Beans of Wisdom

A great—and free—way to nab the 411 on your chosen market is to check with the folks who write the book on such things: the Census Bureau. Expert information is just a phone call (or mouse click) away, thanks to the U.S. Census Bureau Contacts, a booklet that lists experts on any census topic you can imagine plus their phone numbers. Go to www.census.gov or call 301-457-4100 to request this booklet.

Finding competition, on the other hand, is much easier. Just look around as you drive in your city and nearby towns. Ask your friends, your hairdresser, your doctor where they buy their coffee. Search the Internet and scan the Yellow Pages for shops within a certain distance of your home. Don't automatically assume that you'll open the coffee bar in your hometown. The perfect opportunity might actually be five or fifty miles away, but you won't know—or know of competition to that opportunity—unless you broaden your scope and survey the wider world around you.

Sussing Out the Competition

Before you hang out your shingle, you need to know all about the other shingle-hangers in your area. Scope out the competition, and learn what you can from every operation, both successful and not-so-successful.

Visit coffee shops incognito—that's Latin for "wearing a rubber nose and glasses"—and check out their products and services.

You might feel like avoiding shops that always seem empty, but you can learn as much from the wannabes as from the winners. Are they in the wrong part of town? Do they charge too much? Do their products taste "off"? Is the music too loud? Knowledge is everywhere, if you know how to look. Be sure to note basic information such as:

- What products they offer aside from plain ol' joe

- How much they charge for various products

- How many employees they have

- How long they've been in business

- Which hours and days they're open

- Whether they offer catering or delivery

- What the décor looks like

- How many customers the shop seats

Coffee Quips

"COFFEE.EXE is missing. Insert cup and press any key."
—Anonymous

Make a chart that lists competitors down the left side of the page, write the items you want to compare (hours, prices, etc.) across the top, then add your super-secret spy data where the spaces intersect. Not only will this keep your findings organized and easy to read, but you'll likely pick up ideas on what will and won't work at your business.

Don't limit your research to prototypical coffee shops. Coffee is sold in gas stations, convenience stores, bookstores, restaurants, supermarkets, and many other locations. If a business sells coffee—even coffee you'd dismiss as undrinkable swill—it's serving some portion of the coffee-buying public that you want to make your own.

Doing the Math: Projecting Income and Expenses

You can paint a pretty picture of your business-to-be, but the oil that blends the paints, as it were, is the financial data. If you don't include numbers in your business plan, you're leaving out the most important information: the stuff that tells you whether or not you have a chance of making money.

Counting Costs

Much as we hate to bring out clichés, you have to spend money to make money. Starting a business requires much more than the purchase of raw materials, and this section is where we start to see these costs add up.

Expenses come in two types: start-up costs, which are typically one-time payments before you open the business, and operating expenses, which roll around on a regular basis, both before and after you open. Examples of start-up costs include:

- ◆ Business registration fees
- ◆ Business licensing and permits
- ◆ Rent deposits
- ◆ Purchases (equipment, promotional materials, uniforms)
- ◆ Utility set-up fees (phone, electric, water)

The list of start-up costs will vary widely depending on what you want your coffee bar to look like; what regulations your state, county, and town have; and so forth. Want customers to sit in vibrating chairs at solid marble tables? Write that down in the business plan—but be sure to note which expenses can be altered (in case marble tables turn out to be a wee bit expensive) and which can't, such as registration costs.

As with start-up costs, your list of operating expenses will start small, then grow as your vision of the finished coffee bar becomes clearer. Operating expenses you definitely need to account for include:

- ◆ Payroll for you and your staff
- ◆ Rent and loan payments
- ◆ Phone and utility bills
- ◆ Advertising
- ◆ Janitorial and food-handling supplies
- ◆ Food and drink

Adding up these expenses lets you know how much dough you need to get the doors open in the first place, and how much you need to make each month to keep them that way.

Income-ing!

As you can see from the lists above, the cost of the food and drinks you sell is only a tiny part of your total expenses—and yet the sales of said food and drink must support everything else. Quite a job for some brown liquid and a few bagels!

While your sales revenue naturally starts off at $0, a *market-based sales forecast*—that is, a formula that estimates how much your business could sell—will give you and your banker a rough idea of your income in the months and years ahead. (Don't have a professional banker yet? In Chapter 5, we'll try to convince you to find one.)

To figure out the numbers in your market-based sales forecast, sharpen up your math skills on this formula:

Sales forecast = market size × growth rate × market-share target × average sale × average number of visits

This formula has a lot of variables for you to fill in. Here's what the terms mean in more detail:

♦ *Market size* is the number of potential customers within your area.

♦ *Growth rate* is an estimate of how much the industry is expanding each year.

♦ *Market-share target* equals the percentage of the entire market that you expect to capture.

♦ *Average sale* is how much a customer typically spends each time he or she purchases something.

♦ *Average number of visits* is an estimate of how often a customer enters your store in a specific time period (week, month, quarter, etc.).

Beans of Wisdom

The best thing you can do with your conservative forecast is make it even more conservative by cutting it further by 25 percent. Yes, really, a whole quarter of your expected income. Better to be pleasantly surprised than unfortunately undercapitalized.

Don't overestimate your sales forecast by thinking you're going to nab half of your competitor's customers or that your store will be so wonderful that people will visit at twice the national rate. Be realistic, and accept that business growth will take time. Your forecast might indeed be accurate for sales one year from now, but at first, business will be much slower than you'd like.

Digging Up the Data

We've thrown a lot of numbers at you in the past two sections—well, a lot of potential numbers anyway, with average sales and registration fees and so forth. Now it's time to fill in those blanks.

For information on the market size, growth rate, average sale, and average number of visits, talk to coffee trade associations, industry suppliers and distributors, market research firms, the U.S. Census Bureau, and even other coffee businesses in non-competing areas.

Included below are a few coffee industry organizations and a sample of the information they have available to members and members-to-be.

- ◆ **National Coffee Association of U.S.A., Inc.** The NCA provides CoffeeTrax, a quarterly statistical report on the U.S. coffee market, free to members and for sale to nonmembers.

- ◆ **Specialty Coffee Association of America.** The SCAA sells reports that contain information such as roaster/retailer operating ratios and gourmet retailer market surveys.

- ◆ *CoffeeTalk Magazine. CoffeeTalk*'s "Java U" offers a custom service that provides detailed financials based on actual market figures and your specific information.

Contact information for each group, as well as many other coffee-related organizations, can be found in Appendix C.

Show Me the Money ... Please

To pay for start-up costs, you'll need to dip into a retirement account or college savings fund (sorry, Junior!) or, as is more likely the case, take out a business loan. Your ability to pay off that loan, as well as all the rest of your operating expenses, will depend on your sales revenues.

Contents May Be Hot

Even if your family boasts a platoon of rich aunts and uncles, think twice before you borrow money from relatives to start a business. Otherwise, you risk turning every holiday gathering into a discussion over whether you're running the business properly, using their money wisely, and so forth.

A Little Help from Your Friends

You'd think that a solo business owner would do all the initial grunt work, well, solo. Not so, amigo. No matter how much of an independent self-starter you are, you can and should rely on lots of other people—lawyers, accountants, bankers, insurance agents, and even friends and family—to get your business up and running.

Don't feel weak because you ask others for help; instead, realize that you're doing everything possible to make your business succeed. Uber-entrepreneur Oprah Winfrey might stand alone on stage and in her magazine, but she has a million assistants doing her bidding behind the scenes.

We'll explain how to hire lawyers, accountants, and other professionals in Chapter 5, but thankfully some advisors don't charge by the hour for their advice. Your personal life and the business community at large abound with individuals willing to help an up-and-comer (that's you) start off on the right foot.

> **Beans of Wisdom**
>
> Don't feel that you have to create a formal mentor-mentee relationship in which you sign a contract that binds you for life. All you need is someone—or a few someones—whose opinions and experience you trust and whom you can contact when you have a problem or a question. Keep their numbers on your cell phone and touch base often.

Mind Over Mentors

You might picture a mentor as some all-knowing, ultra-wise being who has answers to the questions of life, the universe, and everything, but the reality is much plainer than that.

A mentor is simply someone you trust, someone with an interest in you and your business, someone who will say that she likes this logo over that one and urge you to drop a troublesome supplier before you lose your sanity. A mentor can be a friend, spouse, sibling, parent, local business owner, professional (a lawyer or accountant, say), or even another coffee bar owner.

Positive Peer Pressure

Peers are those people who are already doing what you long to do. They're running their own companies and trying to make a living outside of big business. "Peers?" you grumble. "You mean *competitors!* Why should I network with them?"

Why? Because they've been there, done that. If they're in business, they've either done things right or learned from their mistakes. (Okay, they could be really, really lucky, but let's give them the benefit of the doubt.)

Any business owner—whether a coffee bar owner or not—can be a valuable resource for an emerging entrepreneur such as yourself. Other business owners have been through the start-up phase and may have tips on how to hire good employees, deal with suppliers, handle difficult customers, and market a small business.

Being active in the business community and networking with other business owners will keep you up-to-date on industry happenings, generate new ideas for running your business, and give you sympathetic ears to bend when your friends are sick of hearing about the supplier from hell. To get in on the networking loop, you can:

♦ Attend networking events such as those put on by your local Chamber of Commerce.

♦ Talk to other business owners in your area.

♦ Participate in online discussion groups for business owners, whether coffee-centric or more generally focused.

Don't worry about feeling shy or embarrassed about your status as a newbie on the business scene. Every entrepreneur started in your position and received lots of help on the way to a positive bottom line. All you have to do is ask questions, and they'll gladly overwhelm you with tales from the front lines.

Even if you gain no useful information from your peers, talking with them spreads the word about your business, and they in turn might plug your coffee-klatch skills to their clients, customers, friends, and family.

Going Before the Board

More momentous than a mentor, more pressing than your peers—we advise you now to take on an advisory board.

No, we haven't mistaken you for Microsoft or IBM. Advisory boards aren't solely for international conglomerates with more money than they know what to do with. An advisory board is simply a group of people who offer advice on running a business, and since you plan to run a business, it wouldn't hurt to have a bunch of smart people watching your back.

An advisory board might include your lawyer and accountant (folks we'll discuss hiring in Chapter 5), professionals in related fields (such as restaurant owners), mentors, public relation experts, and other small business owners.

How do you form an advisory board? Just ask people you trust and whose opinions you value whether they'd like to serve on your board. You're already paying your accountant and lawyer for their advice. If you feel bad asking others to advise you gratis, offer them free gift certificates or catering in exchange for their time. Whenever you meet as a group, treat them to a cup of coffee or a nice meal.

When asking for a person's help, be sure you both understand what this responsibility will mean. Will you contact him only when you have a question, or do you want to meet at regular times? Unlike large companies that force the CEO to speak before the board, you can make your advisory board as formal or informal as you like.

If you do opt for something more formal and corral these folks in the same place at the same time, play the role of professional businessperson to the hilt by:

♦ Creating an agenda that outlines the major points you want to cover.

♦ Sending your advisory board copies of the agenda beforehand.

♦ Giving an overview of the points you want to cover at the start of the meeting, then discussing them one at a time.

♦ Allowing a certain amount of time for table talk over each issue, tabling the issue for a later date if it's not resolved in that time.

♦ Using a tape recorder, or having someone take notes old-school style with a pen.

> **Beans of Wisdom**
>
> For more on writing business plans, surf on over to the Small Business Administration and check out its advice at www.sba.gov/starting_business/planning/basic.html.

Pulling It All Together

If you've followed everything above, you now have a mountain of information towering overhead and threatening to bury you. Time to dig out the gold, toss the dross, and whip that material into a presentable plan! A business plan typically has seven parts:

1. **Executive summary.** The executive summary gives an overview of your entire plan, highlighting the key strategic points. You typically write this section last but present it first.

2. **Company description.** Just what it sounds like—a description of your company including your vision and mission statements, a company overview, and its legal structure (discussed in Chapter 5).

3. **Products & services.** This section details which products (specialty coffee, biscotti, homemade donuts) and services (catering, delivery, custom baking) you'll provide customers, as well as how much they'll cost and what research and development you've done to support these offerings.

4. **Marketing.** Here you define the market you'll be operating in (the coffee-drinking public), the type of client you expect to serve (your target market), your competition (The Bitter Cup Coffee Bar), and your strategy for attracting clients (handing out flyers to customers of The Bitter Cup when the owner isn't looking).

5. **Operations.** This section describes your business's physical location, any equipment and inventory you need, and any other applicable operating details, such as a description of your workflow—that is, how your business will perform its day-to-day activities.

6. **Management.** Here you outline your key employees (starting with you, the keyest of the key), external professionals (accountant, lawyer), the members of your advisory board, and your human resource needs (how many staff members you'll need to start operations).

7. **Financials.** The nitty-gritty of the business plan, this contains your financial projections for expenses and income and how long it will take your business to become profitable—that is, to pay off your start-up loans and support itself.

While this is the end of the business plan chapter, you haven't necessarily reached the end of your business plan. Every other chapter also contains information and advice that will affect your business plan.

As we said several pages ago, don't think of writing your business plan as a straight path from A to Z. Heck, the path contains lots of points that aren't even letters! Start your plan now, and by the time you work through the rest of the book, you'll have everything set to go.

The Least You Need to Know

- ◆ A business plan is a blueprint for your business to help you stay on track and apply for business loans.

- ◆ Visit your potential competitors to scope out their prices, hours, marketing, and other business details.

- ◆ You need to define your target market, determine how you'll differ from the competition, and project your income and expenses.

- ◆ Choose someone whose abilities and opinions you trust to be your mentor.

- ◆ An advisory board of mentors, professionals, and other entrepreneurs can lead you through the landmines that confront new business owners.

Chapter **5**

Getting Authority on Your Side

In This Chapter

◆ Your lawyer, accountant, and banker

◆ Business structure basics

◆ Registering your business

◆ Insuring future success

We're going to assume, just for one moment, that you didn't earn a law degree, work as a banker, study accounting, and master the ins and outs of insurance before you set your sights on opening a coffee bar. Perhaps we're mistaken. If so, we apologize and suggest skipping the rest of this chapter.

If, however, you aren't fluent with the worlds of law, banking, accounting, and insurance, you need help from those who are. Managing a business on your own is one thing, but handling all the legal nitty-gritty that comes with managing a business can be an enormous time suck that does little to help you achieve your long-term goals.

By hiring professionals in these fields, you can focus on your core business while knowing that everything behind the scenes is on the up-and-up. As your business changes and grows in the years ahead, you'll return to these pros again and again to reevaluate how you keep records, file taxes, hire employees, and more.

The Pros of Pros

Did you ever run into a random hair salon because you *had* to do something with your hair *right then*—and walked out looking like a throwback to the big-haired, frizzed-out '80s?

If you hire a lawyer or any other type of professional discussed below without first checking them out, you could end up with a lot worse than a bad hair day. We're talking about taxes and lawsuits here!

Ask to meet with the professional for a consultation—many will do this free—and make sure that she has experience with small businesses like yours. Expect the professional to pepper you with more questions than Barbara Walters: Where do you want to be in five years? What are your goals? How do you expect to reach those goals? What are your major concerns? What do you expect from a lawyer/accountant/banker/insurance policy?

These questions aren't tip-offs to a nosy personality. If the pro is going to help your business succeed, she needs to know what you want to succeed at. (And if a professional doesn't grill you, that could be a sign that she either doesn't know your industry or can't be bothered to find out more about you. Neither situation is good.)

> **Beans of Wisdom**
>
> Although you might feel like deferring to the experts on complicated matters, keep in mind that they work for you, which means you have final say on everything. Have them explain the risks of taking or not taking their advice, but make the final decision on your own. Don't follow their advice blindly ...

Don't be afraid to ask a few questions yourself as well. You're the one writing the checks, so consider asking the following:

- **Are you experienced?** Have you done any of the tasks that I'm asking you to do, or is this new ground that you're learning on my dime?

- **Are you well-connected?** It's unreasonable to expect you to know every single fact in your field, but do you have a network of peers to turn to for those times you're in the dark?

◆ **Do you have other clients in my industry?** Having other coffee bar clients is good (as long as they're in different towns), because you'll be able to offer better advice.

◆ **Can you teach me what I need to know?** I'm hiring you for your knowledge, but I don't want you to keep it all to yourself. Can you explain things so that I know what's going on?

The professional should explain her fee structure so that you understand it, and she should have time to address your concerns. A professional who keeps interrupting your meeting to answer the phone and deal with crises is throwing up a red flag that should cause you to flee the room. Ask for referrals, and then call at least two of them to make sure the pro is up to doing the job.

Finally, make sure you feel comfortable working with the professional. Her brilliance might be awe-inspiring and the referrals worthy of being etched on her grave, but if she's brusque and unpleasant, you might be reluctant to call and ask for help when you really need it—which defeats the purpose of hiring her in the first place.

Landing a Legal Eagle

Despite confusing similarities between the two, real life is not like the movies. On the screen, lawyers spend all their time chasing down murderers to protect an orphan or representing town folk who sue evil corporations for poisoning the local drinking water.

In real life, lawyers create and interpret contracts and leases, defend you in legal actions brought against you, offer legal advice on topics such as hiring and firing employees, register and ID your business, and help you choose the right business structure. (More on these last two topics later in this chapter.)

In other words, lawyers spend much of their time doing incredibly boring things in exchange for large sums of money. By hiring a lawyer, you place a layer of insulation between you and mind-sucking tedium, thus allowing your brain to focus on more interesting and useful topics—topics that will hopefully involve those large sums of money mentioned above.

Beans of Wisdom

Try to find a lawyer who has experience with small businesses like yours. He'll be more familiar with your needs and can offer better advice on hiring employees, finding the right business structure, and more.

Not sure where to inquire to find your John Q. Esquire? Start with sources like ye olde Yellow Pages and recommendations from friends and family. If these don't pan out, contact specialized organizations with attorney listings such as:

♦ The American Bar Association (www.abanet.org)

♦ The Martindale-Hubbell Law Directory (www.lawyers.com), which specializes in lawyers for small business

♦ The West Legal Directory (www.lawoffice.com)

♦ Find Law (www.findlaw.com/business.html), which also offers a helpful small business center

With any lawyer you hire, as with the other professionals recommended in this chapter, keep accessibility in mind. Can you consult him by phone, or will you have to visit him at his office? If so, how far away is the office, and do the business hours clash with when you need to be behind the counter?

Accounting for Taste

Bean counters get a bad rap in our society. People call them "bean counters," for example, instead of accountants and dismiss them as drones who do nothing more than add and subtract columns of numbers.

In fact, having an accountant can be the difference between a coffee shop owner who tosses profits around in joy and one who gets tossed in the slammer for tax fraud. An accountant can compile and explain financial statements, design an accounting system to ease year-end financial reporting, keep Uncle Sam off your back by helping you pay the correct type and amount of taxes, tell you whether that fancy new home coffee maker is a legitimate business expense, and work with your lawyer to decide what type of business structure you should have.

> **Beans of Wisdom**
>
> Even with an accountant keeping your finances on the level, you should learn how to read financial statements so that you'll always know how your business is doing. Check out *The Complete Idiot's Guide to Finance and Accounting*, by Michael Muckian (Alpha Books, 2003), for more help.

Good accounting can't save a coffee shop that serves bad coffee, but a good coffee shop can still go bust if the owner doesn't know how to handle money. Costs can rise above income, for example, so that each sale brings a loss instead of a profit; or tax penalties for misfiled forms can plant a business so far in the hole that the sun never hits its door again.

As with your search for a lawyer, start in the Yellow Pages and with recommendations from friends. If those sources don't help, use the "find an accountant" link for the National Association of Small Business Accountants (www.smallbizaccountants.com).

Insuring Success

You may be the most careful and all-around wonderful coffee shop owner this side of the Mississippi, but one claim of personal injury, bodily injury, or sexual harassment can empty your bank account in a flash.

Comedians might have mocked the woman who sued McDonald's for serving overly hot coffee, but the lawsuit itself wasn't a frivolous matter. The jury ruled that the fast food giant had engaged in reckless conduct and issued a $2.7 million punitive damage award. The award was later lowered to $480,000, but that's still enough to wipe out almost any small business—and probably yours.

Protecting your personal and business finances requires insurance, and an insurance agent will tell you which types and how much coverage you need—before you open and as your business changes over time. Agents are typically independent business-people who work for several companies that provide different types of insurance. One agent should be all you need to find liability insurance, health insurance, and other policies.

Aside from checking the usual sources, visit the Independent Insurance Agents & Brokers of America online (www.iiaa.org) and search for agents by name, location, or area code.

Storm the Banks

If you're like most small business owners, you have a bank but no banker. Most likely, the last time you dealt with a banker was when you played Monopoly 10 years ago. Unlike the easy-going, here's-your-$200-for-passing-Go ways of youth, bankers in the real world individually handle accounts for bank members and assist those members in getting credit, avoiding fees, and enhancing business opportunities.

The best way to find a banker who will help keep the money flowing is to ask other coffee shops, restaurants, and small business owners whom they use, then research the banks to make sure they fit your needs. Does the bank offer online service? How long does it usually take to approve a loan? How much red tape will you have to go through to, say, replace a missing ATM card? Interview bankers at your banks of choice, and then pick the one you feel the most comfortable with.

Many small business owners don't bother with bankers, and when they do, they don't understand how to cultivate an alliance with them. Follow these tips to build a good relationship with your banker—after all, a good rapport is like money in the bank!

◆ Invite your banker to tour your facilities.

◆ Let your banker know when something important occurs, such as gaining new market share, reaching a profit goal, or facing a new competitor.

◆ Don't ask for favors at the beginning of your relationship. Create goodwill first by giving the bank your business and trying to bring in other accounts.

◆ If business setbacks occur, try to determine the cause and develop a plan of action before contacting your banker. (Once you have a plan, though, give your banker a call. He'll want to know about potential financial problems ASAP, not months after they develop.)

> **Contents May Be Hot**
>
> While you want the banker to be familiar with your business and its particular needs, don't invite him or her to tour the shop immediately before applying for a loan. You don't want to look like you're pleading for sympathy or special favors.

Many small business owners feel (wrongly) that they need to "fight" their banker to win approval for loans and credit. Try to avoid creating such a relationship. Instead, recognize that a banker who trusts you and your business is on your side; he'll go to bat for you to get lower interest rates or a credit line extension. You're not fighting an institution; you're working with a business partner to achieve a goal.

Should You Go It Alone?

So let's jump back to the beginning of the chapter when we considered your past work history. Maybe you did take one of those tax preparation classes from H&R Block, or perhaps you were a lawyer before you decided to pull drinks rather than push papers. Will you save money by handling the accounting or legal tasks yourself?

It depends. Every hour you sweat over tax filings or contracts is an hour that you're not building your coffee bar business. Sure, you may save $50 by filing that form yourself, but in effect you're *losing* money at the same time because you could be thinking up ways to sell more products or network with other business owners.

Even more importantly, when you're dealing with employees and customers, you're building goodwill. While you're struggling with a form, you're building nothing but a headache.

Coffee Quips

"The coffee is prepared in such a way that it makes those who drink it witty: at least there is not a single soul who, on quitting the house, does not believe himself four times wittier than when he entered it."

—Charles de Second at Montesquieu

If you're cash-strapped when you first start out, it might make sense to do as much on your own as you can. But as soon as you're able, we suggest hiring professionals to do their thing, so that you have time to do *yours:* sell coffee and build your business.

Structuring Your Business

Businesses don't append titles like "Inc." and "LLC" to their names because they sound cool. Those little words are shorthand for the business's legal structure, which affects how much the business pays in taxes, the amount of paperwork the owners have to do, the personal liability they face, and their ability to raise money for their business.

Don't feel that once you've chosen a business structure, you're stuck with it for all time. You can move from one to another, although the ease with which you do this will depend on what you're changing from and what you're now becoming.

Liability, taxation, and record-keeping are the most important factors to keep in mind when choosing among business entities. Here's a brief look at how the most common forms of business entities differ.

Sole Proprietorship

This is the simplest and most common way that entrepreneurs organize their businesses. You are the proprietor—a fancy Latin way of saying "owner"—and you have complete control over managing every aspect of the business.

Control is good, right? Well, control can come back and bite you, because financial control of the business is also your responsibility. You are personally and solely liable for all financial obligations, which means that if someone sues your business and wins, your business *and* personal bank accounts have to ante up the dough. If the business goes bankrupt and you still owe money, your future wages from a completely unrelated business must pay off your debts.

Now, with that warning in mind, let's consider the benefits. First, handling tax matters under sole proprietorships is fairly easy because you can file a Schedule C with your individual income tax return. Tax-filing software can make this process so simple that you might be able to complete the tax forms on your own. You should still run them past your accountant so she can double-check your work, but this will save you money.

The second real benefit of being a sole proprietor is the ease with which you can start and end a business. Sure, you need all sorts of licenses to sell food and drinks—a topic covered later in this chapter—but the business itself exists as soon as you say it does. If you want to use your child's college fund as business capital, you don't have to write yourself a loan; you just use it. (Convincing your spouse that this is a good idea is an exercise we'll leave to you.)

Partnership

A partnership is akin to two or more sole proprietorships smooshed together with the "sole" aspect tossed out. Partners share the profits (and suffer the losses) together, and they typically sign contracts that detail how to split funds among them.

As with a sole proprietorship, partners enjoy ease of tax filings but suffer from the threat of being personally liable for all financial obligations of the business.

Of greater concern is how partnerships change over time. A year or two after opening, one partner might feel he's doing all the work while netting only half the earnings, or the partners might disagree on how to expand the business, who to promote to manager, or what to add to the menu.

To avoid these pitfalls, partners need to decide who will handle which responsibilities long before the business opens. Ideally, the partnership contract they sign should spell out exactly who does what for how much of the profits.

More importantly, the contract should include a method for revising the contract should the work situation change over time. If, for example, one partner is hurt or killed in a car accident, what happens to his share of the business? If a partner decides a coffee career doesn't suit him any longer, how much will it cost to buy him out?

By confronting these issues early, preferably with a lawyer to get everything in writing, you'll avoid arguments and lawsuits in the long run.

Corporation

By legal definition, a corporation functions just like a person. When the owner of a corporation buys something by using money from the business, the object purchased is owned by the corporation itself and not the business owner.

Similarly, the corporation itself makes a profit or loss, is taxed on earnings, and is held legally liable for its actions. If the corporation is sued, only items owned by the corporation are at risk, not the personal finances of you and other co-owners.

You're not completely off the hook, of course. The corporation will pay you a salary, and you'll still owe taxes on that income; you can be personally sued for wrongdoing; and so forth. What's more, running a corporation requires an intense amount of paperwork, paperwork best handled by legal and accounting experts.

Contents May Be Hot

As your business grows, your accountant and lawyer must be able to adapt to your growth. If they work only with small businesses, you may need to find someone else. Susan knows a coffee shop owner who learned this the hard way when his accountant insisted that he didn't need to incorporate his business. The owner was eventually hit with a huge tax bill that could have been avoided had he incorporated!

Limited Liability Company (LLC)

An LLC walks the fence between incorporation and sole proprietorship. Profits and losses pass through to the owners—thus avoiding the "double taxation" involved with corporations—yet owners are shielded from personal liability for business debts.

Just as you share benefits, however, you also share drawbacks. LLCs require more paperwork than sole proprietorships or partnerships, and they expire with the owners, unlike corporations, which can "live" nigh unto eternity. If you dream about going public in the future and selling shares of stock, you're best off forming a corporation instead of an LLC.

Checking Your ID

The state, local, and federal governments employ more than 21 million people in the United States, and to give all those folks something to do, you as a business owner must apply for numerous licenses, permits, and ID numbers. The exact requirements will vary depending on your city and state, but we've included an explanation of the most basic licenses and numbers below.

Employer Identification Number (EIN)

The EIN—also called a federal tax identification number—identifies your business in its current legal structure. If you formed a sole proprietorship, you can use your Social Security number as your EIN; if you chose a different structure, the EIN effectively serves as the business's Social Security number.

Apply for an EIN online with the IRS (www.irs.gov), or call the IRS's Business & Specialty Tax Line (800-829-4933) to apply and say "hi" to one of the millions of folks working behind the scenes.

Business License

No matter which part of the country you live in, you'll almost certainly need to secure a business license to keep the local government at bay. If the business falls inside the borders of an incorporated city, for example, you need to contact the city for a license; if it lies outside city limits, the county government is likely your license source.

You can contact your city or county government for information on business licenses, but if you feel all 21 million government employees might be on lunch break, visit the Small Business Administration (SBA) online and use its links (www.sba.gov/hotlist/license.html) to find business license forms for nearly every state.

Certificate of Occupancy

While setting up shop, you might take over an existing business and use it exactly "as is." If you want to set up in a new or renovated building, however—one that doesn't come as you envisioned it in your dreams—you'll need to apply for a Certificate of Occupancy from the building or zoning department. Again, the SBA link in the previous paragraph will lead you to the appropriate forms for most states.

Fictitious Business Name

In their quasi-personlike status, corporations already have a name under which to do business—that is, the name of the corporation itself.

You, as an individual, are not doing business under your name because few people would enter a store labeled "Herbert Terwilliger" and expect to find coffee for sale. Since you're doing business under a fictitious name, you must apply for a license to do so from the appropriate local government office.

Food License

If you sell perishable foods, such as fresh coffee instead of canned, or baked cookies instead of powdered and freeze-dried ones, then you need to obtain a food license from the city or state or both. Don't think that you can get away with selling 400 cups of coffee under the counter each day. Word will surely get back to the authorities ....

Contents May Be Hot _____

We'll talk more about finding a location in Chapter 7, but now's the time to mention that many cities require you to get a zoning compliance permit before you open shop. Be sure to ask city hall whether you need this permit before you sign the lease; otherwise, you could be liable for a location where you can't even do business!

Reseller's License

Since you're purchasing items from a wholesaler—such as coffee beans or bagels and brie—to resell to others, you first need a reseller's license, which is also known as a seller's permit or sales tax permit. That's right, you have to collect sales tax on (nearly) everything you sell; we'll cover the tax topic in loving detail in Chapter 18.

These six licenses and permits will get you started, but consult your lawyer (that fellow or lady we suggested you hire a few pages back) or speak with a few of those millions of government workers in your area to find out exactly what's required to open for business in your town.

The Least You Need to Know

♦ Small business owners need a complement of professionals like lawyers, accountants, and bankers to help them start and run their businesses.

♦ An insurance agent will help you decide which kinds of insurance policies you need and help you get the best rates.

◆ You need to decide on a business structure that will work best for your business; a lawyer can help you.

◆ Make sure you have the right licenses, IDs, and permits before hanging your shingle.

Chapter 6

A Rose Is More Than a Rose: Branding Your Business

In This Chapter

♦ Naming your baby business

♦ Creating a customer-grabbing logo

♦ Color Me Beautiful

♦ You™

Can you imagine customers referring their friends to "that coffee shop, um, what's-it-called, on Main Street"? Probably not. That's why you need a name for your business that will lodge squarely in your customers' craniums and be at the forefront of their thoughts at all times.

Similarly, boasting a strong logo—a graphical depiction of your business— will also aid customers in remembering your business and what you stand for.

Your business name and logo should convey everything that's good about your business—what makes you unique, why customers should buy from you instead of anyone else—while at the same time telling potential customers that you sell coffee. It may sound hard, but don't despair—we'll show you how it's done!

Strike Up the Brand

Throughout the 1990s and into the new millennium, businesses began paying more and more attention to their *brand*—that is, to their corporate identity, to the essence of who they are, what they do, and how they do it. Examples of popular brands include the Nike swoosh, the Coca-Cola red-and-white "wave," and yes, the green-and-white Starbucks siren.

Why do these businesses and thousands of others care so much about making their brand well known? Two reasons, the first of which is differentiation, the ability to stand out in the marketplace. If you see a swoosh on a product, whether it's a sneaker, a shirt, or a golf club, you know that the item is a Nike design. Not Adidas, not Reebok, not anyone else.

Whether that's good or bad will depend on your past experience with Nike, your concern over sweatshop labor, and other factors, but the important thing from Nike's point of view is that everyone in the marketplace can recognize their products—and that ties into the second benefit of branding. If a company spends the time creating a coherent image and packaging it into their advertising and product design, they can create more effective marketing campaigns that will likely result in better sales.

Instant Facts

Business Week rated Coca-Cola the world's most valuable brand in 2003, estimating that the brand itself—not the soda-producing machines, factories, or any other equipment, but simply the essence of the brand—was worth more than $70 billion. That's a lot of bottles of fuzzy brown liquid!

To continue using Nike as an example, the company used the phrase "Just do it" so regularly in its advertising campaigns that it's now impossible to use the phrase without thinking about the company. Writers even write sentences such as, "As Nike says, 'Just do it'"—as if no one else in the history of the English language had ever uttered that phrase! Say "the next generation," and Pepsi comes to mind; mention that a burger has "two all-beef patties," and who will think of anything other than McDonald's?

While international companies have millions of dollars to spend to place their brand in the public eye, you as a small business will likely budget a tad less towards brand creation. That's okay—no one expects you to compete with the big boys in terms of dollars spent. As long as you offer quality products, you'll be well on your way to success.

That said, whether or not you intend such a thing, your business name, logo, colors, advertising, and more will work together to make up your business's brand and its image in the marketplace and surrounding community. This means you need to consider the following sections carefully, with an eye towards long-term use and consistency. We'll bring up these issues in more detail in each section.

Playing the Name Game

Step number one in creating a business name that will have customers lining up on the street is deciding what you want your name to communicate.

While building your business plan in Chapter 4, you focused on the target market you want to serve and researched the size of that market. Now you need to decide how you want to position yourself within that market.

By "position yourself," we don't mean standing upright behind the counter or sitting with your legs crossed on a park bench. No, you need to position your coffee bar in the mind of the buying public: Is the coffee you offer exclusive to the area? Do you make your own blends? Are your products expensive, modestly priced, affordable, cheap? Are you open before dawn, after midnight, around the clock? Will you provide live music, a place to study, a shelf of books or games to borrow?

These are just a few of the questions you can ask about how you want to be viewed by the market at large. Ideally, your name will convey all this information in as few words as possible so that customers know what to expect when they enter your shop.

Contents May Be Hot

Be cautious about choosing names that constrain you to a certain location or type of business. If you name your business Boston Beans, for instance, how might this name affect you down the road if you expand to nearby towns or move your business out of Boston? What if, after opening The Cheap Cup, you discover that customers are hankering for pricey gourmet beans?

Question Yourself

Continuing in our Socratic vein of self-examination, we have yet more questions for you to ask yourself. As you do, write down at least 10 names that reflect your answers.

♦ What problems do I solve for my target market? Do I help them wake up and warm up in the morning, provide them with affordable indulgences, help them brew the perfect pot at home, offer types of coffee they can't find anywhere else?

- What words or phrases appeal to my target market? Words like "hot," "brewed," "fresh"?

- What are the biggest benefits that my business brings to customers?

- What kind of atmosphere should people expect to find in my shop?

- What kind of name would differentiate me, in a positive way, from my competitors?

Once you have a list of names written down, run them by friends, family, and potential customers. Which names make people want to come to your shop and sample your wares? Which names make them scrunch up their brows in confusion?

If possible, stop people on the street who know nothing about you and the business you plan to open and ask them for an opinion after giving nothing more than the name. You might love "The Perfect Pot" for your business-to-be, but they might wonder whether you're opening a coffee bar, a pottery store, or something that belongs in Amsterdam.

Say the names out loud, and 86 those that don't roll off the tongue. Imagine the name on business cards, on a sign, on letterhead, or in a newspaper article. Pretend someone at a party or on an elevator asks the name of your business. Can you imagine answering the phone with this name? If not, ditch it and move on to the next. Many naming experts say that your business name should use real words instead of made-up monikers like Kodak and Skechers. Why do some companies get away with invented names while you have to stick to boring ol' real words? Simple—you can't afford it. Those firms have multimillion-dollar marketing budgets to plant their invented handles in the minds of consumers. You, on the other hand, probably lack the millions of bucks needed to get customers to remember that Drinqs or Zelpod is a coffee bar.

> **Beans of Wisdom**
>
> Still having trouble coming up with the perfect handle for your business? You might consider hiring a professional naming or branding company. These can be costly, but they'll help come up with a name with impact, can show you how the name will look on signs and promotional materials, and can assist you with trademarking and registering.

Marking Your Territory

Once you finally find the perfect name for your coffee pot of gold, consider whether you want to trademark your creation. A trademark is any word, image, or combination of words and images used to distinguish your business or service from any other business or service.

Trademarks are why people named "McDonald" shouldn't name a business after themselves. In 2003, for example, nationwide lingerie retailer Victoria's Secret sued a small adult novelty and gift shop named Victor's Little Secret. This despite the fact that one of the co-owners was actually named Victor! The U.S. Supreme Court eventually ruled that there was no confusion between Victor and Victoria and threw out the lawsuit, but it's unlikely that you want to risk a drawn-out court battle simply to name a business after yourself. (We're talking to you, Duncan Pete Starbuck!)

You don't need to trademark your name, but doing so ensures that other businesses in the same industry can't use it for themselves. This exclusivity might not be important to you now, but if you want to expand your business later, you don't want to unexpectedly find competing shops with the same name where you plan to expand.

You can submit a trademark application to the U.S. Patent and Trademark Office (USPTO) by mail or in person. Call the USPTO's automated telephone line at 800-786-9199 (toll-free) or 703-308-9000 to request a printed form. Request applications and file by mail by writing to:

> Commissioner for Trademarks
> 2900 Crystal Drive
> Arlington, VA 22202-3514

You can also file a trademark application over the Internet through the Trademark Electronic Application System (TEAS) available at www.uspto.gov/teas/index.html.

If you submit the application without the help of a lawyer, you're responsible for complying with all requirements of the trademark statute and rules. If you do use a lawyer, you'll avoid this grunt work as the USPTO will correspond with only the lawyer, but of course, you'll pay a bit more.

Beans of Wisdom

In Chapter 5, we suggested that you hire a lawyer to handle all your legal mumbo-jumbo, but you can easily search through lists of trademarks to make sure the one you want isn't already taken. Visit the USPTO online at www.uspto.gov and explore the Trademark Electronic Search System (TESS), which contains more than three million pending, registered, and dead federal trademarks. Use Internet search engines such as Google (www.google.com) and Yahoo! (www.yahoo.com) as well to scan the online world for anyone who might be using your desired name.

And speaking of pay, as of the start of 2005, submitting a trademark application costs $335. For up-to-date information on costs, call the USPTO at 800-786-9199.

Logo-a-Go-Go

If you're driving with kids down a Florida highway and spot a sign that has a black circle with two smaller black circles above it, be prepared for lots of screaming from the back seat. You're getting close to Disney World, and the kids can hardly wait.

A business's *logo* is shorthand for the business itself. The silhouette of Mickey Mouse is one of the world's most recognized logos, and as soon as most people see three black circles in a certain arrangement, they automatically think about Disney, vacations, overpriced souvenirs, and long, long lines for amusement park rides.

As a coffee shop owner, you can use a logo to give your business an image of substance and stability while grabbing past and future customers with a visual hook that connects the act of consuming coffee with your business. While not essential, a logo gives a business a more professional look.

Logo Logistics

There's more to choosing a logo design than pasting clip art of a steaming coffee cup onto your business card. Your logo needs to convey important information about your business beyond "Me sell coffee." A gym, for instance, might use a vibrant design to convey health and vitality, whereas an accountant will choose something more conservative to radiate seriousness and trustworthiness.

You want the logo to reflect the true image of your coffee bar, the image that you developed earlier in this chapter while deciding on a name. Ideally, the logo will work together with this name to reinforce the brand image you want customers to have about your business.

Keep in mind, though, that a logo has its limits. You might decide that the perfect logo is a four-color design of an Italian woman quaffing espresso and holding a croissant and only later discover that when you fax a customer your menu or copy your logo on a black and white copier, that beautiful logo ends up looking like a big coffee stain.

To be successful, a logo must be:

- **Appropriate to your business.** Beans, coffee cups, coffee pots? Good. Flowers, puppies, power tools? Bad.

- **Readable and memorable.** When potential customers see your logo, they must be able to understand what they're looking at, read the name of your business, and remember what the logo stands for. If you plan to open near a busy road, your logo needs to be simple enough that drivers can spot it, even while in motion. If you're located in a pedestrian mall, something a bit fancier and more eye-catching might be appropriate.

- **Reproducible.** While similar to readability, being reproducible means that the logo works at all different sizes and looks crisp whether in color or in black-and-white. The more colors and detail you have, the harder and more expensive it will be to reproduce on napkins, in advertisements, and anywhere else you want it to be. Test your logo to make sure it will look good on business cards, faxes, menus, signs, and the Internet.

- **Unique.** If your logo resembles the logo of, say, a business that rhymes with Farbucks, customers might have a hard time distinguishing your products from a competitor's—until the lawyers shut you down, that is.

- **Professional and not trendy.** You don't want to look like a here-today-gone-tomorrow business, so make sure your logo conveys stability and professionalism. Don't mimic a design or color that's popular now or else your logo will quickly become dated and make your business look out-of-date as well.

Remember, you don't have to answer all the questions about your business in your logo. You'd be hard-pressed, for example, to express the concepts of Italian, fresh, pastries, coffee, coffee gifts, and gourmet in one simple design.

Pinch Your Pennies

Déjà vu time—as we said in the previous section, there's more to choosing a logo design than pasting clip art of a steaming coffee cup onto your business card. Unless you have a background in graphic design, you need to hire a professional designer if you want your logo to look, well, professional.

Coffee Quips

"To drink is human, to drink coffee is divine!"

—Unknown

Don't fret that you have to lay out a huge wad of cash, though. You're not Coca-Cola looking for a new concept for an international marketing campaign; all you need are a few designs based on the concepts you already have. You can even contact art and design schools to find a student who may design a logo for you cheap or perhaps in exchange for an endless supply of "study fuel," a.k.a. coffee.

What Color Is Your Business?

Colors convey emotions, so the color you choose for your logo and your shop is an important aspect of your image. To help you choose colors for your logo, letterhead, signs, tables, floors and so forth, check out this list of popular colors and the emotions they convey.

♦ Red is an attention-grabber that makes people look immediately. Red symbolizes fire, heat, passion, excitement, power, and aggression. It can elevate blood pressure and respiratory rate. Hmm, sounds a lot like caffeine!

♦ Blue is peaceful and tranquil, and it relaxes the nervous system. At an extreme, the color represents solitude and depression, such as in the expression "feeling blue."

♦ Green is a neutral, relaxing color and can communicate the idea of life, renewal, hope, vigor, nature, or money. This may be a good color for an environmentally friendly shop that sells, say, free-trade coffees and uses recyclable paper goods.

♦ Black is the color of authority and power, but in large doses it can represent somberness and mourning—not necessarily a good mix with coffee, no matter how black you serve it.

♦ Yellow conveys brightness, playfulness, creativity and warmth. Yellow is the most visible of all the colors, which is why traffic signs are in this color.

♦ Purple, the color of royalty, conveys luxury, wealth, and sophistication as well as passion and romance. This may be a good color for a shop selling pricey luxury items.

♦ Brown, the color of earth and wood, is solid, reliable, neutral, comfortable. It also symbolizes credibility, strength, and maturity.

As with your business name, you can trademark your logo to ensure that no one snatches your awesome design, and the trademark application process is the same.

Some companies have even gone so far as to trademark a particular color! This makes sense when, in the public mind, brown equals UPS delivery, but you have nothing to worry about—at least until you deliver coffee coast-to-coast. Then you might reconsider ....

The Least You Need to Know

- ◆ Your business's name, logo, and colors all need to work together to create a brand image.

- ◆ You need a name for your business that people will understand and remember.

- ◆ A graphic designer can help you create a logo that will symbolize your business and bring in customers.

- ◆ Trademarking your name and logo ensures that no one else can use them.

- ◆ Colors convey emotions; the colors you choose for your shop, logo, and letter-head are an important aspect of your business.

Chapter 7

Location, Location, Location

In This Chapter

◆ Where do you want to be?

◆ Mapping it out

◆ Spy vs. Spy: Checking out the competition

◆ Proposing to the landlord

One of the most important decisions you'll make—after deciding to start a business, that is—is where you'll base your operations. How much space do you need? Do you want to be in the suburbs or the big city? How much rent can you afford? Do you want to be in a mall, strip mall, city street, or office complex?

Not to put any stress on you, but the future success of your business depends on finding a good location. If, for example, your downtown location ends up with less foot traffic than you expected, you'll have to pour money into marketing to get folks to stop by. If you set up in a strip mall with a supermarket that shuts down six months later, you might have to contemplate shutting down yourself.

It sounds like way too much thinking for someone who hasn't had their morning cup of coffee yet, but that's okay. In this chapter, we'll tell you how to develop criteria to analyze locations and prepare a proposal for the landlord.

Where to Get Started

In the movies, the entrepreneur passes by a building with a "for rent" sign, walks in, and starts her business—with great success, of course! But this ain't the movies, and in real life, you'll rarely find your perfect location with a "for rent" sign hanging in the window.

Deciding where to start can be daunting. After all, you have a whole city or town (or more) to choose from! We suggest you start by mapping out a large area to find out where the most profitable locations lie—and by "profitable" we mean "bearing lots of potential customers."

In your "war room" (i.e., your office or living room) put up a large map of your city or town. Armed with a bunch of stickers in different colors and a copy of the Yellow Pages, put stickers of one color on the map for businesses that attract the same sort of clientele that you're hoping to target. For example, if you want to attract families, put stickers on baby stores, toy stores, and family restaurants. If you want to target students, put the stickers on colleges, bookstores, libraries, hip retail stores, and so on. Put stickers of another color on businesses that compete with yours.

Do you see any areas where a bunch of stickers seem to converge (even competitor stickers—we'll talk more about this later in the chapter)? These are the areas where you want to start looking for your perfect location.

To Mall or Not to Mall: Choosing a Location Type

Now that you know where to start looking, you need to decide what type of location you're looking for. Not all locations were created equal; they differ by rent, traffic patterns, accessibility, upkeep costs, and more. Here are the pros and cons of the various options.

Shopping Malls

You'd think a place with all that walk-by traffic would have great potential for a coffee shop. Sadly, that isn't so. People tend to do their shopping *after* the peak coffee-drinking time of the day—malls usually open no earlier than 10 in the morning, after all—and many people won't be tempted to stop shopping to enjoy a cup of coffee in your store.

But that's merely the beginning of the drawbacks. Rent, which is typically charged on a price-per-square-foot basis, can be extremely high in the mall; it's a very competitive place to be. If the rent is low, there's probably a good (and by good, we mean bad) reason for it. You have to contribute to the mall's media fund for advertising and marketing, and that fund goes toward marketing the mall in general, not your store in particular. You also have to pay for common area maintenance (more on this later), which can be pricey. With their fountains, landscaping, and huge parking lots, malls are expensive to keep up.

Contents May Be Hot

You can't count on gaining a loyal clientele at a mall, unless it's the employees of the other stores. After all, would you fight traffic, find parking, and navigate the mall just to get a cup of coffee?

On top of everything else, the mall's hours are set in stone, and you must obey them. Are they open seven days a week from nine to nine, including most holidays? Then so are you—and you have to pay for the labor to staff the store every hour the mall is open, even when it would be more profitable for you to close your doors.

Despite all the doom and gloom in the preceding paragraphs, malls can sometimes support a coffee shop based solely on the volume of traffic, especially during the holidays. Few other retail organizations draw thousands of people to one location on such a regular basis. Rather than set up an entire store, though, you might be better off running a coffee cart only during certain times of the year. We'll discuss cart opportunities a bit later in this chapter.

Strip Malls

Strip malls are shopping centers in which all the stores are set along a strip and are accessible from the outdoors. Strip malls have great potential for coffee shops as the storefronts are usually visible from the street, and there's ample parking. There's generally good foot traffic, too, especially if the strip mall has a popular "anchor" (that's the big store at the end), such as a grocery store or a good bookstore.

Rent and maintenance costs at a strip mall will be lower than at a traditional shopping mall, and you're usually free to set your own hours. In short, by giving up a portion of the foot traffic generated by traditional malls, you also give up almost all of the drawbacks of these malls. Sounds like a good deal to us!

Office Buildings

An office building can be an awesome place to start a coffee business, especially if it has access to the outside for additional walk-by traffic. You have a built-in customer base, and you can expand your profits by offering catering to the businesses in the building. For example, some businesses may want you to supply coffee and pastries for their Monday morning meetings. You can also offer gift baskets, which are popular gifts from businesses to their clients and from employees to bosses and vice versa.

One disadvantage might be hours. If you're limited to being open when the building is open for business, you may miss out on key coffee-drinking times of the day, such as before work (especially if you have outside access and rely on walk-by traffic from people who don't work in your building).

> **Beans of Wisdom**
>
> For either a storefront location or a strip mall, think about the possibility of including a drive-thru to catch customers on the go. You might be able to overcome a shortage of parking spaces simply by letting customers stay behind the wheel!

Storefront Locations

Storefront locations—that is, a business in a building that faces the street—are excellent for coffee shops. You can open and close when it works best for you. You can do cross-promotions with other businesses on your street. You benefit from walk-by and drive-by traffic. The rents are often cheaper than in a mall.

One sticky point may be parking. If there's no separate parking area for your store, see how street parking is during your hours of operation. No one wants to circle the block five times to get a cup of coffee.

Carts and Kiosks

You can dip your toe into the coffee business, so to speak, by opening a trial location in a mobile cart or semi-permanent kiosk. Many shopping malls, for example, allow vendors to run carts during the holiday season to take advantage of the increased foot traffic. (Malls aren't playing Santa, mind you; they still charge dearly for the space.)

Since carts have very limited space, you'd need little more than an espresso machine, a couple of brewing carafes, a stocked refrigerator, and supplies to get started. This means your initial investment costs would be far lower while you get the hang of the business. Kiosks tend to be larger than carts, but they're usually located in a secure permanent location such as a park or next to an office building downtown.

While these locations cost far less for the initial set-up, they offer poor working conditions since you're confined to a very small space for most of the workday—not to mention dealing with the weather, if you're outdoors. You tend to work alone, which increases boredom, and you lack real opportunities for growth. Finally, expanding from a cart to a brick-and-mortar location requires almost as much work as starting from scratch.

Other Locations

Some coffee shops start within other businesses. For example, you can open a shop in a:

- Gourmet shop.
- Superstore.
- Convention center.
- Gym.
- Theme park.
- Hospital.
- University campus.
- Bookstore.
- Tourist stop.
- Museum (like Susan's business!).

You're guaranteed walk-by traffic, and you don't have to worry about competition or the lack of it. The main business will usually have vast parking facilities, although you might be required to contribute towards their upkeep.

The disadvantages can come if the business you're affiliated with is weather-dependent, such as a zoo or theme park, or if the business itself isn't doing very well (since you're relying on their customers for *your* business). Sure, a university campus will supply a steady stream of needy students during the semester, but how will your business survive the summer months when they've all gone home to Mom and Dad?

How to Judge a Location

It would be nice if finding a business location were like finding an apartment. Big, sunny, free utilities? I'll take it! But in reality, you need to use many criteria to judge a potential location.

Size

Sure, the location may seem to be the perfect size now, but you also need to keep in mind that you may want to expand your business further down the line—you'll need someplace with the potential for expansion. You'll also need plenty of room for storage and a workspace for you and your employees. Do you plan to offer entertainment or hold workshops? If so, you'll want to be able to rearrange the seating area to accommodate such uses.

Atmosphere

Sunny, spacious, and clean? Great. Dank, dark, and gloomy? Not so great. Of course, you can change a lot of the characteristics of your chosen space with cleaning, remodeling, and redecorating, but you don't want to spend thousands upon thousands of dollars trying to turn a completely inappropriate location into a space that's cozy and inviting for your customers (and your employees).

Rent

Rent comes in two types: a flat rate, where you generally pay by the square foot, and a percentage basis, where you pay a base amount of rent plus a prearranged percentage of your monthly receipts.

Don't automatically discount a place with high rent. Many desirable locations have high rent because business is so good in that area that competition keeps the rates up. If your rent is $1,000 per month and you can count on 1,000 customers who spend an average of $3 per visit, you have $2,000 after rent (not including food costs). If your rent is $10,000 per month and you can count on 10,000 customers who shell out an average of $3 per visit, suddenly you have $20,000! Makes the higher rent worth it, doesn't it?

> **Beans of Wisdom**
>
> Negotiate for 90 days of free rent while you set up shop; most landlords will agree to this.

Term

The term is how long the lease lasts. For example, you may have a one-year term or a two-year term. You probably don't want to get stuck with a very long lease in case (goodness forbid) you should have to close the business; but at the same time, you don't want to go for a very short lease and then find out that the landlord won't renew it—or that you want to sell the business but can't find a buyer because your lease is about to expire!

A good bet is a shorter lease with a renewal option (say a minimum of three years to offset the cost of improvements you made), and a guaranteed rate for rent increases over a set period (such as five to ten years).

Visibility

The nicest store in history won't succeed if no one knows you're there. You usually need a location that's visible from the street, preferably one that's right on the curb. When you find a place, walk or drive down the street and see from how far the shop is visible. Can you see the store? How about the signage? When you walk by the store, are there nice, big front windows that show you what's inside? A store that's 70 feet wide and 10 feet deep requires a far different approach than one that's 10 feet wide and 70 feet deep.

Convenience

Would you take a left turn across busy traffic to score a cup of joe? A lot of other people wouldn't, either. That's why you need a location that's convenient to the types of customers you want to attract. For example, if you want to cater to busy execs on their way to work, you need to be on the right side of the street on their way to work. If you want to cater to students, you need to be convenient to pedestrians (so they don't have to dodge traffic going from the campus to your store), and even have room out front for bike racks. In most cases, you need ample parking as well.

To place your store right in the path of customers, you can visit the city or county planning department and review traffic flow maps that show how many cars travel on which streets at what times. For decades you've been driving over those black rubber cords stretched across the streets. Since the maps are public information, you can ask for a copy and put to use the information that you and thousands of other drivers created.

Instant Facts

Many times competing businesses feed off of one another, which is why you'll often see Burger King, Wendy's, and McDonald's all in a row, or three gas stations at one intersection. If this strategy works for the big boys, you'll probably want to consider it as well.

Competition

You need a location with no other coffee shops around, right?

Wrong-o. If there are no other coffee shops around, there's probably a good reason for it. Maybe the citizens in that area aren't interested in gourmet coffees and teas, or maybe there's not enough walk-by or drive-by traffic. In any case, you want to see thriving businesses in the area you plan to inhabit. Don't worry about the competition. As we discuss later in this chapter, you can stake them out to uncover their strengths and weaknesses, and use this knowledge to your advantage.

Signage Laws

Some cities have signage by-laws that require you to keep your signs at or below a certain size or that restrict you from using certain types of signs. You certainly don't want to spend $2,000 on a sign only to be told that you're not allowed to put it up! Check city by-laws for signage restrictions, and talk to a sign company in your area that's created signs for local businesses. Chances are, they have a good knowledge of city by-laws.

Electricity

Make sure the electrical capacity in your chosen location can handle your coffee equipment such as brewers, roasters, and so on. You probably need an electrical system that can handle at least 220 volts because most espresso equipment requires a lot of juice. Talk to an electrician to find out if a location has the potential to handle your electrical equipment.

Tenant Improvement Allowances (TI)

Tenant Improvement Allowances are funds that the landlord gives to you to build or improve your business. These improvements—a resurfaced wall, perhaps, or updated insulated wiring—will stay behind if you ever leave the building, thus providing him with a more attractive space for later candidates. Landlords who have many people bidding for their space are less likely to offer TIs, but it never hurts to ask.

Common Area Maintenance (CAM)

Common Area Maintenance is money you pay to maintain the building site. This includes such services as window washing, trash removal, and security. The contract your landlord offers should spell out exactly what the CAM pays for so that you know what you'll receive for this money. The contract should also detail procedures to follow in case you find the services haven't been provided.

Ideally, you want to keep the CAM as low as possible. In some cases, you might be able to arrange for window cleaning and other maintenance needs yourself, which will allow you more direct control over the look and cleanliness of your business.

Courts in some states have ruled that landlords must reveal the costs behind CAM fees to their tenants. The idea behind this ruling is that landlords can't use CAM fees to boost their own profits; they must use the fees only to cover their own (reasonable) costs for the upkeep on their facilities.

Contents May Be Hot

Scan contracts from your landlord to find out whether CAM fees and other expenses are charged on a leased or leasable basis. If the fees are based on a leasable formula, then your costs will be the same no matter how many other stores he owns are vacant. If, however, the fees are based on the amount of space currently leased, you'll pay more if one or more locations are vacant as the landlord is spreading the maintenance costs among his current tenants. Argue for a leasable formula so that your costs don't fluctuate due to happenings outside your control.

Real Estate Taxes

As with CAM fees, the landlord will charge you a portion of the entire real estate bill based on the percentage of space your shop occupies.

Washrooms

You'll probably be required by city health codes to have at least one washroom, and some areas will require you to have two. Make sure that the area either has the washrooms you need or has the space to build them, taking into account the need for handicapped-accessible spaces.

Using these criteria plus the map you created in your "war room," narrow your selection down to five or six places. Just like when you apply for college, you probably will have a first choice place, but you also want to have backups in case that one falls through.

Scoping Out the Competition

As we mentioned above, you actually want to find a location that has some competition. This indicates that your chosen area can support a business like yours. Just keep in mind that you can face two kinds of competitors: direct and indirect.

Direct Competitors

Direct competitors are those that are competing for the same coffee dollar that you're going after. This means other coffee and tea shops.

Go through the Yellow Pages and make a list of direct competitors in your area. Then hit the pavement and visit these shops, asking yourself these questions:

 ◆ What are the competition's strengths? Do they have excellent customer service, superior product, great prices, a wonderful location?

 ◆ What can you do in your own business concept to combat these advantages?

 ◆ What are the competition's weaknesses? Do they have surly baristas, ugly décor, bad coffee, a location that requires customers to go through an obstacle course to reach it?

 ◆ What can you do in your own business concept to take advantage of these disadvantages?

Every business has a weakness, no matter how profitable it is or how popular it seems. Don't be afraid to take on one of the big league coffee chains if you can provide customers with a better retail experience, whether in terms of atmosphere, taste, price, or convenience.

Indirect Competitors

Indirect competitors are those who are competing for the same general food and beverage dollar, such as donut shops, bakeries, and sandwich shops. Find the indirect competitors in your area and ask yourself the same questions that you asked about your direct competitors above.

Don't forget that these competitors can actually be your customers in some cases. Perhaps you can sell fresh-roasted beans at wholesale prices to a sandwich shop. If a local bakery doesn't serve coffee, or if the coffee it does serve is less than ideal, approach the owner with an offer to provide coffee for his business. Perhaps you can even work out a co-marketing agreement in which he sells your coffee and you feature his pastries.

If you focus solely on the individual customer, thus selling only one cup of coffee at a time, you'll miss opportunities to sell lots of coffee in places you never would have thought possible.

Dealing with the Landlord

Once again, we wish renting a business space was like renting an apartment, with nothing but a simple application to fill out. If your references check out and you haven't actually destroyed any of your former dwellings, you're in, as they say, like Flint.

But a business landlord has a lot more to think about than an apartment landlord. An apartment landlord wants to make sure that you'll take good care of the apartment and pay your rent on time. A business landlord wants to know that, too, but he also needs to make sure that your business will benefit the other tenants in his building, that he'll recoup any money he gives you for improvements, and that your business won't fail, leaving him to find another tenant *tout de suite*.

The Proposal

Though it's not required, a proposal will answer the landlord's burning questions and also help you stand out from the other businesses that want to rent the space. In your proposal, you'll want to address:

- The business concept.
- What the business will look like. For this section, you can include photos and illustrations.

- How your business will add to the value of the site and to the other tenants.

- What types of customers you plan to attract.

- What products and services you'll be offering. For this, you can include a copy of your planned menu with products, services, descriptions, illustrations, and prices.

Beans of Wisdom

Don't go to too much effort reinventing the wheel. You can lift much of the information you need for your proposal straight from your business plan.

Dropping off or presenting your proposal to the landlord is a great opportunity to make a positive impression. Dress to impress, and don't press the landlord for an immediate answer. If he has any doubts whatsoever, he'll be likely to answer with a big, fat no. Instead, give him a chance to internalize all the information you've offered, and get back to him at a later date.

Negotiating the Lease

Congratulations! You've found the perfect place, and the landlord is interested in negotiating a lease with you.

Hand the landlord a list of things you'd like him to supply you, such as Common Area Maintenance waivers, Tenant Improvement Allowances, free rent for the first month (or few months), and so on. The landlord will likely cross off some of the requests, but not all of them, leaving you both happy.

Keep in mind these negotiation tips to make sure you and the landlord both get the best deal:

- Never be the one to offer to split the difference; wait until the landlord offers, and then do so.

- Never negotiate by telephone; it's easier to communicate in person.

- Don't haggle too much; a frustrated landlord may just walk away.

- Get everything in writing, right now.

- Make sure you have enough time to negotiate; if you're in a rush, you may not get the best deal. Never reveal any deadlines you may have.

- If you make a concession, ask the landlord to make one, too.

- Keep an open mind. If the landlord can't offer something you want, maybe he can offer something you'll like just as much that you hadn't thought of before.

- If this is your first business, don't be surprised if the landlord asks for a personal guarantee.

- Make sure the lease is assumable in case you decide to, or need to, sell the business.

Remember that lawyer we suggested you hire in Chapter 5? Well, bring her back into the picture, because she can help you understand and negotiate the lease.

The Least You Need to Know

- When choosing a location, you need to keep many criteria in mind, such as rent, visibility, convenience, signage laws, and electric capacity.

- You don't want a location that has no competitors nearby; on the contrary, you want to know that your chosen area can support a business like yours.

- Shopping malls are not the best place to start a coffee shop; strip malls, office buildings, storefront sites, and areas within other businesses are much better locations.

- Though it's not required, creating a proposal to present to your potential landlord can help you seal the deal.

- Hone your negotiation skills; you may be able to get your landlord to agree to pay for bonuses like improvements or give you free rent while you build or improve your location.

Part 3

Setting Up Shop

Once you have a plan, you need to act on it: building the counters and shelves, arranging the tables and chairs, and buying the equipment that will make your drinks—that is, your *dreams*—come true. This part explains the principles you should keep in mind while bringing a two-dimensional plan into three-dimensional life.

No matter how enthusiastic you might be, though, you can't do it alone. You'll need a well-trained crew to handle all the business you can expect, and we'll cover how to hire, train, and (should the situation arise) fire employees.

Chapter 8

Planning Your Décor

In This Chapter

- ◆ Like it or not, you have style
- ◆ The two most important design decrees
- ◆ Through the looking glass
- ◆ Piecing together the design puzzle

Every business, whether the owner has thought about it or not, has a style, a look that tells first-time customers and passers-by what to expect when they come through the doors. The style might not be obvious or important to customers, but it's there all the same, shaping the image of the business in their minds.

Let's look at a couple of examples: Wal-Mart presents a no-frills style that embodies its low-cost approach. Its buildings are supremely uninteresting, saying to customers, "We don't spend any more than we have to on our look, and you can expect the same when you shop here."

The restaurant chain Bugaboo Creek uses thick wood planks for its walls and ceilings and animated animal heads and fake trees for decoration, presenting customers with a hearty, backwoods feel that complements the huge meal portions. The manly-man nature of the restaurant is evident even in the small details. Buttering bread isn't normally a task for tough guys, but the impressively wide knives on hand—knives that look capable of skinning a buffalo—make it tough and cool.

We can't tell you what style to choose—well, we could, but you might not be a fan of the sixteenth century Azuchi-Momoyama Period in Japan—but we can advise you on what to avoid and what to keep in mind as you design your dream domain.

Design Principles

To begin with, let's assume that you want to create a style rather than randomly assemble whatever's closest to hand. You could, of course, buy a half-dozen non-matching couches and tables at Goodwill, throw velvet Elvis paintings on the walls, and call it a day. For some coffee bar owners, adopting a haphazard (and dirt cheap) style will be completely satisfying—and this style might be perfect for the market of college students and night owls they're trying to attract.

For the rest of us, however, we need to take more care with our choices because we want customers to view our shop in a certain light. We want our business to be comforting, inviting, energizing, efficient, or any of a hundred other adjectives. With that goal in mind, let's cover a few design basics before we get down to the details.

"So I Shouldn't Choose the Suede Seat Covers?"

If you're torn between two or more choices, pick the one that's easiest to clean. You might not realize it now, but you're going to do a lot of cleaning in the months and years ahead. You'll clean tables, chairs, floors, windows, espresso machines, bathrooms, counters, garbage cans, napkin holders, and much, much more.

> **Beans of Wisdom**
>
> Ask manufacturers for sample fabrics, tiles, and whatever other design elements you're considering, and then run these samples through a gantlet of spilled drinks, mashed-in chocolate cookie crumbs, and concentrated floor cleaner to find out which items resist stains best.

Your business serves things to eat and drink, after all, and if the tables, chairs, floors, and so forth aren't clean, customers are unlikely to stick around to find out if the food and drinks are equally unclean.

Your design decisions will directly impact how easy or hard it is to keep your coffee bar clean and inviting. Pick a funky textured surface for tables, and you'll need more elbow grease to keep them spotless.

The more decorations you place on the walls, the more dusting and wiping down you need to add to the cleaning schedule.

Buying for Tomorrow, Today

Unless you plan to serve ten million customers the first year and retire, you need to think about how the design you choose in the present will affect the decisions you can make in the future.

If, for example, you choose an unusual table design, how easy will it be to find replacements should a table fall apart or you move to a bigger location? Can you buy this table from more than one supplier so you're not stuck if the original supplier goes out of business?

You might like the look of a particular kind of mug, but the edges chip easily or the special glaze requires that the mugs be hand-washed. Does the coolness of the design outweigh the potential replacement costs in forthcoming years or the added cost of labor needed to wash the mugs?

Outside Looking In

Everyone knows that first appearances can be deceiving—and yet we judge people, places, and things on first appearances just the same.

Prospective customers will approach your coffee bar the same way. If the outside of the shop doesn't welcome them, they'll never experience your rich-tasting coffee or the comfy lounge chairs you spent so much time looking for. They lose, you lose—everybody loses but your competition!

With this thought in mind, approach your location from every possible direction and consider what you can do to make your shop more inviting.

Sign of the Times

If you followed our advice in Chapter 7, you've investigated the town's signage laws and know how many signs you can put up in which sizes.

Laws give only a starting point, of course. Ask yourself questions to determine what you really need for signage. How will customers approach your business? If they drive down a one-way street, perhaps you can tilt your largest sign so that it faces traffic.

If you have a mix of auto and foot traffic, you want to place a sign in the window at a height so that both pedestrians and auto passengers can see it. You can also consider neon "open" signs or custom boxed signs that are lit from within.

Does your town allow sandwich boards on sidewalks? If so, you can advertise daily specials or simply tell the world you're open for business.

Signs are all about being visible, so be sure to include your logo on the sign to give customers a visual hook. Use the same lettering style on your sign that you plan to use in the rest of your marketing materials, and choose a color scheme that can easily be read from a distance.

Window Dressing

While you want signs in windows so that passers-by can learn about your business, you don't want to cover up every inch of glass with come-ons and pitches. By letting people see into your shop, you're inviting them in and giving them a taste of what you have to offer.

Walk by the windows and see what parts of the store are visible from the outside. Make sure that whatever you put in those locations—a stage for musicians, comfy chairs, nude models—will draw customers in. Restaurants do this by always filling the tables by the windows first. They seem to be saying, "See, other people eat here—why not you?"

> **Beans of Wisdom**
>
> Clean windows show customers that a business takes care of its surroundings. While you can easily hire a window washer to come by once or twice a week, you (or an employee) can clean the windows yourself just as easily with nothing more than a squeegee, a lint-free cloth, and a bucket of soapy water.

Dining Room Design

Once customers pass through the doors, what will they see? The counter with your smiling face behind it? Precisely arranged rows of tables and chairs? A potted plant that blocks off a quarter of the room?

Again, the details of the room will depend on the style you want to present: solid wood tables that call to mind home comfort, or smaller, metal and plastic tables that customers can push together; a drink bar where customers can watch your employees do their magic, a refrigerated dessert cabinet that customers can eye while waiting for drinks, or both; wallpaper, wainscoting, or a simple paint job.

Whatever you choose, keep in mind the need for easy cleaning and long-term use. This means, for example, that carpets are definitely out since spills are a sure thing in a liquid-heavy environment. Hardwood floors are a good choice, but a ceramic tile floor is your best bet for quick clean-ups and a long lifespan.

Pull Up a Chair

Depending on the space available, you'll want to provide customers with a mix of tables that accommodate two, four, and sometimes six customers. You might place raised bar tables in one area, and chairs with small side tables in another.

Sit in the chairs and test them for comfort. Do they have enough back support? Will customers stick around long enough to order a second cup, or will they be calling for a stretcher instead?

Whatever furniture you choose, know that the Americans with Disabilities Act requires restaurants to make at least five percent of their tables accessible. By law, the tops of these tables must be between 28 and 34 inches above the ground with a minimum of 27 inches of clearance for legs and knees. Similarly, at least one section of the serving counter must be no higher than 34 inches.

To satisfy both the easy-clean and long-life provisos at the beginning of the chapter, make sure the legs of both the tables and chairs are padded so they don't scratch the floor. More importantly, laminate the tables (and counters) so they don't expand, contract, or absorb stains.

> **Beans of Wisdom**
>
> For more guidance on how to make your coffee bar accessible to everyone, you can read the entire Americans with Disabilities Act online (http://www.usdoj. gov/crt/ada/smbusgd.pdf) or your lawyer can advise you on particular sections relevant to your business.

Climb the Walls

Walls usually aren't too exciting. They hold up the ceiling—for which we are ever thankful—but no one's going to write an epic poem memorializing that feat. That's okay—you don't want your walls to be too colorful and eye-grabbing. They're merely the backdrop against which business is conducted and drinks are drunk.

When it comes to dressing your walls, wallpaper can be a fine choice if you install a chair guard in all seating areas to minimize damage and you keep an adequate supply of replacement rolls on-hand (for the damage that will inevitably occur).

To avoid the time and cost of replacing wallpaper, you might opt for an old-fashioned paint job or perhaps a faux finish to add depth to your walls. Decorate with framed artwork or posters that explain the coffee-roasting process—whatever it takes to match the mood you want to create.

Another possibility is to install a shelving unit (or slotted wallboard that holds brackets and shelves) so that you can show off retail wares, such as French presses, teapots, or bags of whole roasted beans. We'll cover retail possibilities in more detail in Chapter 15.

Creating Ambiance: Lights, Color, Action!

With the right approach, your coffee bar will be more than just a place to grab a cup of joe to go. Think about how you can personalize all the details of a business that might normally go unnoticed.

At the end of Chapter 6, we already discussed colors and the associations attached with each of them. Aside from your logo, perhaps you can add color to the edges or tops of tables, around doorframes, in pictures and artwork on the walls, or on the aprons employees wear at work.

A good design principle is to use three colors, with 70 percent of the space being one color, 20 percent a second color, and the final 10 percent reserved for the third color. Working within this plan keeps a space from having a monotonous checkerboard look with colors alternating regularly or from having a room dominated entirely by one color.

Aside from color, let's look at other factors that can add to (or subtract from) the environment you're trying to build.

Tunes in the Room

When you think about setting a mood, whether romantic, festive, or trendy, you often think in terms of music. The right tunes can go a long way towards cementing the style you want, and you can go all out with an installed multi-speaker system or as low budget as a boom box and your personal collection of CDs.

Two great sources of music are Internet radio stations and Muzak (yes, the elevator music people). Thousands of Internet radio stations exist, many of them highly specialized in the type of music they play. Want to stick with alternative country, early twentieth century blues, or lounge-style electronica? No problem.

Although most people don't know it, Muzak produces far more than watered-down classical tunes. The company offers a subscription service that provides targeted programs of music similar to today's Internet radio stations but available from one source.

Whatever music set-up you decide on, remember that the goal is to make customers feel welcome. Keep the volume low enough that they can talk, study, and place orders.

Hit the Lights

If you've ever worked for a long period of time under fluorescent lights, then you already know that you should avoid using them—unless, of course, you think customers want a side dish of headache with their drink.

Naturally you'd prefer to use natural light (a.k.a., the sun) to set your shop aglow, but not every location comes blessed with large windows. Besides, natural light won't do much for you in winter months or during the late-night "hanging out" hours. To supplement whatever natural light you have, choose comfortable, soft lighting that allows patrons to read for hours without eyestrain.

If you install a drop-ceiling to cover wires or avoid heating a large unused space overhead, you'll likely want to install light fixtures at the same time so you can hide the wiring. Don't forget that lighting can be more than merely functional; we've run across many eating establishments that use hanging lights with fancy glass sconces or elaborate painted paper shades, conveying style through objects normally dismissed as mundane.

Clear the Air

Ideally, customers will enter your shop, breathe deeply the aroma of heated cinnamon rolls or your latest bean blend, and exclaim, "Man, that smells good!"

To keep those smells fresh and at the forefront of your customers' noses, ask employees to forgo perfumes and colognes that might compete with the smell of your goods. (You'll have the added benefit of avoiding possible allergic reactions from sensitive customers.)

Contents May Be Hot

Smoking in eateries and coffee bars is now forbidden in many states, eliminating a major source of nasal obstruction. If smoking isn't taboo in your town, you need to decide whether customers can light up after their lattés or whether the practice will drive off more people than it will attract.

Cue the Supporting Actors

You've set the stage and have the props in place; now what about the actors? Many coffee bar owners are comfortable allowing their employees to wear whatever they want. After all, coffee bars are meant to be relaxing, right?

While there's nothing wrong with that attitude, imagine if you did require employees to wear some type of uniform, whether something as simple as black pants, a white shirt, and an apron, or a more elaborate custom-designed outfit.

To begin with, customers would always know who to approach with questions or orders, whether your employees are behind the bar or cleaning tables. The bigger effect, however, might be on the employees themselves. By requiring them to wear uniforms, you enforce a more professional standard and remind them that they're in the shop to serve others, not to goof off.

How far you want to go with a uniform will depend on your budget and your desire to create a unified look. Employees can be expected to provide their own black pants and white shirts, for example, whereas you would have to spring for customized T-shirts that bear your coffee bar's logo.

Aprons are a worthwhile expense, both to provide employees with a visual hook that customers can easily recognize and to protect them from spills while working. You can have the shop's logo embroidered or silk-screened onto the aprons, or you can simply adorn the aprons with homemade buttons. Button machines are fairly inexpensive, allowing you to create pins for your employees.

The Least You Need to Know

♦ Whether you intend to create a style or not, you will have one—so don't leave it up to chance. Think about how you want customers to see your store, then make it happen.

♦ Before purchasing anything, ask yourself two questions: how easy is it to clean, and can I buy it again in the future?

♦ The outside of your shop is your most important advertisement, so keep it neat and clean while still telling potential customers what's inside.

♦ Think in terms of style as well as functionality. Everything in your coffee bar contributes to your overall image.

Equipping the Shop

In This Chapter

◆ Hardware, hard choices

◆ What your shop needs now

◆ How to choose a supplier

◆ Buy or borrow: which is better?

Turning your coffee bar into a house of style will create an environment that customers will appreciate each time they stop by—but they're not likely to enter more than once if you lack the equipment needed to put cups in their hands and coffee in their bellies.

Although you could make do with an old Mr. Coffee and mugs purchased from the Salvation Army, we suggest putting a wee bit more time and thought into how you equip your surroundings. Operating a modern coffee bar requires a wide variety of machines and tools to satisfy every customer's desires.

What You Can't Live Without

Some equipment and furnishings are more essential than others. Floors, for example, are extremely useful in keeping all your stuff from falling to the center of the earth. While the exact list of equipment you need will vary depending on which food and drinks you serve (topics we'll cover in Chapters 12 through 15), some pieces of equipment are absolute must-haves.

As you shop for the items in this chapter, be sure to consider the following:

- **Electrical requirements** Espresso machines, for instance, can require 115, 220, or 240 volts, and high-volume, high-power dishwashers might also need more juice than the 110 volts available from a standard outlet. You'll need to consider these electrical requirements when you design the kitchen and create counter space (a topic we'll cover in Chapter 10).

Contents May Be Hot

Make sure that all warranties cover retail or business use of the equipment. If you find out after the machine breaks down that the warranty covers only household use, you might be stuck shelling out for a new machine.

- **Warranties and service plans** Does the retailer or wholesaler who sells the equipment also service it, or will you have to ship the equipment away for service? Can the retailer recommend local shops that can help you out in a crisis? (Not that your machine will ever desert you in a time of need, we say with fingers crossed while knocking on wood.)

- **Color, design, and cost** With that pesky style issue now under control, you need to consider the look of the equipment in addition to whether it gets the job done and fits your budget.

Coffee-Brewing System

Call us crazy, but before you can sell coffee, you have to make it. And since you hope to make a living doing so, you'll probably need something with a bit more oomph than a single 12-cup machine.

You could go the old-fashioned route and buy two or three brewers with hot plates that hold multiple glass carafes. This set-up is still common in convenience stores, all-night diners, and other locations that don't rely on coffee sales for their main source of income. Coffee made this way tastes fine, but the air contact and constant heat ages the coffee quickly, leading to a lot of waste on slower-selling decaffeinated and flavored coffees.

A better choice is a system that brews directly into airtight thermal carafes. Coffee brewed this way retains its original flavor for up to three hours, which reduces both waste and labor costs (since an employee won't have to remake specialized coffees every hour or so).

Brewing systems are either in-line—that is, hooked directly into the plumbing system so they can draw water as needed—or pour-over, which works exactly like it sounds. Choose between the two options based upon, first, your potential remodeling costs if you need to run water lines to accommodate an in-line system, and second, your expected level of sales. Pour-over systems are more hands-on, so if you're setting up in a high-volume location, you might prefer in-line.

You'll want to purchase at least twice as many carafes as the number of coffee types you plan to offer each day. If, for instance, you'll serve a medium roast, a dark roast, a special blend, and a flavored coffee each day, purchase at least eight carafes so that you can brew up a second batch before the first carafe runs dry.

> **Beans of Wisdom**
>
> Label the carafes permanently so you always put the same type of coffee in them. This is especially important for flavored coffees; the flavor tends to remain in the carafe no matter how much you clean. Stick regular coffee in a flavored carafe and your customers are sure to taste the difference—and not in a good way!

Espresso Machine

You have two major choices when purchasing an espresso machine—how many *groups* the machine handles, and how *automatic* it is.

Espresso machines typically come in two-, three-, and four-group models, which means the machine can make two, three, or four servings of espresso at one time. Choose the number of groups based on your budget and expected sales volume.

The machines also vary in how much attention they need while making espresso. Manual espresso machines require you to heat the water separately, then squeeze the water through the coffee by pulling down on a lever—and this is where we get the phrase "pulling a shot." Unless you're trying to build a strong upper body, we suggest passing on these machines, as the quality of the espresso will vary from shot to shot.

Semi-automatic machines take the hard labor out of the process. You push a button to both start and stop the flow of water through the grounds, which makes for reliable water pressure while letting you control the extraction time. This is the most common type of machine used in specialty coffee shops. It will provide the best espresso once you learn how to use it correctly.

Fully automatic machines require only one button push as both the water pressure and the extraction time are regulated. These machines generally come with buttons for single espresso, double espresso, short espresso, and so on, so you can pick the serving to match the order. Restaurants that don't hang their reputation on the quality of their espresso tend to favor these machines because they're easiest to operate.

Super-automatic machines grind the beans, pump the water, and (in some cases) clean themselves. This sounds like everything you need, but you probably don't need to purchase a machine this elaborate. A semi-automatic machine should be perfect for your shop.

The espresso machine will come with at least one steaming wand and a hot water tap. We'll tell you how to shoot the shots in Chapter 13.

> **Instant Facts**
>
> Most espresso machines sold in the United States are Italian, which makes sense since espresso originated there. Contrary to Italian taste, however, Americans prefer to use steamed milk in nearly all espresso drinks, which means that your steam wands and valves will require more maintenance than those of an Italian café owner.

Grinder

To make superb coffee, you need to grind the beans in-house since they lose their flavor quickly after being chopped up. A *batch grinder* holds exactly the right amount of beans to make one pot of coffee—but if you opt for a thermal carafe brewing system, you need to verify that a batch grinder will work for you.

As with the coffee carafes, you should purchase two grinders so that you can reserve one solely for use with flavored coffees. What's more, espresso grinders grind the beans much finer than coffee grinders, so you might need yet another grinder, depending on the model you choose.

Scale

If you sell coffee beans—whether roasted or green—you'll absolutely need a scale, one labeled "for legal tender" so there's no question about proper measurements and one shaped so that you can easily pour beans into the bag for delivery.

Even if you don't sell green beans, a scale is still vital for measuring beans before you grind them. For most people, repetition is boring; for great coffee, repetition is the key to success.

Refrigerator/Cooler

You need at least one refrigerator up front to hold the milk and cream you'll use while making drinks. If you plan to offer food, you might need a larger fridge to hold meat and sandwich fixings that aren't being kept in the prep area.

If you sell soda and other bottled drinks, you must decide whether to purchase a second cooler to place near the counter so that customers can pick out their own drinks, or use one refrigerator for both purposes. The first option costs more, yet encourages spur-of-the-moment sales since the sweet, refreshing drinks are right in front of your customers. The second option is better for tight budgets or tight operating quarters.

> **Beans of Wisdom**
>
> All equipment you purchase for the coffee bar should bear an NSF label to show that the design was inspected and met the standards of the National Sanitation Foundation. For more information on NSF standards, visit http://www.nsf.org.

Food Display Case

Any business that sells coffee should also sell tasty accessories, such as cannolis, chocolate-chip cookies, or cheesecake. Your choice of foods for sale will determine what type of display case you need.

By sticking with biscotti, brownies, cookies, and other room-temperature–safe goodies, you can use countertop displays or plates covered with glass domes. For cheesecakes and pies, you must use a refrigerated display case, preferably one that circulates air to avoid condensation inside the case. In general, stick with glass over plastic, as glass is more scratch-resistant and holds up better over time.

Dishwasher

You'll use paper cups for to-go orders, but unless the shop is little more than a drive-thru window, you'll have plenty of plates, mugs, glasses, and other dishes and silverware to clean. Heck, the number of spoons you'll use behind the counter might be enough to merit a dishwasher.

You can try to get away with an employee in rubber gloves and an apron, but that's hardly cost-effective. Invest in a high-temperature, fast-running automatic dishwasher that can handle your needs. Choose high-temperature over low because such machines have a shorter drying cycle, use less water, and remove grease and lipstick without resorting to chemicals.

An automatic dishwasher is yet another item that needs access to water lines, drainage, and (in some cases) high-voltage wiring, but the benefits are worth the trouble.

Cash Register

Sure, you *could* run a business with a cigar box and a calculator, but the harm done to your business would cost far more than the price of a good cash register.

In addition to automatically determining sales tax and showing the proper amount of change a customer receives, electronic cash registers allow you to print out data that divides sales into categories you determine. Want to know how many iced coffees you sold in July? How sales of mochaccinos compare to those of cappuccinos? Whether your brownie inventory matches the number of sales? What sales were between 11 and 11:30 A.M.? The sales tape will tell you everything you want to know.

What's more, once you program it, the cash register will charge (or not charge) sales tax as appropriate and let you know how much to forward to the state tax bureau. Many cash registers can also be used as a time clock, which makes it easy for employees to punch in and out and easy for you to determine who's owed what.

The Best of What's Left

While certain types of equipment are essential for anyone entering the coffee business, what and where you sell will also determine the particular layout of your counters. We'll cover foods and drinks you should consider selling in more detail in Part 4, but for now think about how these machines might blend in with—or break—your budget.

Water Treatment

The bulk of your sales will be coffee and espresso, and the bulk of coffee and espresso is the water used to make the drinks. While coffee's flavor comes from the essences extracted from the beans, that flavor can be destroyed if you make the drinks with bad-tasting water. To counteract water woes, consider using a water filtration system that uses a paper and carbon filter to screen out foul-tasting and odor-carrying particles.

"Hard" water—that is, water with a high mineral content—is another concern for coffee bar owners because as the water passes through your espresso machine, it will leave mineral deposits that clog the pipes.

You can call the town's water department to ask whether you need to be concerned about hard water wrecking your machines. If so, you might consider attaching a water softener, either one with disposable cartridges or a rechargeable device, to the water intake on your espresso machine.

Smoothie Machines

The range of smoothies you can offer is limited only by your imagination—and, of course, the sensitivity of your customers' palates. Blended frozen coffee drinks are a natural choice for a coffee bar, especially if you're located in a part of the country where the sidewalks sizzle come summertime.

If you have room to set up a second smoothie machine, you could offer fruit smoothies to give caffeine-fearing customers another choice on the menu, or opt for a juice machine to create vitamin-packed beverages.

Blenders

Another cool option you can offer customers are milkshakes, both caffeinated coffee-flavored ones and the more traditional ice cream kind. Be aware that some miracle milkshake makers can cost up to $200, but you can probably make do with a blender in the low double digits, since milkshakes will comprise only a small fraction of your business.

Contents May Be Hot

If you go low-budget on a blender, avoid adding chunks of ice or large ice cubes to blenders whenever possible. Ice can destroy inexpensive blenders quickly.

Ovens, Microwaves, and Grills

To capture the crowd that just wants to grab a drink on the run, you might consider selling more substantial food than mere biscotti, such as sandwiches and wraps.

Depending on how heavily you want to get involved in food preparation, you'll have to consider purchasing a toaster oven (for mini pizzas or grinders), a grill (for grilled cheese and other toasted sandwiches), or a microwave (to melt cheese and heat deli meats). Microwaves, toaster ovens, and grills don't need much space and require nothing in the way of electricity beyond a standard outlet.

Ovens naturally require a more intense dedication of space, not to mention access to natural gas or propane. You might also need an additional license from the city waste department if you plan to pour grease from cooking down the drain. Consider these drawbacks carefully before jumping into this side of the food biz. (We'll lay down the legal nitty-gritty about food sales in Chapter 15.)

Finding Suppliers

While you could enter a department store and purchase an espresso machine off the shelves, that's probably not the best way to equip your store. For one thing, these machines aren't made to handle the high volume you're going to demand of them. Two to three shots a day, yes; two to three hundred, not really.

Of greater concern is the level of support that the manufacturer of this equipment can offer you. If your coffee machine breaks down at home, you simply do without until you can go to the store and buy a new one. If the coffee-brewing system that pumps the lifeblood of your business breaks down, you need a replacement and you need it now.

When you start talking with equipment suppliers, keep the following in mind:

◆ **Evaluate the supplier from the first "hello."** Everything the supplier does tells you about the level of service you can expect. Does the supplier answer the phone in a courteous and professional manner? Does he answer politely, even when you're only calling to ask questions, or does he bark, "Call me when you're ready to buy," and hang up? Does he return your phone message after an hour—or a week?

◆ **Insist on a demonstration.** Whether you meet with a supplier in a retail location or at a showroom, try out the machines so that you can see how each one handles. Have him demonstrate the different features and explain why they'll benefit you. Ask whether your employees can receive training directly from his company instead of second-hand through you.

- **Ask for references and call them.** Any supplier with a good track record will have satisfied customers he can offer for references. Don't just take him on his word, though. Call these folks up and find out how the supplier has treated them throughout their relationship, especially in emergency situations.

- **Remember that price is only part of the picture.** Suppliers who boast of nothing more than low, low prices usually have nothing more to offer. While the thought of saving a few—or a few hundred—dollars might be enticing, don't think of this purchase as a one-shot deal.

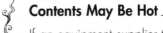

Contents May Be Hot

If an equipment supplier tries to pressure you into making a deal, even going so far as to offer a special discount if you sign that instant, that's a sure sign of someone to avoid. They're clearly more concerned with their bottom line than yours.

Aside from the need for servicing and maintenance, you want to think of yourself as partnering with the supplier to build a stronger company. If you move to a bigger location or want to open a second store at some point, your supplier will be ready to help you upgrade equipment or otherwise support the expansion. When you win, he wins, too, and a sole focus on low prices usually undermines this relationship.

Buying, Leasing, or Renting?

For some equipment, the decision to rent or buy is obvious. After all, paying interest on a $50-100 scale doesn't make much financial sense. (You could ask your accountant to verify this, but that would also set you back a few clams you didn't need to spend.)

Costlier purchases, such as a decent-sized refrigerator or a top-of-the-line espresso machine, run into the four figures, and that might be hard to cough up all at once. You can cover these costs in a few different ways:

- **Borrow funds for all equipment purchases.** In Chapter 4, which covered how to create a business plan, we included equipment among your initial costs. If you've followed this example, then you should have the funds for equipment already on hand.

- **Take out individual loans with equipment vendors.** Vendors may or may not be as competitive as banks and other financial institutions when it comes to setting interest rates for loans. We've seen cases where equipment vendors charge

0 percent interest over the first 12 months of the loan, and other cases where the interest rates would make you grow pale and dizzy.

◆ **Find vendors that offer free equipment.** Some food and drink vendors will provide free equipment, but naturally there are strings attached, starting with the requirement that you carry that vendor's products, usually on an exclusive basis, and post the vendor's brand on the equipment and possibly the outside of the store.

The vendor might also set "sales goals" that require you to purchase a minimum amount of product every sales period. If you don't sell enough, say, bottled iced tea to meet the quota, tough beans: your contract says you have to buy it anyway. The contract will also require you to stick with the vendor for a certain number of months. Combined with the purchasing requirements, this nets the vendor a certain amount of money, thus paying for the "free" equipment he provided.

◆ **Lease equipment instead of buying it outright.** No one ever said that you had to shell out for equipment all at once. You could decide to lease certain items on a month-to-month basis, which would almost definitely be cheaper than the monthly cost of repaying a loan. At the end of the lease period, you will typically have the option to buy the equipment at fair market value or for a token $1 payment.

While leasing is cheaper on a monthly basis compared to a loan, the cost is generally higher in the long run because—as with the debate between apartment rentals and home ownership—if you don't buy, you'll have spent a lot of money with nothing permanent to show for it. And if you do buy, you'll pay more than you would have by buying the equipment up front.

Renting equipment might make sense, though, if you're unsure how large a cooler you need or whether you need a two- or three-group espresso machine. If you can test out this equipment and see whether it meets your needs, it might be worth the added expense of a month or two's rent on top of the price of the equipment itself.

The Least You Need to Know

- Make sure that any equipment you purchase is labeled for retail or business use.

- Equipment is only as good as the warranty behind it. Talk with a vendor's current customers to find out whether the support and emergency service he provides matches the claims he makes.

- Make a list of specialized equipment needs (electricity, water, gas) while you're shopping, because you'll need to lay out the kitchen to meet these requirements.

- You have more choices when purchasing equipment than cash, check, or charge. Talk with vendors about financing and see what kind of deals they can offer.

Chapter 10

Kitchen and Restroom Layout and Design

In This Chapter

- ◆ Show customers where to go
- ◆ Speed and efficiency: your two design goals
- ◆ Balancing storage and style
- ◆ Lessons for the loo

Ideally, customers at your coffee bar will be able to enjoy their drinks and snacks and relax in an inviting environment in the company of friends. When designing your dining room, which we talked a bit about in Chapter 8, this means focusing on style and comfort.

Style and comfort are also important when you design the kitchen and counter areas, but here comfort has a somewhat different meaning that won't be satisfied by plush chairs.

No, in this case, comfort means the ability to know how to order and where to pay. Customers hate having to guess where the line ends or how to pick up their drinks. If you do a good job laying out the kitchen, you can keep the line of customers flowing smoothly and put their minds at ease.

The same goal applies to the space behind the counter as well. Your employees should be able to work around each other with ease so that they can serve customers quickly and safely.

Carving Up the Counter Space

Whatever the size of your shop, most of the action—both monetarily and physically—will take place in an area roughly 50 square feet in size: the counter and the space on both sides of it. Customers order goods and employees make them. If you design the counter well, this system will flow smoothly and make everyone happy.

For the Customer

From the customer's point of view, three things happen at the counter: he orders a drink, he pays for the drink, and he picks it up.

You want to make this process flow as smoothly as possible, which means dividing the counter into clear, distinct regions. Pick one end of the counter to be the place to order, preferably the end nearest the door since that's where customers will naturally drift, and deliver the goods at the other end of the counter.

Customers at this part of the counter, as well as those in line, should be able to see the entire menu from this location. If they have to move back and forth along the counter to see the menu, they'll take longer to order and disrupt the flow of business. They'll also make it more difficult for arriving customers to see where the line is. Chaos ensues!

> **Beans of Wisdom**
>
> As with the tables and chairs in your business, the Americans with Disabilities Act requires that your counter be accessible to all. In particular, this means making a portion of the main counter between 28 and 34 inches high and at least 60 inches long. The counter where customers pick up food must be similarly accessible.

The cash register can be located at this same spot or a bit further down the counter. Again, the idea is to keep customers moving, so if one customer moves to the side to pay, the next customer can place her order, depending on how many employees are working.

When customers order, tell them where to wait for their goods (thus encouraging them to slide down the counter) or invite them to sit and you'll bring their order to them.

For You

Although you want customers to find their way around the counter quickly, you also want to use this space to sell goods. You can achieve this in a number of different ways:

- **Feature the food.** Use food display cases, which we describe in Chapter 9, to display cookies and other nonrefrigerated goods on the counter. With different-sized cases, you can rearrange them often to make the choice of offerings look fresh each day. Having many cases also allows you to easily adjust the goods you offer based on sales. Caramel Brownies not selling? Wash out the case and try Rocky Road Brownies instead.

  You should also arrange beverage coolers and refrigerated display cases so that customers pass them as they approach the counter. Customers won't automatically buy everything they see, but if they never see goodies—or see them only after ordering—you probably won't get the sales you expected.

- **Set out samples.** Chop up cookies and coffee cakes into small portions and offer a plate of samples where customers place their orders. Sure, they know you're doing this to boost sales—not out of the goodness of your heart—but sometimes the samples taste so good, they happily succumb to your mercantile desires.

Contents May Be Hot

Don't try to pass off day-old goods as samples. If what your customer tastes isn't the very best you have to offer, you risk turning away future sales.

- **Sell other services.** Do you offer classes on how to roast coffee beans? Will you create a custom blend for a wedding present or anniversary gift? Tell customers about these services by placing flyers in a small counter display. Such displays are good for hiding the ugly backsides of cash registers where other displays won't fit.

Whatever you place on the counter, though, be sure to leave space where the customer orders, pays, and picks up the goods. Don't make them guess. Design the counter so they know where to go.

Laying Out the Prep Area

Now let's look at the space behind the counter. You and your employees will spend most of your working hours in this space, which makes it imperative that the space be well-organized. You don't want to have to say "excuse me" every time you turn around because you bump into someone.

What's more, the space needs to facilitate speed and efficiency so that customers get their drinks quickly. The slower your delivery time, the lower your sales volume in any given time period.

What's Front and Center

The most important question to start with is also the easiest to answer: Where do you place the espresso machine? On the main counter between where customers order and pick up drinks.

Placing the espresso machine here eases the flow of customers down the counter, while allowing the employee working the machine to hear orders as they're placed and start working on the drinks.

Never place the espresso machine on the back counter because employees must then turn their backs on customers to make drinks. Not to mention, of course, that customers would see exactly what goes on in the making of an espresso. (We're not worried about protecting trade secrets here—only that the process is messy and will diminish the romance of the finished product.)

Beans of Wisdom

If you use paper cups, use a magic marker to label the cup with the customer's name. In addition to helping your employee place the drink in the hands of the proper owner, this builds a more personal relationship with customers. Soon you'll remember their names *and* their favorite drinks!

Along the same lines, you want to place the coffee carafes on the front counter so that employees can dish out the drink and hand it directly to the customer. The shelf holding the carafes might need to be lower than the counter so that employees and customers can see each other eye to eye.

Keep espresso cups, coffee mugs, and saucers close at hand so employees don't even need to take a step while they prepare the drinks.

Milk, cream, sugar, and other coffee condiments should be placed either on the main counter past where customers pick up drinks or at a separate station nearby. Whichever you choose, make this area wide enough so that more than one customer can use it at once. Place a garbage can inside the counter with a hole over it, so customers can dispose of their stirring sticks and teabags without having to touch or see a garbage can.

What's on the Back Counter

Once you know where to place the espresso machine, you need to find a spot for the coffee-brewing system, grinder, and scales. Unlike the espresso machine, the brewing system can go on the back counter since employees won't be attending to specific customers while using it. The brewing system requires special electrical and plumbing hook-ups, so keep that in mind when deciding where to place it.

Blenders, smoothie machines, microwave ovens, grills, and other food and drink preparation equipment can all go on the back counter. Each of these machines requires an electrical outlet, and some require more than the standard 110 volts, so work closely with your contractor or electrician to meet these needs. Place grills and ovens apart from other machines so that you have all the hot stuff in one place.

Store mugs, plastic cups, plates, and so forth next to the machines where they'll be used. Employees shouldn't have to walk back and forth for supplies. This will slow delivery time and increase opportunities for bumps and spills.

In addition to the plumbing hook-up for the brewing system, you'll want to have a sink installed in the back counter so that employees can wash their hands regularly and clean up spills more easily.

Contents May Be Hot

Installing a hand sink isn't just a good idea; it's the law. Contact your local health department for advice on where hand sinks should be placed in relation to food preparation areas.

Don't fill every available space with equipment. You want to leave room for food and drink preparation and for people to put boxes when they're bringing goods and supplies out from the back room.

What's Stored Away

The espresso machine, the brewing system, the cash register: everything in the prep area is on counters, ready to be used, and underneath the counters lies ... what?

Well, everything you don't need on hand: paper products, straws and stirrers, napkins, paper towels, and much, much more. Use the under-the-counter space for cabinets and shelves to hold extra supplies. Don't use open shelving as a single spill (and there will be a lot more than just one!) could ruin lots of goods.

Label the cabinet doors with what's inside. Sure, you may know the contents of every cabinet, but new employees won't, and making them hunt for extra napkins so they can refill dispensers is a waste of time.

Depending on the counter layout, you might also place a small refrigerator under the brewing system or espresso machine so that milk, cream, and half-and-half is always within reach. Again, the goal is always to improve efficiency and lower the customer's wait time between order and pick-up.

Behind Closed Doors

The layout of the front and back counters aims to have the equipment accessible, the supplies organized and labeled, and the employees working smoothly without interruption. All of this should apply to your back room as well.

Practical, Not Pretty

The heart of the back room is possibly the least glamorous, yet most needed element of any dining establishment: the sink and dishwasher. We don't recommend serving everything in disposable packaging—customers prefer the solid feel of ceramic, glass, and plastic—so you'll deal with a lot of dirty dishes.

As with the hand sink in the prep area, you should contact the local health department to see how many and what type of sinks you need to install in the back room. Triple sinks are commonly required, with the sinks divided into washing, rinsing, and sanitizing stations. The health department will likely have rules on where to locate the mop sink as well.

In addition to cleaning dishes, you'll use the back room to store lots more supplies: paper towels, toilet paper, and everything else that's too big to fit underneath the service counters. Again, label every shelf so that employees know where to find supplies as well as where to put them when restocking.

Keep black markers handy, perhaps on strings hanging from different shelves, so employees can mark boxes that are otherwise unlabeled. This will make it easier to quickly find, say, plastic lids for large cups versus small ones. Labeling should also speed the counting during inventory time.

Give Them a Break (Room)!

Depending on the size of your location, you might devote space to an office or break room. Such a room will give your employees a place to escape the sales floor during their meal breaks and let you write up bank deposit slips or make phone calls without interruption.

Keep in mind that you can't treat an office the same as a break room. If employees can eat lunch in your office, for example, you need to keep business and employee records under lock and key so they can't peruse information they shouldn't see, such as a co-worker's rate of pay. If the office is locked when you're not in it, you don't have to worry about such things.

Whether or not you set up an office or a break room, you will need a safe place to store money—rolls of change, the day's receipts, and paychecks—and what could be safer than a safe? Find room for the safe in the office, if possible, but if you don't have an office, the break room or back room will have to do.

Whatever you decide, don't forget that you won't sell anything from the office and you can't seat customers in the break room. While you'd like to create a safe haven for yourself and employees, devote enough space to the business end of your business first.

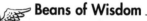

Beans of Wisdom

Many health permits require lockers or some type of secure area where employees can safely store their coats, hand-bags, and backpacks.

Bathroom Basics

Finally, we arrive at the room that no one likes to think about, but all of us turn to in time of need. As with an office or break room, bathrooms take up space that could otherwise be devoted to customer seating or shelves of merchandise, yet bathrooms are essential to keeping customers happy.

You could set up a bathroom that's accessible only to employees, but all this does is either annoy customers, who will leave instead of sticking around for refills and treats, or annoy you, when customers inevitably beg and plead for access.

To avoid that uncomfortable feeling that comes with escorting someone through your functional but, let's face it, unattractive back room, go through the trouble of installing a bathroom for your customers. Depending on the size of your location and the percentage of customers you expect to eat in-house, you might even have separate bathrooms for men and women.

Once again, be sure to contact the local health department to find out what they require in a bathroom in terms of size, handrails, water usage, and so on before you actually start to build.

Don't let the bathroom look like an afterthought when compared with the rest of your shop. Carry the style and design of the coffee bar into the bathroom, repeating colors, for example, or using mirrors that match those in the seating area. Whatever design you choose, remember to choose materials that allow for easy cleaning.

The Least You Need to Know

- ◆ Organize your counter so that customers entering the shop instantly know where to order, where to pay, and where to pick up drinks.

- ◆ Use the counter to display goods and inspire purchases without blocking sales and delivery.

- ◆ Arrange equipment so that employees have everything they need within reach to minimize accidents and speed up service.

- ◆ Work with the local health department to find out what sinks, plumbing, and fixtures are right for your location.

- ◆ Design a publicly accessible bathroom that matches the style of the entire business.

Bringing On a Crew

In This Chapter

- ◆ Hiring helpers and signing on supervisors
- ◆ Grilled well-done: interview techniques
- ◆ Payment means more than just money
- ◆ Back to school: training employees
- ◆ When to say goodbye

When it comes time to staff your coffee bar, you'd probably prefer to clone yourself a half-dozen times and be done with it. After all, you know how you want customers treated, you know the cleaning and restocking procedures. You know everything that needs to happen to make the coffee bar a success, and you know you'd do a great job.

Unfortunately for you, science has yet to reach the point where clones of yourself can work the cash register and empty the garbage cans while you—the original you, that is—count the profits in the backroom. Think of it as a blessing in disguise, though. Imagine the trouble you'd cause by listing yourself seven times on tax forms, not to mention the threat of mutiny if you ever slighted one of your other selves!

For the time being, you have to stick to hiring people who don't make you think you're looking in a mirror. We'll help you interview these prospects, train them, figure out what to pay them, and—should they not prove to be your equal—nudge them on to greener pastures.

All Hands on Deck!

Believe it or not, it's bad form to walk into a competing coffee shop and shout, "Who wants to quit this dump and come work for me?" Besides, anyone who would leave their current employer that way would likely turn traitor on you just as quickly.

You'll have much better luck finding potential employees the old-fashioned way: through newspaper ads, online job boards, and word-of-mouth through family and friends. When you place ads, outline exactly what you need in a worker—availability in the mornings, for example—so that applicants won't be surprised later.

Each potential employee should fill out an application before you even consider hiring her. The application should have room for contact information, employment history, education, and pay expectations.

The application is your first step toward dividing applicants into two categories: "Maybe" and "Not on Your Life." If an applicant can't fill out the application properly, for example, she probably won't be able to handle a cash register or complete sales logs. If her past jobs all lasted less than a month, she might be too flaky to trust with the responsibility of opening or closing the shop.

> **Beans of Wisdom**
>
> While you can interview applicants anywhere, if you meet them in your coffee bar, they can see where they'll be working and how things are run. This gives them a chance to ask questions, thus potentially impressing you with their smarts and curiosity, or ignore what's going on around them—which will give you an entirely different impression.

A Queue of Questions

You've probably been in the interviewee hot seat a number of times. Now it's your turn to ask the questions and try to determine who's telling you the truth—and who's telling you what you want to hear.

Call all applicants who sound promising, even if you have fewer positions to fill than the number of applicants. After all, you never know who will have found a job in the meantime and who won't work out.

Not sure how to conduct an interview? Don't worry—the applicant will likely be more nervous than you, and by following the advice below, you'll learn everything you need to make the right hiring decisions for your business.

Write Out Your Questions

Ask questions that explore an applicant's work history while simultaneously answering how the applicant will help you. Avoid asking questions that can be answered with a simple "yes" or "no." Sample questions might be:

- What experience do you have in food service and customer service?

- What was your worst working experience, and why?

- What are your two main strengths and weaknesses?

- Why are you interested in this job?

- How would you describe your current job and supervisor?

By writing down your questions, you can refer to them during the interview to help you remember what to ask and to ensure that you ask everyone the same questions so that you can compare apples to apples. Having the application as well as an applicant's work history in front of you can inspire questions you might not think of otherwise.

Contents May Be Hot

Ask about an applicant's skills and experiences only as they relate to the job. Don't ask whether the applicant plans to have children, whether he's married, whether he's ever filed a workers' compensation claim, whether he's a citizen, when he was discharged from the military, whether he's been arrested, or what his race/creed/color/religion/national origin/age is. These types of questions can be considered discriminatory, and federal laws prohibit discrimination against job applicants based on gender, race, disability, religion, marital status, and so on.

Get a First Impression

Don't feel that you have to jump into the interview right away. Try some small talk first to break the ice and put the applicant at ease. One way to do this is to describe your business and the positions for which you're interviewing. Explain what traits are most important to you: customer service, for example, or teamwork and mutual support.

While you're doing this, notice details about the applicant. Is she groomed and dressed appropriately for your business? Does she smile and look enthusiastic about the job? First impressions don't always tell the whole story, but they help you build a complete picture of an applicant.

> **Contents May Be Hot**
>
> You'll want to take notes during the interview because days later you'll have a hard time remembering who said what, but try not to be too obvious with your note-taking. You don't want the applicant to feel like you're grading her on everything she says!

Shoot the Query ... Then Wait

After you ask each question, pause and give the applicant time to formulate an answer. Don't run together several questions at once because you probably won't get answers for all of them. Ask follow-up questions such as "Why did you do that?" and "How did that happen?" to draw more out of an applicant.

Turn the Tables

Near the end of the interview, ask the applicant whether she has any questions for you. This not only gives the applicant a chance to clarify the job in her mind; it gives you a chance to learn more about her. Does she ask intelligent questions about the training process, or does she ask what you do when a worker's till constantly comes up short?

If you hire this person, you're going to spend lots of time with her and trust that she can present your business to customers in a positive light. You can't learn everything there is to know about a person in a 30-minute interview, but you can often learn enough to know whether this person is someone you want to work with day after day.

Learning Labor Law

Labor law, a.k.a. employment law, is the collective name for thousands of federal and state statutes that govern the rights and obligations involved in any type of employment situation. Labor law regulates everything from the initial hiring process and job duties to minimum wage and collective bargaining rights.

The field of labor law is enormous, far more than we can cover in a few pages. Consult your lawyer for advice, or explore the pages of *The Complete Idiot's Guide to Human Resource Management*, by Arthur R. Pell (Alpha Books, 2001), to learn about your obligations as an employer.

Show Them the Money

Job applicants will naturally be curious about payment. They're not volunteering to feed starving children, after all! They expect to be reimbursed for their effort, and you should have a figure in mind for each position that you're filling.

There's more to paying wages than handing out a simple per-hour rate, though. Workers' compensation insurance, unemployment taxes, Social Security taxes, and more all figure into the equation.

Giving the Government Its Due

Government taxes add an additional 20 to 35 percent onto the cost of an employee's gross wages, so the more you offer an employee, the more you'll hand over to Uncle Sam as well. These costs include:

◆ **Workers' compensation insurance.** Workers' comp, as it's known to fans and friends, covers your employees' costs if they get sick, injured, or even killed on the job. The benefits of workers' comp include medical expenses, lost wages, vocational rehabilitation, and death benefits. Workers' comp protects you as much as your employees. Before workers' comp existed, a serious injury to an employer could shut down the business. Now, lost wages, rehab, and so on are paid for by the insurance, no matter who's at fault.

◆ **Social Security and Medicare taxes.** Not only are you required to withhold 7.5 percent of your employees' paychecks to pay for their Social Security and Medicare taxes—you must match those contributions dollar for dollar. If one employee pays $30 a week in Social Security taxes, you must pay that amount as well. Add that cost up for all employees and you're talking serious spending.

> **Beans of Wisdom**
> Workers' comp requirements vary from state to state, so call your state's insurance commissioner for more info. (You can find the phone number in the blue government pages of the phone book.) Your insurance agent can also help you with the details.

◆ **Federal unemployment taxes.** Most employers have to pay federal unemployment taxes because the qualifications aren't that hard to meet: either pay wages totaling $1,500 to all employees in one quarter, or have at least one employee working on any given day for 20 (not necessarily consecutive) weeks in a year.

If you meet either of these standards, you must pay a flat rate of 6.2 percent on the first $7,000 paid to each employee for both the current calendar year and the following year. This tax covers unemployment compensation for workers who have lost their jobs. States often have their own unemployment tax, so contact your accountant or the state's department of labor for more details.

Check, Please

Okay, the government taxes tell you how much to add on top of your pay. Now for the harder question: How much do you pay? You want to be able to offer an hourly rate that will leave your employees tickled pink without putting your business in the red.

To begin, go back to your business plan (developed in Chapter 4) to see how much you allocated towards the cost of employees. If you offer, say, $7 per hour—and government taxes push that figure to $8.50 per hour—how many hours of help can you afford? Is this realistic? Are you offering too much per hour? Did you underestimate how much help you'll need?

Contact coffee bars in noncompeting areas to find out how much they pay and how many employees they use during each shift. Use this information to adjust your business plan (if needed) and guide you in determining a per-hour rate for each employee.

Sign Them or Ship Them?

Should you handle the coffee bar's payroll on your own, or should you hire an outside payroll company to handle the burden? As with the issues of hiring a lawyer and accountant (which we discussed in Chapter 5), the answer is: it depends.

Have you researched the federal and state tax issues thoroughly and know exactly how much needs to be withheld from each employee's check? Do you save more money handling the payroll yourself than it would cost for an outside company to do it? Do you file payroll taxes with the IRS promptly? If the answer to all these questions is "yes," then perhaps you should keep hold of the checkbook.

If the answer is "no"—or if you want to offer employees direct deposit or track sick hours and vacation time easily—consider hiring a payroll company that's national in scope and can assign an account representative to work with you.

More than Money

Money is good for lots of things, such as being exchanged for goods and services. Okay, that's basically the definition of money, but motivating employees and keeping them happy takes more than just dough.

Even if you pay sky-high wages, if you let customers treat your employees badly or you don't praise them for a job well done, they will be miserable. And they won't be miserly with their miserableness: they'll generously share it with customers, who will soon feel equally miserable when they think about entering your coffee bar. Soon miserableness will abound, and health authorities will move in and set up barriers to keep it from spreading further.

Don't let this happen to your coffee bar. Keep your business a pleasant place to work with a private, clean space for employees to take breaks in and a small fridge to store their lunches. Keep the surfaces clean and the air fresh. (Admittedly, they'll be doing much of the cleaning and freshening, but give them the tools to work with.)

Take the attitude that they're working *with* you, not *for* you, and treat them as equals as much as you can. Start football pools, if they're interested, or let them come to work in costume on Halloween. Be flexible with the work schedule to accommodate unusual circumstances rather than dogmatically insisting that they work the same hours and the same days no matter what. Ask them for suggestions when problems arise.

Offer generous praise when they do good work, and if you want to go a step further, put the praise in writing or reward them with gift cards to local businesses or extra time off with pay. Provide employee discounts on the products you carry. Sure, they might prefer to have a permanent pay increase, but these steps will make your appreciation clear and keep them on your side.

Barista Baccalaureate

Training your employees is the best business investment you'll ever make. It's the ol' "teach a man to fish" parable writ large. Once you train an employee, she'll have that knowledge forever. More importantly, she'll be able to pass that knowledge on to new employees, leaving you free to do things like count your money.

Reaching that point of autonomous and self-perpetuating systems doesn't happen overnight. You must have a willingness to train employees from the moment they start working with you. Don't half-explain a task, and then say, "Never mind, I'll do it," or else employees will take the wrong lessons from your training: that you don't trust them and that you will take over any job that's slightly difficult.

Train them right, and they'll have confidence in their abilities. What's more, their confidence will be deserved because they will have mastered every task you could ask of them.

Creating a Training Manual

Imagine taking an eight-hour crash course on how to run a coffee bar. How much do you think you'd remember about foaming milk, refilling the supply cabinet, running the register, cleaning the tables and floors, and rotating the baked goods? Not enough to do it right the next day, most likely.

That's why you should write an employee training manual that spells out your business procedures. Whenever an employee wonders how to maintain a piece of equipment or void a transaction, he can flip open the book and find the answer.

> **Beans of Wisdom** _____
>
> Writing all the procedures of your business for a training manual will show you where they may be lacking. Maybe you don't have any procedures in place for handling customers who get ill, for instance, or perhaps you'll discover the need for a chart that shows who's responsible for cleaning what each day. Sometimes you learn what's missing only by writing down what you already know.

Here are a few of the procedures you'll want to include in your training manual:

- **How to clean:** Who is responsible for cleaning each section of the coffee bar? How often should cleaning take place?

- **How to maintain equipment:** Who cleans and repairs equipment? How often does maintenance take place?

- **How to take money:** Do you accept cash, checks, credit cards? What are the procedures for each? How do you handle register mistakes?

- **How to answer the phone:** What's the procedure for taking messages? Do you want your employees to answer with "Good day, this is Tony at The Perfect Brew. How may I help you?" Then write it down!

♦ **How to handle an unsatisfied customer:** Do you give her a free cup of coffee? Issue a refund? Call in the supervisor?

Your training manual should also contain information on benefits like vacation time and medical leave, policies on drugs and weapons in the workplace, details about lines of authority (i.e., who reports to whom), rules regarding lateness and attendance, info about disciplinary actions, expectations for your employees (such as how often they'll be reviewed for job performance), and information on regulatory compliance such as the policies you have in place to comply with the Americans with Disabilities Act and other regulations.

In short, the training manual should detail the goals you have for your business and explain the policies necessary to make it happen.

Training Trials

If you've ever worked as a schoolteacher—or even better, substituted for a schoolteacher—you know how hard it is to clearly and cleanly give directions for anything. If you haven't worked as a teacher—hoo-boy, it's time for you to learn about teaching!

There's more to training employees than explaining a procedure once and leaving them on their own. Different people learn in different ways, and for you to succeed as a teacher, you need to find what works for each person. For one employee, you might be able to simply give verbal directions; for another, you might have to draw a diagram; for a third, you might have to lead him through the procedure the first time.

Once you're aware of each employee's learning style, you'll know how to teach him— and you'll know how others can teach him as well. Here are a few specific training techniques to get you started:

♦ **Role-play.** The thief has just picked the lock on the treasure chest when a gargoyle lumbers into the room with slobber dripping from its fangs and ....

Forget Dungeons & Dragons. By role-play, we mean acting out with an employee situations that might arise during a workday, such as a peeved customer who received whipped cream he didn't want or a customer who complains about the music in your shop. (Of course, these situations will never arise in *your* shop, but it never hurts to be prepared.)

Acting out these types of situations gives the employee a chance to discover or remember the right solution before he's faced with it in real life. Role-play helps you evaluate his strengths and weaknesses, so that you have him share the former and work on the latter.

- **Monkey see, monkey do.** Have the new employee closely follow a more experienced worker (or you), copying everything in order to learn how things are done. It never hurts a table to be cleaned twice, after all, and you can always give away the practice drinks he makes, thereby building customer satisfaction at the same time!

  Switch roles after doing an action twice, and have the new employee lead the master, talking his way through the procedure out loud in case the master needs to jump in.

- **Assign a mentor.** Ask an established employee to become the new guy's best buddy until he can work on his own. In addition to freeing up your time for other tasks, having an employee serve as a mentor shows that you value her knowledge and trust her judgment. Give her guidelines on training if she's never worked with anyone before, and then send her on her way.

> **Beans of Wisdom**
>
> The mentor experience commonly teaches both employees new things. The newcomer learns everything about the business from scratch, while the old hand refreshes knowledge she might have forgotten and learns how to take more responsibility for others.

Even when you have employees experienced enough to be mentors, don't disappear into your office. Work the floor with your employees to see what you can learn from them and to correct them when they take shortcuts that might hurt the business or customer relations.

Crying "Fire" in a Crowded Coffee Bar

No matter how careful you are during your hiring procedures, employees don't always work out. Some turn out to be lazy, some steal, some are rude. Whatever the reason, you need to let them go, and by "let them go," we mean *fire them*.

Don't think you can go firing people willy-nilly, though. That's a sure-fire recipe for legal trouble with a capital L. Just as there's a legally proper way to hire someone, the law also dictates when and how you can let people go. We'll explain the details below in addition to giving tips for how to say good-bye the politest way possible.

Is the Law on Your Side?

When you hire an employee, you should explain that the position requires the person to do X, Y, and Z. Effectively, you're making a deal with that person: "You do X, Y, and Z, and I will pay you for doing so." If that person repeatedly fails to do any one of these tasks, you have the right to replace him with someone who will.

You're allowed to do this because—unless you've signed a contract stating otherwise—you've hired the person on an "at will" basis, which means that either one of you can terminate the employment agreement at any time for nearly any reason. (You can't fire an at-will employee, for example, if he files workers' comp claims, reports you to a state agency for violating the law, or breaks up with you after the two of you start dating.)

Even without a written contract, if you told an employee that his job would last at least X months, then you need justifiable and documented reasons—such as dishonesty, theft, or misuse of trade secrets—for letting him go earlier.

Contents May Be Hot

If you're unsure whether you have the right to fire someone, discuss the situation with your lawyer to make sure you're staying on the right side of the law.

"This Will Go Down in Your Permanent Record"

You might have laughed when a high school teacher threatened to note your note-passing in your permanent record, but she actually had the right idea. By documenting your history of insubordination, the school would have a better case against you later should it need to expel you. (Thankfully, we all grow out of that stage.)

As the owner of a small business, you should take a lesson from that teacher and record violations by your employees, along with whatever actions you took to fix the problem. If, for example, an employee repeatedly handles food without gloves despite your warnings, you'll have a much stronger case for firing her if you've documented each disciplinary problem.

Don't keep this record to yourself, though. Develop a plan for handling employee violations, such as a "three strike" policy, and include details of the policy in the training manual. When you hire employees, tell them about the policy so they can never argue that they were blindsided by your accusations.

Saying Good-Bye

The day has finally come. You've warned so-and-so repeatedly that he can't put his lips on the milk foamer, and yet he's still doing it! Before you boot him out, though, run through this checklist and make sure everything is in order for the firing-to-come:

◆ **Have you given him warnings?** Make sure you've documented this employee's past violations. If you grumble quietly to yourself, then fire someone out of the blue, you could face legal action for wrongful termination. By noting violations and making other employees aware of such problems, you also make them feel less threatened because they know you've given the employee sufficient opportunity to fix his mistakes.

If, however, you catch an employee in the act of pocketing money from the till or doing something else illegal, you don't really need to give him a second chance.

◆ **Is this really necessary?** Is the violation serious enough that it warrants firing? Is the employee leaving milk unrefrigerated, which risks bringing health inspectors down on your head, or is he not stocking the Styrofoam cups in the order you prefer? Firing an employee often has a traumatic effect on the rest of your staff, so make sure this step is necessary.

◆ **Are you sending mixed messages?** Don't tell an employee that he's doing great and is a super-nice person to work with, and then hand him his hat and shoo him out the door. The employee might feel that he's being fired unjustly and file a wrongful termination suit. After all, why would you compliment him so much if he were really that bad?

Lay out the reasons for the termination and stress the opportunities you gave for improvement, without hinting at anything positive about the employee's performance. Keep calm if the employee lashes back at you or tries to argue about what a good worker he is. Don't argue back; merely restate your decision and let the employee know that's the final word.

◆ **Are you being mean?** Although this person has disrupted your business through his actions, don't make the firing a personal assault. Keep things on an "all business" level. Leave insults and jabs out of the conversation and stick to the facts of his work violations.

Much as you might dislike it, you will have to fire employees at some point. While we hope your good hiring practices will make the practice rare, knowing how and when to let go is an important skill that every business owner must learn.

The Least You Need to Know

♦ Hire (and don't hire) employees for the right reasons, such as their knowledge of food preparation or their hours of availability. Leave personal feelings out of the decision.

♦ Figure out the true cost of an employee's hourly pay and budget for that amount.

♦ Train employees to the point of self-sufficiency, and then teach them to train the next wave of employees.

♦ Document job violations so that employees will know what to do to keep their jobs, or why they're being fired.

Part 4

Eat, Drink, and Be Merry: Choosing Which Products To Sell

Finally we get to the meat of the matter, if you'll forgive the expression: the stuff that goes in the cup. Part 4 covers the different types of coffee; how beans are sorted, graded, and prepared; and how to create coffee drinks like lattés and cappuccinos. And where coffee goes, milk must follow, whether it's steamed, heated, or frothed.

Not everyone digs coffee (gasp!), so we include information on tea—its history, the different types available, and how to prepare the perfect cup—as well as many other drinks, from soda to smoothies.

Who brings all these goodies to your shop? Lots and lots of suppliers, all of whom you'll learn to deal with in this part. We'll also cover how to price your products, in case you'd care to earn something from all this effort.

Chapter 12

Complete Coffee Compendium

In This Chapter

◆ What's in a bean?

◆ How to dress a bean for dinner: roasting, decaffeinating, flavoring

◆ How to store coffee

◆ Brewing the perfect pot

Planning your décor and hiring friendly employees are essential to the future success of your coffee bar, but let's face it: what's going to draw customers through the door—and more importantly, keep them coming back—is the smell and taste of coffee. If you can convince them to hand over their cow, um, cash for a handful of beans, you'll have customers for life.

Sounds simple? If only it were that easy! You have dozens, if not hundreds, of different types of coffee to choose from, each with its own flavor, aroma, and body. Don't worry, though. By the end of this chapter, you'll be well on your way to becoming a coffee connoisseur!

Java 101

In our quest for the perfect pot of coffee, let's begin at the beginning, with the bean itself. Each coffee bean is actually the seed of a coffee cherry, the fruit of the coffee tree. Most coffee trees grow near the equator, but with a lot of care, they can be raised in other locations.

Coffee beans come in two major types. No, not ground and instant, although that's what we thought while growing up in a world without coffee bars. In fact, the two types of coffee beans are *robusta* and *arabica*.

Robusta beans, which are native to West Africa, grow at low altitudes and are less prone to disease than arabica beans. While this makes them cheaper to grow than arabica, robusta beans have a harsher taste and up to twice the caffeine, so they're used mostly in mass-produced, supermarket blends of coffee.

Arabica beans, by contrast, are grown at altitudes of 3,000 to 7,000 feet above sea level, which makes them expensive to grow and harvest. Despite their high cost, specialty coffee bars prefer arabica beans because they have a smooth, rich taste that can't be matched by robusta beans. Anywhere from 60 to 85 percent of the world's coffee production is in arabica beans.

> **Instant Facts** _____
>
> Get ready for some science talk. Coffee trees and bushes belong to the botanical family Rubiaceae, which is made up of more than 13,000 species of flowering plants including gardenias and Cinchona, which produces the malaria treatment quinine—if only coffee cured diseases! Aside from arabica and robusta, more than 20 other types of coffee exist, such as liberica, dewevrei, racemosa, stenophylla, and zanguebariae. These other types account for less than 1 percent of the world's production of coffee.

A pound of coffee contains roughly 4,000 coffee beans, and with only two seeds in each cherry, 2,000 cherries must be picked for each pound of coffee. That's a lot of picking! Unripe green berries, ripe red ones, and overripe black ones may show up on the same branch, which makes coffee bean picking a very time-consuming task.

The seeds are removed from the fruit by either a wet or dry process. In the wet process, the cherries are soaked until the fruit comes off and leaves behind *washed coffee*. For the dry process, which produces *unwashed* coffee, the cherries dry in the sun or in dryers, and then machines strip the dried fruit from the beans.

Coffee beans can have no more than 11 to 12 percent moisture, so after processing, they must dry anywhere from six to fourteen days before they are cleaned once again, inspected for damage, and packed for shipping.

Decaffeinating Details

To many people, decaffeinated coffee is like a car without an engine—it might look good on the surface, but it won't get you where you want to go. These folks use caffeine to get them moving in the morning or to push them through a post-lunch slump.

Not everyone appreciates the buzz that caffeine provides, though, and thankfully science has figured out how to separate the cof from the caf. You won't have to decaffeinate the beans you buy from suppliers, but in case you want to explain what goes on behind the scenes to your customers, here are the different decaffeinating processes and how they work:

- ◆ Methylene chloride (DCM) processing

- ◆ Ethyl acetate processing

- ◆ Carbon dioxide (CO_2) processing

- ◆ Water processing (also known as Swiss water processing)

In most instances of methylene chloride (DCM) processing, the beans are soaked in DCM, and molecules of caffeine bond with molecules of methylene chloride. The beans are then washed to remove the DCM, which is carcinogenic in large doses. (Roasting the beans burns off any remaining DCM.)

The chemical ethyl acetate is found naturally in certain fruits, so using ethyl acetate for decaffeination is sometimes labeled a "natural" process. As with DCM processing, the coffee beans are soaked in ethyl acetate and the caffeine bonds with the chemical.

In carbon dioxide processing, the CO_2 is compressed into a near-liquid state and combined with the coffee beans. As with the other processing methods, the caffeine molecules

Instant Facts

The caffeine removed from coffee isn't thrown away, but is instead added to medicines, soft drinks, and other products. Believe it or not, less than 5 percent of the caffeine in a regular cola drink comes from the kola nut itself. The rest of the caffeine in the drink comes from coffee that has been stripped of its natural buzz.

bond with the CO_2 and are removed. Carbon dioxide is found in coffee beans to begin with, and any CO_2 remaining behind has no effect on the taste of the finished product.

In water processing, coffee beans are soaked in hot water, which absorbs both caffeine molecules and "flavor" molecules, the oils and other components of the beans that give them their particular taste. The water-caffeine-flavor solution then passes through a carbon filter that removes the caffeine but leaves the other elements untouched. The beans soak in this solution again to reabsorb the flavors and oils.

Calling coffee "decaffeinated" is not quite right, because this coffee will still contain some caffeine, no matter which processing method is used. Federal regulations in the United States allow products to contain up to 2.5 percent caffeine and still wear the decaffeinated label. Turns out the car has a bit of "go" power after all.

How to Judge the Beans

Determining whether a batch of beans makes good coffee or not isn't just a matter of brewing up a pot and giving it a taste. Taste alone isn't a true measure of quality. Instead, you have to take a closer look at the beans themselves.

Each country that produces coffee has its own guidelines for quality, but rather than compare dozens of different guidelines, let's look at those created by the Specialty Coffee Association of America (SCAA) for use by member coffee bars that roast their own beans. To start, we have a list of primary and secondary defects to look for when examining a coffee lot.

SCAA Green Coffee Classification

Primary Defects	Number of Occurrences Equal to One Full Defect
Full black (discolored bean)	1
Full sour (a bean that has a fermented odor or taste)	1
Pod/cherry (whole cherries including the shell)	1
Large stones	2
Medium stones	5
Large sticks	2
Medium sticks	5

Secondary Defects	Number of Occurrences Equal to One Full Defect
Parchment (the membrane that surrounds the bean)	2–3
Hull/husk (the dried pulp of the cherry)	2–3
Broken/chipped	5
Insect damage	2–5
Partial black	2–3
Partial sour	2–3
Floater (lighter than normal)	5
Shell	5
Small stones	1
Small sticks	1
Water damage	2–5

So one large stone, while not desirable, does not equal one primary defect in a coffee lot. Eight beans damaged by insects (yum) equals anywhere from two to four secondary defects, with the amount of damage to each bean determining the actual number.

In addition to spotting these defects, you need to measure the size of the beans to make sure the coffee hasn't been "cut" with a cheaper grade. Why does size matter? Beans grown at the highest altitudes—the most arabica of the arabica, as it were—are denser and larger than beans grown at a lower height. These beans are also thought to have the best flavor, so in general, bigger is better when it comes to coffee beans.

To measure bean size, you filter them through screens of size 18, size 17, and so forth down through size 14, where "18" means "18/64 of an inch," "17" means "17/64 of an inch," and so on. Beans in one lot should be the same size so they'll roast uniformly. (You don't necessarily need to buy screens for your own use, but we want you know what the numbers stand for.)

Beans of Wisdom

While bigger is generally better, good tastes can come in small packages. Peaberry coffee, which comes from cherries that have only one seed instead of two, is often a delight in the cup!

Taste

Taste or flavor is the combination of the following three characteristics, as well as how well they're balanced, describing the overall sensation of the coffee.

- Acidity is a feeling of dryness at the back and edges of your mouth, which, unlike sourness, is a good thing. Without the pleasing, astringent tartness of acidity, a coffee would taste flat.

- Aroma adds subtle touches such as nutty or floral to the basic taste sensations of sweet, salty, sour, bitter, and umami (a meaty flavor associated with proteins).

- Body refers to the feel of the coffee in your mouth, how heavy or fluid it feels. If you dilute two coffees with milk, the one that retains more of its flavor has a heavier body.

Grades

With all these details in mind, here are the SCAA grade guidelines from best to worst when examining 300 grams of hulled coffee:

- **Grade 1—Specialty Grade:** No primary defects, 0 to 3 full secondary defects, sorted with a maximum of 5 percent above and 5 percent below specified screen size or range of screen size, and exhibiting a distinct attribute in one or more of the following areas: *taste (flavor)*, *acidity*, *body*, or *aroma*. Also must be free of *cup faults* and *taints*. Zero quakers (that is, unripe, blighted, or underdeveloped coffee beans) allowed. Moisture content between 9 and 13 percent.

- **Grade 2—Premium Grade:** Same as Grade 1, except maximum of 3 quakers and 0 to 8 full secondary defects.

Java-nitions

Cup fault or cup taint are general terms for any problem with the taste or odor of coffee. Examples of faults include grassy (too much nitrogen in the beans while the cherries matured), green (not enough heat during roasting), hidey (breakdown of fats during the drying process due to too much heat), and tipped (charred bean tips due to heat being applied too quickly during roasting).

- ◆ **Grade 3—Exchange Grade:** 50 percent above screen 15 and less than 5 percent below screen 15. Maximum of 5 quakers. Must be free from faults. 9 to 23 full defects.

- ◆ **Grade 4—Standard Grade:** 24 to 86 full defects.

- ◆ **Grade 5—Off Grade:** More than 86 full defects.

These grades are based on 300-gram samples from much larger lots, but they should be good indicators of overall quality. If you do limit yourself to using only specialty grade beans, you'll pay a premium for the quality, but you can turn that cost into a marketing advantage. Post signs in your coffee bar that explain the grades and boast about the standards you keep to give customers the best coffee possible!

The Roast with the Most

Roasting coffee isn't like roasting a side of beef—you can't throw it in the oven for an hour. Beans are small and cook quickly, so like people on a caffeine buzz, they have to be in motion at all times. Typically, you roast coffee in a rotating metal drum over a heat source such as a gas flame. The air temperature inside the drum falls between 400° and 500° Fahrenheit, with the specific temperature being determined by the experience of the roaster, the type of beans being processed, and the desired roast.

How the Pros Do It

During the roasting process, the beans lose more of their moisture, so the finished batch will weigh less than when it started. The beans also lose a bit of protein, traces of different chemicals, and roughly 10 percent of their caffeine. Sugars and other carbohydrates in the bean are caramelized—that is, burned—and this darkens the bean and adds flavor.

After seven minutes of roasting, while changing from bright green to yellow to light brown, the beans have cracked and swelled in size as the moisture has been driven out. American mass marketers usually stop with this "light" or "cinnamon" roast, with dry, lightly roasted beans.

At the nine- to eleven-minute mark, called "medium" or "city" roast, the beans gain a bit more sweetness as the sugars caramelize. The flavor of these beans is stronger than lightly roasted ones, with the aroma, acid, and body all gaining strength.

After 12 to 13 minutes, the interior of the bean reaches 400° Fahrenheit, and an oily film starts to appear on the bean's surface. The sweetness of the caramelized sugars overtakes the bean's aroma, and the oil gives the bean a somewhat spicy taste. This roast, known as "dark" or "French," is common in Europe but only came to prominence in the United States thanks to specialty coffee stores in the Northwest.

> **Instant Facts**
>
> In France's colonial days, the French roasted their coffee extremely dark to mask the poor flavor of the robusta blends that came out of the country's colonies in West Africa. Today, "French Roast" refers to any dark roasted coffee, whether the beans are arabica or robusta.

Fourteen minutes into the roasting process, the beans stop cracking and the sugars begin to carbonize—that is, turn to carbon—and taste smoky. The surface of these "Italian" or "espresso" beans looks very oily, and the flavor reaches a nearly burnt intensity.

The operators of roasting machines sample the roasting beans continuously—smelling the changing nature of the sugar, listening for the crackle of the skin as the oil starts to escape—and when the beans reach their moment of perfection, the operator dumps the beans into a cooling tray and blasts them with cool air to keep them from cooking any longer.

How You, the Pro-to-Be, Can Do It, Too

How do you get to Carnegie Hall? Practice, practice, practice. The same spirit holds true when learning to roast your own coffee beans.

View your first efforts as experiments, and keep a notebook to record the type of beans used, the preheating time, time in the heater, chilling method, and so forth. You never know which batch will turn out perfect, and when that happens, you don't want to have to guess at how you got them.

While you can buy a roaster that handles large quantities of beans—and you'll definitely need to purchase a roaster if you decide to self-roast in your store—you can experiment with a much simpler tool: a hot air popcorn popper.

Try to use a popper that heats from the side of the popcorn reservoir instead of the bottom. This will reduce the danger of fire that might result from overheated beans. You will also want to roast outdoors if possible; chaff from the green coffee beans will fly out during roasting, and the roasting smell—while delightful initially—becomes stale quickly inside your home.

Okay, with green beans and a colander or sieve at hand, plug in the popper and let it heat up briefly. Pour in green beans until they stop swirling; you don't want to add too many or the ones on the bottom will burn. As the beans start to dry out, they'll start churning once again.

Wait for the first crackling of the beans, and then listen for the second crackling a minute or so later. Start timing from the start of this second crackling, and roast for an additional one to three minutes, depending on how light or dark you want your coffee to be.

When you decide to stop roasting, dump the beans into the colander or sieve and swirl them around in front of a fan to cool them down and stop the roasting. In addition to fanning, you could sprinkle them with water, although this shouldn't be necessary. Once they cool, you can pack them away or jump down to the section on grinding and put them to use right away.

Storing Coffee

Okay, we have a heaping pile of roasted coffee beans—now what? Roasted beans, when exposed to air, stay fresh for only 7-10 days, so you need to get them into storage pronto, preferably into something airtight.

Some roasters solve this problem for their customers by packaging beans in a coffee bag with a one-way gas valve that lets gases escape from the beans—thus allowing them to reveal their optimal flavor as chemicals from the roasting process escape—but keeps outside air from reaching the beans. If beans aren't packaged in this type of bag—or once they're exposed to air after being in airtight bags—they begin to deteriorate, with dark roast beans being the most vulnerable.

In a retail environment, you're most likely using beans quickly and not having them sit around for weeks waiting for their moment in the sun. Customers who purchase whole beans from you will go through their supply more slowly; offer them these storage techniques so the fine coffee they bought from you will keep its great taste longer:

- Keep the beans whole until you're ready to use them. While whole beans stay fresh for a week, ground coffee starts losing flavor an hour after grinding.

- Store the beans in an airtight container, preferably a glass jar with a rubber gasket, and take out only as many beans as you need for each grinding and brewing session. Coffee cans with plastic lids aren't airtight, so send them to the recycling bin and get with glass.

◆ Don't store coffee in the refrigerator, even in an airtight container. The "oils" in coffee aren't oils at all (fooled ya!) but rather water-soluble substances that absorb surrounding moisture and odor. Refrigerators, strangely enough, tend to be both moist and odiferous, so unless you want a "Colombian and Leftover-Chinese" blend, keep the coffee out of the fridge.

◆ Place coffee in the freezer only if you plan to store it longer than a week. Use freezer bags and remove as much air as possible. Remove coffee from the freezer as you need it, and don't try to refreeze it. Light roasts fare better than very dark roasts, but all types of coffee can suffer from freezing as the oils may break down in the freezing process.

Around the World in 80 Coffees

In addition to different grades and roasts, coffee comes in hundreds of different varieties, each with its own special blend of taste, acidity, body, and aroma.

One way to label a coffee is with the name of the country where the beans were picked. Non-European country names, such as Kenyan, Mexican, or Ethiopian, let the buyer know that these beans were all part of one crop in this one country. European names, as we mention in the roast section, refer to the darkness of the roast and not the country of origin, which is why you find French Colombian coffees on supermarket shelves.

Market names are another way to label coffee, with the market being a single town, province, state, port, or landmark that somehow relates to the origin point of the coffee. Moshi, for example, is a large city on the south slope of Tanzania's Mount Kilimanjaro, and beans grown on the mountain carry the market name "Moshi."

Even more specialized than market names are estate names, like Nicaraguan Santa Lucia Estate and Jamaican Blue Mountain Mavis Bank Estate. A coffee that bears an estate name has been grown—and most likely processed—entirely on a single farm or estate. Since a coffee's flavor varies depending on the soil and altitude it grows in, an estate coffee is prized because buyers know exactly what they're getting from one batch to the next.

A flavoring agent can be added to almost any coffee, and the coffee name will naturally include that flavor to attract the attention of those customers eager for a taste of vanilla, chocolate, cinnamon, raspberry, amaretto, or dozens of other nuts, spices, and fruits.

> **Beans of Wisdom** _____
>
> The newest label to hit the coffee world is "Fair Trade," which can be applied to any type, roast, or grade. After petroleum, coffee is the most-traded commodity in the world, and with volume comes a push for cheap labor and low costs. Roasters who promise to pay coffee growers a set price (rather than wildly fluctuating market prices), provide credit at fair rates, and develop long-term relationships can earn their products a "Fair Trade" certification. Offering Fair Trade coffee can be an excellent selling point, depending on the political make-up of your marketplace!

"Organic" and "decaffeinated" are two more labels that might accompany a coffee's place of origin, roast, grade, and flavor. For a coffee to be labeled organic, one of several international monitoring agencies must verify that no harmful chemicals were used during the beans' lifespan.

Blending In with the Crowd

You'd think that with hundreds of combinations of flavors, roasts, and types of coffee, eager bean buyers would be satisfied. Not a chance! Many types of coffee hit a drinker's sweet spot in, say, taste and acidity but not aroma, or they have body but lack taste. No coffee is all things to all drinkers.

To solve this problem, roasters and coffee dealers offer a variety of *blends*—that is, mixtures of two or more coffees that are designed to create a better drink than any of them offers on its own.

Coffee drinkers might not be familiar with the sharp, medium-bodied taste of Yemen Mocha or with the smoother, richer Java Arabica—but they've all surely heard of, if not tried, Mocha Java, a blend created from one part Yemen Mocha and two parts Java Arabica. Mocha Java provides a taste experience that doesn't exist in any single coffee, and that uniqueness is what makes blends popular.

Another reason for the appeal of blends, at least from a manufacturer's point of view, is cost. Mass-market coffees generally offer a blend of better-tasting arabica beans with cheaper robusta beans to lower their costs while still providing a coffee buyers want to drink.

As you become more experienced with the nature of particular types of coffee, you'll likely want to experiment with blends yourself. You'll notice something in one cup that's missing from another—so what's to stop you from mixing them together? The worst thing that happens is that you spoil a few beans. The best thing, of course, is that you create a house blend that's available nowhere else in the world. If customers want it, there's only one place to go!

If you roast your own beans, you should roast each type of bean individually before blending and grinding them. This process, while more time consuming, ensures that each type of coffee is roasted properly. You don't want to risk undercooking one while scorching another.

The Old Grind

You've picked the beans (from the supplier, not from the tree!), roasted them, and blended them. One more step to go before you can drink the fruits of your labor: grinding.

As we mentioned in the storage section above, coffee begins to lose flavor only one hour after grinding, so it's best not to grind more than you plan to use immediately. This will be tough when you first open your doors for business, but as you gain a sales history, you'll be able to plan a grinding schedule and provide customers the freshest taste possible.

Although mechanical grinders offer several different grinding levels, you generally want to grind the coffee as fine as you can without turning the beans into powder or clogging your brewer's filter. The smaller the particles, the more contact you create between the coffee and the hot water. More contact equals more flavor from the coffee oils being transferred to the water, making a brew that better reflects the nature of the coffee.

A burr or conical burr grinder will be ideal for your business. This device, which crushes the beans between moving and nonmoving surfaces, allows you to grind the beans to a consistent size, which means

> **Beans of Wisdom**
>
> Make sure you match your grind to the type of brewer. It's your responsibility to taste batches and determine whether your grind is appropriate, whether your grinder needs cleaning and adjustment, and whether you need to change the degree of fineness.

your coffee will have a consistent taste. Burr grinders create little heat, so the flavor of the coffee won't be changed during the grinding process.

Avoid blade grinders. Instead of grinding the beans, the blades work like a blender and slice the beans apart. Since the beans move about freely, the blade grinder mashes the beans into a mix of large chunks, small bits, and powder, and the varying bean size will create a different taste with each brew. Even worse, the friction of the blades creates a lot of heat, which can start to cook the beans while they're still being ground. Hardly a recipe for success!

If you're making small pots of coffee to test new blends or offer customers sample tastes, you might consider grinding the beans old-style—with a mortar and pestle. This tool served humans for hundreds of years, and the personal touch allows you to fine tune the grinding to perfection.

Even if you feel that hand grinding is too much of a, well, grind, don't shy away from making mortar and pestles available to customers. Many people feel that homemade cooking is always better, and although they're unlikely to fly to South America to pick their own beans, a hand grinder might be perfect for their kitchen.

> **Beans of Wisdom**
>
> If you serve flavored coffees, consider purchasing a separate grinder for these products so that the flavors don't taint the regular coffee. Flavored coffees have their fans, but folks who prefer the plain stuff usually can't stand any hint of flavor.

Preparing the Perfect Pot

After all that roasting and grinding, it's time to finally make some coffee! And what a simple process brewing is at heart: you soak ground coffee in water until the water tastes good. You could get away with just a metal pot, an open fire, and a strainer, but there's probably a law or two against keeping open fires in your store.

While a drip coffee maker is fine at home, in a retail environment you need to think in bigger terms: How many roasts, types, and flavors do I need to offer? How much should I make of each type? How do I make coffee on such a large scale? Let's look at these questions in more detail.

How Many Types of Coffee Should I Offer?

You want to find a balance between providing all things to all people and wasting lots and lots of money by pouring unsold coffee down the drain. The key is to offer variety without overwhelming the customer with coffees that differ only slightly.

Although you can find or make a dozen different roasts, your best bet is to offer only three: light, medium, and dark. You can name the roasts with more specialized terms—light can be "American" or "Cinnamon," medium might be "Full City," and so forth—but be sure to post the generic terms as well, so that customers know how to ask for what they want.

In addition to reducing customer confusion, you also make the job easier for your employees. They'll have only three roasts to match (if you roast your own beans), less chance of mixing up customer orders, and fewer carafes or thermoses to clean.

For the same reasons, you want to stick with only three types or blends of coffee. You might choose to offer one or two different blends daily, to offer customers variety, but most customers value consistency and want the same drink every day. Make sure you don't throw these folks for a loop with your constantly shifting menu.

As for flavored coffee, one or two types should be all you need. This provides customers a taste of the larger coffee world without you sinking too much time and money in brews that lack the widespread appeal of "plain" coffee. What's more, flavors linger in thermoses no matter how much you wash them, so you don't want to invest in 20 separate thermoses for each flavor you carry.

How Much Coffee Should I Make of Each Type?

The right answer to this question will come only with time. The longer your store is open, the more sales data you'll have to draw on, and the more accurate you'll be when deciding how much coffee to make. (We'll talk more about how to use sales data in Chapter 18.)

The answer to this question also depends on which type of brewing system you use. The best system for a retail environment might be one that brews coffee directly into a thermal carafe. Since the coffee isn't exposed to air and retains its heat, it can stay fresh for hours, reducing waste and rebrewing time.

How Do I Make Coffee on Such a Large Scale?

The essence of coffee-making remains the same, whether you're brewing one cup or one hundred:

◆ Grind the coffee immediately before brewing, and grind the beans as fine as you can without losing any through the holes in the filter.

- Use at least two level tablespoons of coffee per six-ounce cup, unless your brewing equipment recommends otherwise.

- Clean the coffee maker and grounds basket after each use; rinse the carafes with hot water before each brew.

- Use fresh or filtered water. Coffee is 98 percent water, after all, so if the water tastes like anything at all, that taste will carry over into the coffee.

  Coffee might taste strong, but it's actually quite delicate. If you boil or reheat coffee, you cook off elements of the flavor and leave more bitter components behind. Storing coffee over a heat source has the same effect. Mixing old with new coffee is another recipe for disaster. Sure, you want to save money by not wasting coffee, but reusing or reviving coffee cheats customers of a clean coffee taste—and will cost you far more in the long run.

- Brew with hot, near-boiling water. Brewing systems are either pour-in, meaning you pour the water into the system before each brew, or in-line, meaning the water is plumbed directly into the machine through attached pipes. In-line systems will heat the water to a pre-set temperature before passing it over the grounds; with a pour-in system, you heat the water yourself before adding it to the machine.

The Least You Need to Know

- The taste of a coffee bean results from where it's grown, how long it's roasted, and when it's ground.

- The less time between roasting, grinding, and brewing, the better the coffee will taste.

- You get what you pay for, so don't buy cheap beans and expect a superior brew.

- You can make your own coffee blends and provide customers a taste they can't find anywhere else.

Chapter **13**

Beans with a Boost

In This Chapter

- The world of coffee drinks
- Pulling the perfect shot of espresso
- Milk madness: Steaming and foaming
- The shot heard round your drink

Regular coffee may still be the king of sales, but the world of coffee drinks goes far beyond "black." Espresso has been around for nearly two centuries, for example, and in an effort to reach new markets, innovative cafés and experimental baristas have come up with all kinds of tasty treats.

Whether you want to create concoctions of your own design or merely satisfy every customer request, let this chapter be your guide to the international world of coffee drinks. Assume the role of drink ambassador and get ready to send customers on a tasty trip!

The World of Specialty Coffee Drinks

Specialty coffees are usually built on a base of espresso with steamed or foamed milk—though some drinks contain no beans at all. Specialty coffee drinks include:

- Cappuccino

- Latté

- Café au lait (this is made with regular coffee, not espresso)

- Hot chocolate

- Flavored steamed milk

- Mocha

- Iced coffee

- Blended frozen coffee drinks

And this list is only the beginning of what's possible! Once you become comfortable making these drinks, you can blend elements from two or more different drinks, search online to find drinks popular in other countries but unknown in the United States, or let customers' tastes guide you in fresh directions.

The Dairy Dilemma

Before we plunge into the drinks themselves, let's look at one of their most important ingredients: milk. Many coffee drinks call for steamed or foamed milk—which we'll describe below—and since the milk holds its heat and texture far longer than the espresso, you'll want to prepare the milk first.

Java-nitions

A whipped cream **dis-penser** looks something like an old-time seltzer bottle, and it uses nitrous oxide **chargers** to blast the liquid cream into its smooth whipped condition and dispense it through the nozzle on top. Load a dispenser with other ingredients, and you can make sweet sauces as well.

But what type of milk should you offer? Milk is named according to its fat content, and there's skim (nonfat), one percent, two percent, and whole. Do you have to offer your customers all of these choices?

Whole milk is the most popular type, with nonfat and two percent tied for second place. If you're in an area with limited competition, you may be able to get away with offering something middle-of-the-road, such as two percent. But if you're in a competitive area or have customers with sophisticated tastes, you may want to offer more choices—and even soy milk, which is a popular option for vegetarians and other health-conscious or dairy-intolerant customers.

Some customers also order their drinks "breve," which means made with half-and-half, so you may want to offer this option as well.

And then there's whipped cream. Canned whipped cream is bad for the environment and is also inferior in taste and texture to fresh, so invest in a *dispenser* and *chargers*, and order fresh pints of cream as you need them.

Steaming and Foaming

Steaming and foaming sound like something you do when you're angry, but really they're the two different ways of preparing milk for specialty coffees. Steamed milk (used in lattés) is merely heated with steam, while foamed milk (used in cappuccinos) is made frothy by mixing air in with the milk. Both steamed and foamed milk are made using the heating wand of your espresso machine.

You've seen the baristas at the local coffee house expertly steam and foam milk—and now it's your turn to learn how!

How to Steam Milk

Believe it or not, you'll use your eyes *and* ears to learn how to steam milk.

1. Fill your steaming pitcher up to three-quarters full with milk. It doesn't matter if you use warm or cold milk, but if you're resteaming milk that has already been steamed, double its volume with fresh, cold milk.

2. Clean the steaming wand of the espresso machine by sending a short blast of steam through it and then wiping it with a cloth that you keep especially for this purpose. (You might consider keeping a pin or needle handy in case the spout does get clogged, although this shouldn't happen with proper maintenance.)

3. Place the steam wand well below the surface of the milk and turn on the steam full blast. Keep the pitcher in one place; moving the pitcher up and down doesn't speed up the process. (And if you lift the end of the wand above the surface of the milk, you'll actually slow down the steaming process.)

Contents May Be Hot

Don't let the milk scald! Scalding the milk, which happens when the temperature hits 200°F (93°C), results in bad-tasting coffee drinks.

4. Use a milk thermometer, which has a clip to hold it on the pitcher, to test the temperature. When the milk reaches 145°F (63°C), get ready to turn off the steam. Heat the milk to just over 150°F (66°C). You'll know it's ready when it makes a sound like an airplane taking off.

5. Turn the steam off, remove the pitcher, and clean the steaming wand with a cloth before the next batch.

Take care not to touch the wand with your bare hands. As you can imagine, all that steam pouring through the wand heats it enough to burn your skin upon contact.

How to Foam Milk

Bubbles, bubbles, bubbles … the bubbles are all-important when you foam milk. Read on to find out how to foam the perfect pitcher.

1. Fill a bell-shaped pitcher (which foams milk better than a straight-sided pitcher) one-third full with cold milk. Milk must be cold to foam. Keep in mind that foaming triples milk's volume. For this reason, you must have plenty of backup pitchers in case you get several orders at once that require foamed milk.

2. Clean the steaming wand of the espresso machine by letting a short blast of steam through it and then wiping it with a cloth.

Contents May Be Hot

Don't move the pitcher around too much, either up and down or around and around. Doing so will result in overly aerated foam with big, fragile bubbles.

3. Place the tip of the steaming wand just below the surface of the milk and turn on the steam. You need to mix air with the milk to create the bubbles, and if you place the tip of the wand just right, the milk will roll in circles as it mixes with air.

4. Gradually lower the pitcher as the top of the milk foams, so that the wand always stays just below the surface of the milk.

To determine how you're doing with the foaming, check out the bubbles. If the bubbles are large and pop quickly, the wand is too far out of the milk. If the bubbles are nice and small, you're on the right track. If you get no bubbles at all, the wand is too far below the surface of the milk or you started with milk that's too warm to foam properly.

Another trick: Let the pitcher sit for a few seconds, then take a spoonful of foam and turn it upside down. If the foam sticks, it's good. If it falls, try again with another batch of milk (and clean up the mess).

5. As with steaming, heat the milk to just over 150°F (66°C), using a milk thermometer to track the temperature.

6. Turn the steam off, remove the pitcher, and clean the steaming wand before the next batch.

With a bit of practice, you can steam and foam milk at the same time. Start by filling a pitcher half-full with cold milk, then follow the instructions above on foaming. The result? A pitcher of steamed milk topped by tiny bubbles of foam. Use a spatula or large spoon to hold back the foam when you need only steamed milk, or use the spoon to push foam onto a drink.

Practice hard enough and you'll even be able to separate the milk from the foam with a simple twist of the wrist.

Hit Them with Your Best Shot

To make many of the specialty coffee drinks we listed above, you need to be able to pull a great shot of espresso. The espresso machine does a lot of the work for you, but you still need to master the basics.

Espresso 101

A good shot of espresso—which is always pronounced with an "eS" and not an "eX"—is created from seven ounces of freshly ground espresso, packed tightly at 50 pounds per square inch (PSI) and brewed with one to one-and-a-half ounces of hot, high-pressure (135 PSI) water for 18 to 24 seconds. Sound like high school science? Don't fret—we'll give you a step-by-step guide to pulling the perfect shot.

Because it's brewed for such a short time, espresso is best made from a dark roast coffee such as a Mexican or Italian roast. Whatever blend you decide upon, make sure you stick with it, as the consistency of your great product is key to keeping customers.

To get the best flavor from the coffee during the short brewing time, espresso is ground very finely. This results in more surface area for the water to come in contact with and extract flavor from.

The reason humans have opposable thumbs is so that we can test the grind of our espresso. Just take a pinch of espresso between your thumb and forefinger and slide it around. If it feels like flour, it's too fine, and if it feels like sugar, it's too coarse. If it feels like grains of sand, it's perfect.

Step-By-Step to Perfect Espresso

When you first try to work an espresso machine, the process will likely seem as clear as mud. Heck, your first pull of espresso might even taste like mud! Don't fret—we'll start by explaining all the terms you need to know, from parts on the espresso machine itself, to supplementary equipment, to what to look for in the cup.

- ◆ A **doser** is a device mounted on your grinder that measures and dispenses ground coffee into a portafilter. (Coffee tastes best when it's made from freshly ground beans, so you'll be using your grinder quite often throughout the day.) **Dosing** is the act of measuring out espresso from your grinder or a stand-alone doser.

- ◆ A **portafilter** looks like a grip on the handlebars of a bicycle. Once the coffee grounds are dosed into a filter insert within the portafilter, you'll tamp the grounds, and then attach the portafilter to a group on your espresso machine.

- ◆ A **tamper** is a hard wood or aluminum, mushroom-shaped tool used to pack the espresso grounds into the portafilter. Avoid plastic tampers as they break and chip when dropped.

- ◆ A **group** is the port on the espresso machine where the espresso is brewed. Espresso machines come with from one to four groups. Hot water runs through the group, over the grounds held in the filter insert, and out the spouts on the bottom of the portafilter into a waiting cup.

- ◆ **Crema** (also *creama*) is the rich, golden-brown foam at the top of a good shot of espresso; this is where the sugars of the coffee are concentrated. The crema should be a quarter-inch thick and last a full minute before beginning to break apart. The characteristics of the crema depend on the grind, the length of the extraction time, and other factors.

We don't expect you to remember all these terms right away, but thanks to the miracle of print, these definitions will always be here should you need them. Now

1. Dose the espresso from your grinder or doser into a portafilter. The doser should be set, preferably by the machine supplier, to dose consistently.

   Never have more beans in the cone-shaped hopper of the grinder than can be used in eight hours, and use ground espresso within an hour. That said, make sure that the grinder contains enough grounds that you'll never get less than a full shot.

   Coffee is moist, so you may have to get aggressive with the doser to make sure you get the full dose. Pull the dosing handle firmly.

2. Place the portafilter on a hard surface—an insulating mat or steel plate works best since countertops can be easily damaged through constant banging—and use the tamper to pack the grounds into the portafilter. Give the grounds a good hard tamp, perhaps even twisting the tamper to flatten the surface.

   An ideal tamp will pack the grounds in at roughly 50 pounds per square inch (PSI); this density will provide the proper resistance to the hot water. Some baristas give the portafilter a shake to dislodge loose grounds from the edges and then give it a second tamp.

3. Fit the portafilter firmly into the espresso machine *group*. If you don't do this firmly enough, the water pressure will push water and espresso grounds out of the sides of the portafilter, which can ruin your shot—not to mention your clothes!

4. Begin brewing within 15 seconds or the espresso will start to deteriorate from the heat and moisture. Yes, it's delicate stuff!

   The ideal temperature for brewing espresso is 195–197°F (90–91°C), and the ideal pressure is 135 PSI. Run one to one and a half ounces of water through the espresso for every shot (about 7 grams). If you have an automatic machine, the machine will run through the right amount of water at the press of a button. If not, you'll need to use a shot glass or timer to make sure you get the right amount.

   Espresso should be extracted (brewed) for 18 to 24 seconds for the best flavor and *crema*. Try to brew the espresso into the cup or glass it will be used in, and serve it within 15 seconds.

5. Remove the portafilter, dump out the grounds, clean it, and return it to its group. The portafilter should always be stored in a group, as this keeps it warm and makes for a better shot of espresso.

How do you get to Carnegie Hall? Practice, practice, practice. Learning how to make espresso takes the same kind of dedication as no one gets it right the first, the fifth, or sometimes even the fiftieth time. Every employee will likely add her own personal twist to the brewing process, but first she—and you—must master the basics.

Beans of Wisdom

The less fat there is in milk, the easier it is to foam. That said, the creaminess that comes with whole milk makes for a drink that's much more flavorful than one made with skim milk. If you ever offer free samples of drinks to entice new customers, be sure to use whole milk so that they experience the richest taste possible!

You Want a *What?*

When is an espresso not an espresso? When it's one of these commonly ordered espresso creations:

- **Double (or *doppio*):** A double shot, for the ultimate pick-me-up

- **Espresso macchiato:** Espresso topped with foamed milk

- **Espresso con panna:** Espresso with whipped cream

- **Americano:** Espresso with hot water added to make strong coffee

- **Espresso romano:** A *demitasse*—that is, a serving—of espresso with a twist of lemon on the side

- **Ristretto:** About three quarters of an ounce of espresso; the first, sweet burst of espresso that comes out of the machine

But wait, there's more! For many customers, espresso is merely the base into which everything else is mixed or added. Learning to pull is the first step; next you start mixing and matching, gaining more knowledge about what espresso can do with every drink.

From Mocha to Iced Coffee: How to Create Specialty Coffee Drinks

You've got the espresso (after enough measuring and timing to make you feel like a scientist), and you've got the steamed or foamed milk. Here's how to put them together to make delicious specialty coffee drinks.

♦ **Cappuccino**   Pour or pull one shot of espresso into an 8-ounce cup. Fill the cup two-thirds full with steamed milk and top with foam. For a large, use a 12- to 16-ounce cup and two shots of espresso. If a customer asks for a "dry" cappuccino, spoon foam onto the espresso and forgo the steamed milk.

♦ **Café Latté**   Pour or pull one shot of espresso into an 8-ounce cup and fill the cup seven-eighths full with steamed milk. For a large, use a 12- or 16-ounce cup and two shots of espresso. (Some baristas add a bit of foam on top, while others insist that it has no place in a latté.)

♦ **Café Latteccino**   As you might gather from the name, this drink blurs the lines between lattés and cappuccinos. To a shot of espresso, add two parts steamed milk and one part foamed milk.

♦ **Café au Lait**   Fill a cup half full with coffee and half full with steamed milk.

♦ **Café Mocha**   Cover the bottom of an 8-ounce cup with chocolate syrup, then pour or pull one shot of espresso into the cup. Fill the cup seven-eighths full with steamed milk, then top with foam or pile on the whipped cream. For a large, use a 12- to 16-ounce cup and two shots of espresso.

♦ **Café con panna**   Pour a shot of espresso, then top it with whipped cream.

♦ **Café breve**   A standard milk-based espresso in which half-and-half is used instead of another type of milk.

♦ **Hot Chocolate**   Use .75 ounces of chocolate syrup for an 8-ounce cup, 1 ounce for a 12-ounce cup, and 1.25 ounces for a 16-ounce cup. Cover the bottom of the cup with the chocolate and fill seven-eighths full with steamed milk. Top with foam or a mound of whipped cream.

Coffee Quips

"Coffee is a fleeting moment and a fragrance."
—Claudia Roden

◆ **Flavored Steamed Milk**   Use .5 ounces of flavored syrup and 6.5 ounces of cold milk for an 8-ounce cup, .75 ounces of syrup and 10.25 ounces of cold milk for a 12-ounce cup, and 1 ounce of syrup and 14 ounces of cold milk for a 16-ounce cup. Pour the syrup and the milk into a foaming container and foam the mixture to a temperature of 160°F (71°C).

◆ **Italian Soda**   Mix one ounce of flavored syrup with mineral water or club soda. You can add half-and-half for a creamy treat.

Flavor Shots

Many customers want more than the perfect shot of espresso, blended with the exact quantity of steamed or foamed milk—they also want it flavored! You can get syrups with flavors that go well in coffee drinks, chocolate, Italian sodas, and foamed milk, such as:

◆ Vanilla

◆ Almond

◆ Mint

◆ Hazelnut

◆ Raspberry

◆ Lime

◆ Orange

◆ Boysenberry

If you have a half-dozen or so different flavors to choose from, your customers should be very happy. Choose half of your syrups from the nutty or sweet side of the spectrum for coffees, such as vanilla and almond, and half from the fruity side for Italian sodas, such as raspberry and boysenberry.

The Least You Need to Know

◆ Foaming and steaming milk is an exact science that you'll need to learn if you plan to create specialty coffee drinks.

◆ Speaking of exact science, pulling the perfect shot of espresso means using the right amount of coffee, the right amount of water, the right brewing temperature, and the right brewing time.

◆ Espresso is a delicate thing; be sure to use fresh beans and grind only what you can use in an hour. Brew espresso within 15 seconds of dosing it, and use the espresso within 15 seconds of brewing it.

◆ Don't forget the flavors! Many customers want their coffee and chocolate enhanced with mint, hazelnut, raspberry, and other flavors. You can also use flavored syrups to make Italian sodas.

14

Tea for Two–or Two Hundred

In This Chapter

- Eye-opening tales of tea history
- How to make green tea black
- Which form of tea for thee?
- Brewing and serving

Let's take a break from our immersion in all things coffee and spend a few pages talking about the world's other favorite hot drink: tea. Not everyone who walks into your store will be a coffee fan, after all, so to keep all your visitors happy, you'll want a variety of drinks on hand.

An obvious choice for a coffee alternative, tea can be served both hot and cold, its preparation requires many of the same items as coffee (clean filtered water, insulated cups, sugar, milk), and it's best taken with a side order of cookies or biscuits, thus boosting food sales at the same time!

Tales of Tea

Tea, known by the scientific name *Camellia sinensis*, has been part of our culinary menu for anywhere from 1,800 to 4,700 years. The origins of tea are unclear, but Chinese legend credits Emperor Shen Nung, who ruled in the 2730s B.C.E., with the discovery.

Supposedly Emperor Nung was boiling a pot of water to drink—boiling would sterilize the water, although germs weren't yet a concern in ancient China—when a leaf from a nearby tea bush landed in the pot and infused the water with its flavor. The emperor tried the flavored water, found it invigorating, and added tea to his stock of herbal medicine. (Would you drink water that had been tainted and discolored by a random leaf? Probably not, but that boldness must be why Shen Nung was emperor in the first place.)

The Japanese offer a competing tale of tea's origin, one that involves Bodhidharma, the man who brought Buddhism from India to China and Japan. Around 520 C.E., Bodhidharma started a nine-year course of meditation, during which he would do nothing but stare at a wall.

Instant Facts

To preserve tea for travel, the Chinese of the tenth through twelfth centuries molded tea into bricks, which were then bartered for other goods. These tea bricks were often mixed with salt, onion, garlic, and dried fish—surely the first power bar known to humanity, but hardly a recipe for success in today's market!

Five years into his mission(!), Bodhidharma grew weary for a moment and closed his eyes. When he awoke, he was so furious with himself for falling asleep that he ripped off his eyelids and threw them on the ground. A plant grew from the bits of his flesh, and he brewed its leaves into a drink that kept him alert through the remaining four years of his meditation.

Putting aside the myths, written records show that tea was part of daily life in China by the eighth century. Chinese merchants spread tea throughout Asia by trading goods with Turks, Japanese, and others.

The Dutch started importing tea from China in the early seventeenth century and made the drink a hit with aristocrats in England. By the 1650s, prices had dropped enough that British coffeehouses were serving tea as an alternative to coffee and hot chocolate. (The more things change ….)

European traders spread the love of tea to North America and throughout the rest of the world. Currently, some 40 countries produce about 6 billion pounds of tea annually.

Learning about the Leaves

As with coffee and its range of roasts, the flavor of a tea bush's leaves depends as much on how the leaves are processed as it does on the type of bush from which the leaves are picked.

In fact, you can take leaves from one bush and process them in different ways to make green, black, and oolong tea. The processing methods mainly differ in how much *fermentation*—that is, how much chemical reaction between air and the leaf's natural enzymes—occurs inside the leaves.

Grilling Up the Green

To make green tea, the freshly picked leaves are steamed or pan-fried, destroying the enzymes and preventing fermentation. Without fermentation, the leaves' oils and antioxidants remain in their natural state, which is why green tea tastes most like the leaves themselves.

Steaming also softens the leaves, which makes it easier for handlers during the next step: rolling or twisting the leaves. This action, performed by machine for mass production batches and by hand for specialty blends, breaks down the cells in the leaves so that the flavorful oils and juices will infuse the water during brewing.

The leaves are then heated again to dry them out, and the rolling/heating cycle might be repeated one or more times afterward to slowly remove the moisture from the leaves.

Contents May Be Hot

You can try to grow *Camellia sinensis* on your own, but be sure to keep a pair of pruning shears handy. In the wild, untended tea plants can grow up to 30 feet high!

Finally, the green tea is graded based on its age and shape. The best grade, Gunpowder, is given to young leaves rolled into tiny BB-like pellets. Other grades include Young Hyson (rolled or twisted middle-aged leaves) and Imperial (old leaves that resemble Gunpowder), but the names might vary depending on the source of the leaves.

Any Color You Like—As Long As It's Black

Black tea is everything green tea isn't. During processing, the leaves are laid out to dry—either in the sun or the shade, depending on the type of tea. Once the leaves have started to shrivel, they're rolled by hand or machine to mix air with the natural juices, and this starts the fermentation process in earnest.

After only a few hours, the leaves have turned a coppery red and are dried to stop fermentation from changing the leaves' taste any further. Once dry, the whole leaves, broken bits, and dust are sifted so that particles of the same size end up together. This process creates a finished product with an even brewing time.

Instant Facts

Sri Lanka, the Indian Ocean island formerly known as Ceylon, once produced only coffee, but in 1869 disease wiped out the coffee bean plantations. Tea was introduced to replace the beans, and today Sri Lanka is the third-largest producer of tea in the world.

Grades for black tea correspond to the size of the leaves or pieces: Orange Pekoe, or OP, refers to whole leaves; broken Orange Pekoe (BOP) is used for large pieces of leaves; fannings is used for small bits; and dust is exactly what it sounds like.

Fannings and dust grades typically end up being used in mass-market tea bags because the large amount of surface area causes the tea to infuse quickly and make a dark cup of tea. As with coffee, though, the large surface area also means that any unpleasant flavors in the leaves find their way into the cup.

Green + Black = Oolong?

Oolong tea falls between green and black in that the leaves are fermented, but not completely, so the leaves carry a mix of their natural flavor and the fermented juices. While green tea is favored throughout Asia and black tea far outsells everything else in the Western hemisphere, the "little bit of this, little bit of that" taste of oolong tea accounts for only 2 percent of the tea sold.

More specialized teas with even smaller market shares (and higher retail prices) include pouchong tea, which falls between green and oolong on the processing scale, and white tea. White tea is processed like green tea—that is, not very much—but the leaves are harvested before they fully open while the buds are covered by delicate white hairs.

Now with Even More Flavor!

As with coffee beans, tea leaves can have flavors and scents added to them to create tastes not found in nature. The Chinese have had flavored tea for at least a thousand years, and their methods still work today, although machines now give the process a bit more oomph.

To create jasmine tea, for example, harvesters gather jasmine blossoms at dawn before they've bloomed for the day. The blossoms are placed on or mixed with dry tea leaves destined to be either green or oolong, and when evening comes, the blossoms open their petals and the tea leaves absorb the jasmine aroma. This process is repeated anywhere from two to nine times to create the desired level of jasmine flavor.

In other cases, such as with vanilla, peach, and orange teas, the flavoring is sprayed on the tea leaves before they're heated. Earl Grey, for instance, is made with oil of bergamot, which is extracted from the peel of the bergamot orange, a sour pear-shaped fruit cultivated mostly in southern Italy. As the tea leaves dry, they absorb the flavor of the oil. Lapsang Souchong, on the other hand, gets its intense smoky flavor by smoking the tea leaves over pine wood. Spiced teas often contain dried spices and pieces of fruit rinds to perk up the flavor and increase the visual appeal of the tea.

Java-nitions

The best-tasting teas are those made from a *fine picking*—that is, a harvest in which only the top two leaves and bud are plucked from the tea plant. A *coarse picking* grabs up to five leaves from the stem, and these inner leaves provide a harsher-tasting tea that usually ends up in *CTC* (crush, tear, curl) products, such as low-cost tea bags.

High on Chai

In many parts of the world, *chai* is simply the word for tea. In the United States, however, chai refers to a specific kind of milky spiced tea that originated in India, where it's known as masala chai.

Typically, chai is made using black tea leaves; some combination of cardamom, cinnamon, cloves, ginger, pepper, fennel, and allspice; warm milk; and a sweetener such as granulated sugar, honey, or a flavored syrup.

Making chai by hand is time-consuming, as different ingredients must steep for different lengths of time and the spices must be strained from the drink prior to serving. Thankfully for busy cafés that can't afford to spend ten minutes on a single drink, dry chai mixes are available that provide a taste nearly equal to homemade.

Chai latté, which is more popular than chai in many cafés, is similar to chai except that it's made specifically with steamed milk instead of milk warmed any other way. We talked about how to steam milk in Chapter 13, and that advice will serve you well with this hip drink.

When Is a Tea Not a Tea?

All teas are herbal since an herb is any plant with medicinal, savory, or aromatic qualities—the very definition of tea, in other words—but not all herbal teas are actually teas. Instead of using the leaves and buds from *Camellia sinensis*, most herbal teas use dried leaves, bark, roots, or flowers from other types of plants.

Rose petals, mint, ginseng, chamomile, and even catnip are all examples of nontea plants that make a surprisingly tealike drink when they're infused in hot water.

A Question of Presentation

We've filled your head with a treasury of tea lore, but now you need to push aside the romance of tea and make a practical decision on how you should sell tea at your coffee bar: In no-name tea bags? Specialty tea bags? Loose in individual teapots? By the pot as well as by the cup? To help you decide, consider the following questions:

♦ **How many customers will buy tea?** Clearly you won't know the answer to this question before you open, but you can estimate the number by examining cafés and restaurants around town. How many types of tea do they offer compared to types of coffee? How do tea sales compare to coffee sales at the local donut shop? Does your town already support a tea shop?

♦ **What image am I trying to project in my store?** If your image is homespun and down-to-earth, customers will welcome commonly known brands of tea bags. If you're aiming more for an upscale image, you need to shy away from supermarket brands of teabags and sell only specialty brands or even loose tea.

With loose tea, you then have to decide whether to use tea balls (stainless-steel, wire-mesh strainers that allow water to circulate through the leaves), opt for filters that fit into teapots, or throw the leaves in loose.

Instant Facts

Thomas Sullivan, a tea importer in New York, invented the tea bag in 1908—but to cut costs, not to boost tea sales. Sullivan regularly sent out large tins of tea to let potential buyers sample his wares. To lower his overhead costs, Sullivan switched from tins to small silk bags that held an individual serving of tea.

♦ **What can I charge for tea, and how long will it take to make?** Serving tea is akin to serving specialty coffee drinks—you make each order individually as the customer requests it. If you decide to carry loose tea, employees need to measure the tea as they make each cup or pot. They'll spend as much time preparing tea as they would making, say, a café latté. Can you charge an equivalent price, or will customers reject the price tag?

Keep in mind that you can choose a combination of offerings—say, loose tea leaves for most drinks but a dry mix for chai—and that you can always change your store's offerings should tea prove to be more or less popular than your research originally showed.

Brewing Basics

The title of this chapter could have been "Separated at Birth?" because coffee and tea share an amazing number of similarities: they're the two most popular hot drinks in the world; their taste depends largely on how the raw materials are roasted and cooked; and flavored versions are becoming increasingly popular.

With all that in mind, let's look at what goes into brewing a cup or pot of tea and see what other similarities we can find.

Making Sure the Medium Isn't the Message

As with coffee (ah-ha!), brewed tea is 99 percent water and 1 percent solids and essences extracted from the raw materials. To ensure that the water (the "medium" that delivers the desired flavor) doesn't distract the drinker from the taste of the tea, you should use only filtered, nonchlorinated water for brewing.

If you have a pour-in brewing system for coffee—that is, one in which you heat water and add it manually to the brewer—you're all set, since you can use the same water source for tea that you use for coffee. If you own an in-line brewing system that heats the water internally, the machine most likely has a separate valve that will issue hot water.

Unfortunately, "hot" water isn't specific enough for our purposes. Different teas require water of different temperatures for optimum brewing results:

♦ Green tea leaves are the most fragile, delivering their best flavor when steeped in water between 160° and 175°F.

♦ Oolongs are best when steeped in water that's around 190°F.

♦ Black teas need water that's heated to a full rolling boil (212°F).

To take the water's temperature, you can use the milk thermometer you bought to help steam and foam milk. With a bit of experience, though, you'll be able to judge the temperature solely by sight and sound. At 160–170°F, the water will be on the verge of simmering, so it should appear somewhat restless. At 190°F, steam will rise from the water and bubbles will come to the surface. A rolling boil is exactly what it sounds like: bubbles tumbling all over each other like children in a ball pit.

Avoid "Pre-Flavored" Cups

If you're a regular tea drinker, you already know that teapots and cups build up a brownish haze over time. What you might not realize is that this haze is more than a mere coloring; this residue adds a slight bitterness to each new cup that you drink.

If you plan to use Styrofoam cups in-house, then tea haze build-up is a nonissue. For those who are using ceramic teapots and cups to satisfy an upscale clientele, make sure to clean them thoroughly with a mild detergent or baking soda to remove the haze.

Measuring Cup Size

At home or in the office, most of us make a "cup" of tea in a standard 8-ounce mug. Tea experts, however, have a different size cup in mind, one that holds only 5.5 ounces.

While you should feel free to ignore the experts and use whatever size cups you wish in your business, keep in mind that all references to cups in instructions for making tea refer only to those holding 5.5 ounces.

Tea, Spoon, Teaspoon

For each cup of water (5.5 ounce cups, mind you) that a cup or teapot holds, add one teaspoon of loose tea or one teabag. With loose tea, use an actual teaspoon when first measuring the leaves, then transfer the tea to the spoons you'll use every day in the shop so that you can eyeball the measurement in the future.

Time for Tea

In general, the smaller the leaf, the faster the brewing time. Tea bags, which use tiny bits of leaves and dust, should brew for no longer than three minutes. Medium- and large-size leaves of black tea should brew for up to five minutes. Green teas should steep from two to three minutes, while oolongs need from four to seven minutes. Brewing time is really the key to tea: brew it too long, and it gets bitter; brew it too little, and you'll have only discolored water with a bare hint of flavor.

You'll likely hand the tea to customers right away, and that's both good and bad. Fast service is good because, like coffee, tea tastes best when consumed immediately after brewing—and you can start serving the next customer and keep the line moving! The bad part is that the customer doesn't know how long the tea has brewed. Color alone doesn't tell the whole story; a tea isn't ready to be sipped just because it's brown. And once the tea is in the customer's hands, he might leave the tea bag or leaves in the cup long past the optimal brewing time, thereby making the tea more bitter.

The best thing you can do—aside from waiting by the customer's table and yanking out the teabag at the proper time—is tell customers how long to wait for the brewing process to run its course. You can also hand out small sand timers that customers can use while in the store.

Instant Facts

Soft water infuses tea more easily than hard. In fact, some experts claim that hard water—that is, water with a high degree of dissolved calcium and magnesium—is completely unsuited for brewing tea. While we wouldn't go that far, we do recommend increasing brewing times a bit if your shop uses hard water.

Milk and More

As with its good friend and arch nemesis coffee, tea can be consumed black or it can be jazzed up with milk—skim, two percent, or full-fat—and sweeteners, whether granulated sugar, sugar cubes, honey, or (as the Russians sometimes like it) with a dollop of raspberry jam. Some tea drinkers also like a touch of fresh lemon juice.

Whether you add these, um, additions to the tea yourself or let customers customize their own tea will depend on the layout of your coffee bar, a topic covered in detail in Chapter 8.

Iced Is Nice

So far we've talked only about the hot stuff, but when the summer months roll around, your customers will likely be far more interested in your selection of iced teas.

Iced tea, unlike its hot, fresh-today, stale-in-an-hour cousin, doesn't need to be made fresh for each customer. Equipment vendors have many styles of iced tea machines that create the drink with nary more than the touch of a button, and iced tea typically retains its flavor for a full 24 hours.

> **Instant Facts**
>
> In the summer of 1904, Englishman Richard Blechynden was hired by Indian tea growers to promote tea at the World's Fair in Missouri. To no one's surprise but his, the hot tea was a sales failure in the steamy American Midwest. Desperate to make sales, Blechynden poured the tea over ice and created a cool treat that was a hit with fair-goers. Despite its origin at the hands of an Englishman, iced tea is difficult if not impossible to find in the United Kingdom.

If you desire—and if you think your customers will appreciate the difference—you can make your own iced tea by hand. Start with one ounce (approximately two table-spoons) of whole-leaf tea and add one quart of water that's only slightly below boiling temperature. Steep the leaves for 3-5 minutes, then strain them out. Add one quart of water at room temperature, and then pour the drink over ice as you serve it.

Sugar dissolves better in hot water than cold, so if your market prefers the sweet stuff, dissolve the sugar in the tea before you add the room-temperature water and serve the tea pre-sweetened. Feelings vary widely about how much sugar is enough—and how much is too much. You'd do best to add no more than one-half cup of sugar and allow customers to sweeten the final brew to their own tastes.

The Least You Need to Know

- You'll probably already have everything you need to make tea except the leaves, so it's a good idea to think about adding tea to the menu.

- Making tea ranges from a drop-dead simple dunk of the tea bag to a carefully tended pot of slowly unfolding leaves, giving you plenty of options for your market.

- Tea comes in as many flavors as coffee, and the growth of chai sales shows a real love for strong-tasting drinks.

- The number of bottled iced teas on the market has grown rapidly, but fresh iced tea is easy to make and serve and the taste far surpasses pre-made tea.

15

The Rest of the Menu

In This Chapter

- Balancing the hot with the cold
- Smooth drinks for health-conscious customers
- Food to fuel sales
- Drinks with a kick
- Dealing to the do-it-yourselfer

To run a coffee bar, you must sell—say it with us—coffee. Since many people will see the word "coffee" and assume that you process the beans in more than one way, you probably want to handle espresso, cappuccino, and other such drinks. Once you decide to sell these, you might as well add hot chocolate and tea to the menu, thereby covering the entire world of hot beverages.

This selection might seem extensive from your point of view—especially when you start teaching new employees how to make it all—but you will inevitably face customers who frown at the menu and say, "Is that all you got?"

To anticipate such demands, as well as satisfy the desires of every young Dick or Jane who comes in with their coffee-drinking parents, you will likely want to expand your beverage line in many other ways. And why stop there? Man (and woman) does not live by liquid alone. Expand your product line to offer an array of goodies and sweets, whether freshly made at local bakeries or pre-packaged from large manufacturers, that customers will order with their drinks. If the market is right, you might even consider adding sandwiches, soups, or other hot foods to your menu.

Before you put on the oven mitts and start making meals, read on to discover the legal ins and outs that come with food preparation.

Cold Drinks, Hot Profits

Coffee-based drinks have an inviting aroma that draws customers off the streets and up to your counter. Cold drinks lack that enticing element, but the ka-ching they'll bring to the register will be music to your ears.

Soft Drinks

Thanks to decades of marketing muscle, Coke and Pepsi are known throughout the world, from the school around the block to villages in far-off lands. Everyone's part of the next generation, teaching the world to sing in perfect harmony. In addition to the cola itself, the parent companies of Coke and Pepsi sell a diverse number of carbonated drinks that satisfy different thirsts.

Selling products made by one of these companies makes perfect sense since customers know and enjoy them. The real question for you is how to sell them: from a vending machine, in bottles, or from a fountain.

Instant Facts

Don't be too surprised if new menu items bring new expenses. The city of Chicago, for instance, adds a nine percent tax onto the cost of syrup used to make fountain drinks. Research potential taxes at town hall to avoid unexpected surprises at tax time!

Offering canned sodas in vending machines requires the least effort from you, as a local distributor will likely provide the machine for free and visit your shop regularly to stock it. With little effort, however, comes little reward. The distributor will keep most of the funds collected by the machine, which means that you're giving up space in your coffee bar to advertise and sell another company's product (through the large, backlit graphic on the vending machine) for a relatively small return.

Selling bottled soda from a cooler offers a better return on the space required in your store because you'll buy the soda directly from a distributor and keep everything that you collect. You'll need money up front to purchase the initial deliveries and storage space in the backroom to hold stock—a subject we'll take stock of in Chapter 17—but after a while you'll be able to use past profits to buy product for the future.

That said, your best bet might be to sell soda straight from the fountain since it costs only about one cent per ounce. Even when you toss in the cost of ice, a straw, and a cup, you'll spend far less preparing a fountain drink than you would on canned or bottled soda. Set up the fountain in the seating area so that customers serve themselves and you can even avoid the labor costs of filling the cups. Admittedly you will have to handle heavy boxes of syrup to keep the fountains running, but the soda companies will handle all maintenance on the machines.

If you do opt for fountain drinks, remember to work the fountain into the design of the shop since additional plumbing and drainage will be needed.

> **Beans of Wisdom**
>
> Don't feel that you have to stick with soda only from the big two. More than 400 kinds of soft drinks are available in the U.S. market. By offering sodas that aren't available in every supermarket and convenience store, you can set yourself apart from other businesses and attract customers who want something cold that's also cool.

Bottled Water and Juices

Aside from stocking the standard sodas, you can pack a cooler with bottled water, plain and flavored seltzers, and multiple fruit juices that package produce in ways that nature never could. The only limitations on your product line are your budget and the size of your cooler.

Keep in mind with all bottled beverages that you're never locked in with your offerings. If, for example, an intense ginger ale just doesn't catch on with customers, clear it out and use the space for a new pomegranate fruit drink or carbonated raspberry soda instead.

Instead of sticking with bottles, you might choose to purchase fresh lemon concentrate (an oxymoron, we admit) from a supplier and make lemonade to order for mere pennies. You can even provide a pitcher of iced water and plastic cups so that customers can help themselves. This practice might cut into bottled water sales, but customers will appreciate access to free water and might spring for a treat instead.

Ask customers what types of drinks they want to see because they might suggest a product line that you would have otherwise never considered. (We'll talk more about customer relations in Chapter 19.)

> **Contents May Be Hot** _____
>
> Fresh-squeezed juice appeals to health-conscious consumers, but wringing out a half-dozen oranges takes a lot of time when the line at the register backs up. You can juice the fruit at the start of the day, but then you have to take great care storing it to prevent microorganisms from setting up house. Check with the local health department before offering fresh juice to see whether you can balance the demands of health and labor.

As with bottled sodas, extra stock of water and juices will require a lot of space in your store's backroom—and the heavy bottles won't fit on shelves, so you'll need plenty of floor space. We're not trying to discourage you from offering these low-labor, high-profit items; we're merely making you aware of all the handling issues they entail.

Italian Soda and Granitas

In Chapter 13, we talked about fruity flavor shots, such as raspberry, orange, and lime. While some madcap coffee drinkers might favor raspberry over almond in their cup, these sweet flavors will serve you—and your customers—far better in cold treats like Italian soda and granitas.

To make an Italian soda, mix one ounce of flavored syrup with mineral water or club soda, then pour it over ice. You can add half-and-half for a creamy treat.

Granitas are frozen, slushy drinks that combine fruity flavor shots with other flavors such as coffee. Unfortunately, to make a decent granita, you need to purchase a granita machine, which tends to cost as much as an espresso machine and yet be unreliable compared with more familiar pieces of kitchen equipment. Research your market thoroughly before making this type of investment.

Egg Creams and Real Cream

Since you already have the flavored syrups close at hand, you might consider adding egg creams to your list of liquid treats. Egg creams, which were invented in Brooklyn and are little known outside New York, are an easy-to-make treat that will delight your customers.

Despite the simple-sounding name, egg creams contain no eggs and no cream; the only ingredients are milk, seltzer, and flavored syrup, most commonly chocolate syrup although other flavors work just as well.

To make an egg cream, take a chilled 12-ounce glass, add one-half cup of cold whole milk, squirt seltzer into the glass until a nice creamy head forms (about one-half cup), and pour 2 tablespoons chocolate syrup in a thin stream through the foam. Carefully insert a long thin spoon through the foam and stir the syrup into the milk without disturbing the head. That's all there is to it!

Aside from drinks that are cream in name only, you might consider stocking extra supplies of milk and cream for retail sale if your dairy source can't be found in a common supermarket. Use creams from a local dairy farm, for example, and you can be sure that customers will want to bring some home for themselves.

Smoothies

We included smoothie machines on the list of equipment you might consider purchasing back in Chapter 9. Now's when we convince you that you want one.

Smoothies appeal to the sweet tooth in every customer, yet they contain light ingredients that appeal to customers who pooh-pooh ice cream and chocolate cookies. You can make smoothies with fresh or frozen fruit, sherbets, sorbets, liquid concentrate mixes, or even vanilla-based powders, with each drink prepared fresh for each customer.

While the range of smoothie flavors is limited only by your imagination—and the gag reflex of your customers—do keep in mind the potential for waste if certain ingredients can't be used for anything else. If an orange sherbet is used in smoothies only twice before it turns icy and frostbitten in the freezer, you're going to lose money on the wasted food.

Instant Facts

Louis Auster, a candy store owner in Brooklyn, is credited with inventing the egg cream in 1890. The drink was so popular that lines of customers would form down the street, and the candy shop would be standing room only. As a result, egg creams are traditionally consumed while standing—never sitting!

A Little Something on the Side

The appeal of adding food items to your menu of offerings is easy to understand. Many coffee drinkers—dare we say most—prefer to have something to nibble on while they drink their cuppa, and rather than sending them to the office vending machine for a three-pack of powdered doughnuts, you can fill the void with goodies of your own.

Don't feel that you must carry food to succeed. In the right location, sales of coffee drinks alone can support your shop. If you've set up in such an area, you might choose to avoid complicating your business by adding in food distributors, buying new display cases, applying for additional licenses from the local government, and so forth.

If, however, sales need a boost to push you into profitability (a topic we'll cover in Chapter 21), or you want to draw in customers who might otherwise opt for chain coffee shops, survey the sections below and learn how you can feature food for fun and profit.

Morning Munchies

For many businesspeople, the day begins with the first cup of coffee—but that coffee rarely flies solo. No, it travels arm-in-arm with a muffin, croissant, cinnamon roll, scone, bagel, or Danish—all hand-held treats that can add a couple of dollars to any coffee sale.

Given the capital costs you would have to pay to start producing these items on your own—starting with a multithousand-dollar convection oven, but also including whisks, mixing bowls, measuring cups, a dozen other items, and the know-how to use them—you should find a local bakery or food supplier that can deliver these items fresh to your door each morning. (We'll cover how to find and judge suppliers of all types in Chapter 16.)

All-Day Treats

In addition to the items listed above, you can offer many other tempting, low-cost impulse foods, such as cookies, brownies, candies, pastries, and slices of cakes and pies, that will attract sales throughout the day. Display these items in the display case that customers pass on the way to place their order and on glass-covered plates near the register. After all, it's hard to sell impulse foods when customers don't have a chance to be impulsive!

Contents May Be Hot _____

You might make the best Rocky Road Brownies in the world, but think twice before offering homemade treats in a retail establishment. Many state health departments require separate food permits for home bakeries and demand inspection of the premises. Some even insist that the bakers establish separate commercial kitchens in their homes. Don't be a show-off if you're flaunting the law!

Full-Meal Deal

If you're feeling ambitious or want to distinguish yourself from the competition, you might go so far as to add complete meals to your menu, such as a sandwich and chips or hot soup with a side of bread.

The easy way to make such meals is to order them from food suppliers in a nearly complete form. You can heat frozen or canned soups in a countertop electric holding unit and order bread from the bakery that supplies your morning pastries.

Food suppliers can also provide panini sandwiches that you store in a refrigerated display case and grill in a panini press as they're ordered. Within minutes, you can serve customers a hot sandwich far superior to whatever cold leftovers they brought from home.

Another possibility for ready-to-eat meals is a local deli willing to prepare and deliver fresh, pre-wrapped sandwiches at wholesale prices each day. You'll have to order enough sandwiches to make it worth the effort, so balance the profits against the potential for waste before jumping into such a deal.

Beans of Wisdom _____

Before adding foods to the menu whenever the urge hits you, make sure that the food license granted to you by the local health department covers such sales. Pre-packaged foods like candy and bagged cookies usually fall under a different licensing category than cookies and brownies, which themselves fall under a different category than refrigerated cakes and made-to-order foods like sandwiches and soup.

Even if these meals are a hit with customers, don't feel that you should necessarily try to do even more, such as offering cold cuts with a choice of toppings or freshly made salads. The purpose behind offering solids to complement your liquids is to provide customers with enough options to keep them coming to your establishment, thus boosting your bottom line.

The last thing you want to do is overburden you and your staff with prep work and the cost of ovens, exhaust vents, and wasted food. A final concern for some entrepreneurs might be sour relations with neighboring businesses that already sell hot meals. If you expand into their turf by offering surf-and-turf dinners, they'll likely find room for coffee and cookies on their menu.

Food Without the Financing

If you want to offer customers something solid to go with their drinks—but you don't want to prepare food yourself—steal a page from the fast-food market and *dual-brand* with a local restaurant.

Dual-branding occurs when two businesses that sell separate product lines come together in one building to create a more attractive draw for customers. Pizza Hut and Taco Bell, both owned by Yum! Brands, Inc., commonly dual-brand with one another; having both businesses in one location provides a greater variety of products for sale without the need for two buildings.

While you're unlikely to convince a nationally known franchisee to split the costs of business with you, you might able to find a locally owned business, such as an ice cream parlor or deli, that will partner up with you. Doing so will likely lower the costs of rent and other utility bills without affecting your level of sales. Even if this option doesn't appeal to you initially, keep it in mind when you start to consider expanding to a new location, something we cover more thoroughly in Chapter 21.

Should You Serve Alcohol?

If you plan to operate late at night in a busy downtown area or near a college campus, you might consider serving alcohol-flavored drinks to provide a cup with a bit more kick. In addition to widening the scope of your menu, you'll also score a decent chunk of change with each sale as customers are often willing to shell out a premium for alcoholic beverages.

Before you go grabbing bottles of Créme de Menthe and Kahlua to dress up the drinks, we need to set up a few legalistic hoops that demand your attention.

Landing a Liquor License

Sales of liquor, even for businesses like yours that won't be dishing out straight shots of whisky, require special licenses from the local government, perhaps from a special alcohol control board.

Many towns are divided into districts that prohibit alcohol sales in certain zones. If you open in one of these "dry" parts of town—next door to an elementary school or a church, for example—you have no chance of garnering a liquor license. If this isn't the case, you might be out of luck simply because the town issues a limited number of licenses, all of which have been claimed.

Instant Facts

Filling out the liquor license application is only the first step in some parts of the United States. In Arizona, for instance, first-time applicants must attend a management training course to learn about their responsibilities as sellers of alcohol in the state.

If a license is available, you'll likely have to post a notice on the store window of your intent to sell alcoholic beverages so that residents in that area can lobby against you, if they so choose.

Staff Spirit

Once you have the liquor license in hand, you need to train your employees on how to handle the hard stuff without running afoul of the law. Ignorance of the legal issues won't protect an employee from being prosecuted or your liquor license from being pulled if the offense is severe enough.

To begin with, aside from the usual regulations that apply to food and drink preparation, employees must now be wary of serving alcoholic drinks to intoxicated customers. If a drunk individual causes an accident after leaving your coffee bar, you or your employees could be held liable or named in a civil lawsuit—even if the drink contained only a trace of alcohol.

You could also be held responsible for alcohol-related crimes that occur in a parking lot adjacent to your shop, even though the lot might not be considered a part of your location.

Since localities generally prohibit underage employees from serving alcohol, you now must consider employee age when making up work schedules to ensure that an employee of the proper age is always on hand to prepare and serve certain drinks.

Inventory control also takes on a whole new meaning once you start serving alcohol. Keep these supplies under lock and key and maintain a rigorous reorder policy, perhaps keeping the empty bottles as a check and balance system.

Instant Facts

Health Communications, Inc., a Washington, D.C.–based organization founded by a former director of the National Institute of Alcohol Abuse and Alcoholism, markets a program called TIPS (Training for Intervention Procedures) that teaches servers and managers how to sell alcohol responsibly. Visit http://www.gettips.com to find training programs near you.

All of these restrictions might deflate your enthusiasm for carrying alcohol-flavored hot drinks, but given the weight of the legal material you're already bearing—food establishment license, reseller's license, business license, business lease, vendor contracts, and so forth—you might consider these limitations merely a few more pebbles on the top of a mountain.

In the right market, these beverages with a bang can really boost your sales volume thanks to the high retail prices that they bring—a boost that might reduce the drawbacks to a mere afterthought. As always, a mix of market research and trial-and-error is the key to knowing what will sell best in your business.

Hardware, Soft Sell

You'll spend a lot of money purchasing equipment for your shop and—assuming you learn how to use it all correctly—your customers will greatly appreciate the investment you make.

Some of them will appreciate it so much, in fact, that they'll want to purchase similar equipment for themselves. Oh, they might not spring for a $1,000-plus espresso machine, but they'll lay out a few hundred dollars for a smaller model. If espresso doesn't grab them, they might still buy a French press, a grinder, or even an old-fashioned percolator.

Where are they going to purchase said items? Why, from you, of course! That's right—in addition to selling the drinks themselves, you should also deal in the equipment that makes these drinks. If you do your job right, your customer base will include dozens, if not hundreds, of particular coffee fans. There's no sense directing them elsewhere to purchase coffee-making equipment if you could be selling the items yourself.

Beans of Wisdom

If you do display espresso machines or other coffee-making equipment for retail sale, make sure that you and every other shop employee know how to use every single machine. Don't force customers to learn how to work a machine from the instruction book; lead them through the works from start to finish. You'll increase your standing as a coffee expert, and they might encourage friends to buy from your store!

Not ready to approach your equipment vendor about selling espresso machines on commission? Maybe you should focus your retail energies on hand-painted coffee mugs, souvenir spoons that memorialize your area, travel mugs, books on coffee, or milk thermometers. The list of retail items that you could sell is far longer than you have room for on your shelves.

In any case, you should absolutely carry retail goods other than food and drinks. Add shelves to your seating area, and decorate them with goods for sale. Otherwise that space is going to waste because no sales will ever result from it.

The Least You Need to Know

♦ If you restrict the menu to coffee, espresso, and tea, you'll also restrict the growth potential of your business. By offering a wider variety of drinks, you can draw customers from a wider retail pool.

♦ Soda, bottled water, and juices are standard fare that no drink dealer should be without, but you can choose from many product lines to match the style and look of your business.

♦ Look for foods you can add to your offerings that will increase sales without substantially increasing labor costs and prep time.

♦ Coffee bars located in areas with college students or an active nightlife can consider serving alcohol-flavored drinks if the hassles of the legal requirements don't outweigh the potential sales boost.

♦ Carry coffee-related equipment for retail sales and cultivate a do-it-yourself attitude among customers.

Chapter **16**

Choosing Suppliers

In This Chapter

- ◆ Taking samples from suppliers
- ◆ Working hard for extra credit
- ◆ Becoming an expert flour arranger
- ◆ Tagging goods and releasing them to the wild
- ◆ How to shop like you've never shopped before

Over the previous 15 chapters we've covered a lot of ground in terms of the food and drinks you can offer customers. In the end, of course, you are entirely responsible for what you choose to serve.

What you cannot do, however, is create those items from thin air. You need clay if you want to shape statues, canvas to paint portraits, and, yes, beans to brew coffee. You will need to purchase every single item that you plan to sell or use in your store from a supplier—or, to be a bit more accurate, many different suppliers.

We covered big-ticket items like espresso machines and refrigerators back in Chapter 9. Now we get to review every minor item you might possibly need to purchase to run a coffee bar. Depending on your product line, you won't necessarily purchase all of these items, but if you ever decide to expand your line of wares, you'll know where to look to find the goods.

Ten Million Beans to Go, Please

Your first concern will naturally be hunting down the raw materials for the finished food and drinks, with the focus on coffee bean importers and developers.

Whichever supplier (or suppliers) you choose will provide the base around which everything else is built. (Appendix C contains a list of bean importers to contact, as well as potential suppliers for most of the other material listed in this chapter.)

Meet, Greet, and Eat

These steps will apply to almost all of the suppliers covered in this section, but to keep our focus, we'll stick to talking about coffee, since that's what's driving your business.

Contact each coffee supplier you find and arrange to meet the salesperson who covers your area. Explain a bit about your business and ask him to bring samples of his company's products to your meeting.

When you meet, offer more details about your coffee bar-to-be, such as your target market of customers and choice of décor. Share your logo and store design, if he's willing to look, and ask for feedback on your ideas. He's likely seen hundreds of stores on the job and he might spot trouble points that would otherwise go unnoticed. Once the representative has absorbed these details, pepper him with questions that will reveal all you need to know about the supplier, such as:

Contents May Be Hot

If a supplier lacks a local salesperson and wants you to order remotely, turn to other suppliers first to see whether they can dig up a contact. You want to develop close relationships with salespeople at every supplier in case you need fast service. Faxing in orders is definitely not the way to go!

- The frequency and flexibility of the delivery schedule

- Whether delivery is available on the weekend in case you run out of product

- The minimum dollar amount of each order

- The availability of discounts based on volume

- Whether the supplier offers special products for Mother's Day or Valentine's Day

- What type of point-of-purchase promotional material is available to boost sales

- Whether free product is available if you want to run in-store tastings or other special promotions

- What makes their product stand out over those of their competitors

- Whether the supplier can provide references from current customers

- What terms they offer new clients—that is, how quickly they ask to be paid for deliveries

Treat the salesperson as a partner in the business, because in all likelihood he'll be able to suggest products that will fit your needs perfectly. He'll also be aware of your competition and will be able to describe how his products differ from what they offer. Listen carefully—take notes even—and you'll understand how to describe the difference to your customers in the months ahead.

Don't just take his word, though. Let him offer product samples based on the market and goals you've described. Ask him to suggest markups for the product so you can gauge what percent of each sale will be profit and judge whether the product is right for your image. (We'll cover pricing in more detail in Chapter 17.)

How to Seal the Deal

Once you've decided that a supplier's products fit within your desired price range and match your target market's needs, it's time to take your hat in hand and ask for credit.

Yes, you'll be borrowing money once again—many times, in fact, as you will have to start relationships with a number of suppliers to locate all the goods you need. Don't worry about sounding needy or cash poor; suppliers are used to extending credit to their customers.

For each supplier, you will complete a credit application to show that you will be able to pay the bills if the supplier does issue you credit. Bills from suppliers are typically due one to two weeks after delivery, which gives you a bit of time to work some alchemical magic and turn those goods into gold. (The business shorthand for this type of arrangement is "net X days," which means that payment for a shipment is due X days after delivery.)

On the application, you'll note details about your coffee bar, give a desired amount of credit, and list prior credit references. If you have no business references, which is quite possible if this is your first business, you may be able to list personal references instead, such as credit card companies or the bank that holds your home mortgage. If you're in this situation, ask the supplier the best way to handle it.

If the supplier turns you down, ask why and see whether you can ameliorate his concerns in the months ahead. He might just be nervous that you have no business experience, for example, and be willing to reconsider your application after you've been open a few months.

> **Beans of Wisdom** _____
>
> Whenever you place a COD order, contact the supplier for the total of the order so that you can have a check ready to hand to the driver. If you do cash payouts from the register, have the delivery person sign your receipt, showing that payment was received. This practice will keep you from having to search for your checkbook while the driver—and lines of customers—wait for you.

Even if the supplier does grant you a credit line, be aware that your first order will still likely be cash on delivery (COD). Once you pass that final hurdle, the credit program will kick in and you'll have a bit of breathing room between delivery and payment from then on.

Three Orders, Over Easy

If you haven't run a coffee bar previously—and we think that's a safe assumption— you probably aren't sure what an appropriate opening order would be. Should you order three types of coffee—or ten? Two bags of beans, or two hundred?

Don't hang the order form on the wall and reach for the darts. Ask the salesperson for advice on how he would stock a location of your size in your area. Admittedly, some sales reps will be quite, shall we say, *optimistic* with their figures as large orders from you equal good vibes for them at headquarters. If you really have qualms about his figures, reduce the numbers slightly or ask about arranging a second order to follow quickly on the heels of the first.

Once you make it past your first few orders, you'll have an inventory to work with and the start of a sales record, both of which will make later orders match your immediate needs more closely. (Sales records, ranging from daily to yearly, are covered in Chapter 18.) Although we don't recommend trying this with your initial order, once you have a handle on what you need, you can solicit prices from multiple suppliers and see who can provide the goods at the lowest cost. You don't necessarily want to flit back and forth from one supplier to another—thus eliminating any loyalty you've established—but shopping by price can sometimes lead you to amazing deals.

Maintain a file for all orders so that you know what's coming in and therefore don't duplicate an order with another supplier. You'll also need the order sheets close at hand to refer to once the goods arrive.

Who's in Charge?

Make sure that your suppliers know which of your employees, if any, are authorized to place orders. In the early days, that's you and nobody else but you, but once you grow enough to hire other managers—a subject covered in Chapter 21—you'll need to give them ordering authority as well.

This set-up prevents employees from calling suppliers on their own and placing rush orders for items that are nearly out of stock. Allowing employees to place orders willy-nilly is fraught with all sorts of negative possibilities:

- You might already have an order on the way, which means you'll now have twice as much stock.

- You've discontinued that product and switched to something else, but haven't yet told the employees.

- You'll have to pay the supplier a rush charge.

- You might not be out of the product after all, and the employee just missed seeing a box in the stockroom.

While you want employees to be smart enough and confident enough to take charge in difficult situations, you don't want their "charges" to end up hurting your business financially.

I'll Stand, You Deliver

When the supply truck pulls in behind your coffee bar, you want the order sheet available to compare what you asked for with what's on the truck. Did you ask for a case and receive only a box, or vice versa? Make a note of it on the shipping receipt. Inspect boxes and bags quickly for tears and water damage. Again, note

> **Contents May Be Hot**
>
> While you'd hate to over-order and have money tied up for months in goods that can't be sold, under-ordering and offering customers empty shelves is even worse. What will they think of a store that has nothing to offer only three days after it opens?

problems on the shipping receipt. If something is completely wrong or unusable, refuse it, note the reason, and have the delivery person take it back.

Have the delivery person initial all the notes you've taken so that you can later request a credit for damaged, missing, and unordered items.

Taking Stock of the Stockroom

All the action might happen in front of the customers, but if you can't do the prep work, the stage will be empty when the curtains go up.

So let's go backstage to where the magic begins: the stockroom. As we explained in Chapter 10, the stockroom is a functioning work area in which practicality always trumps prettiness. You'll need plenty of shelves and open storage units to start with, and in the months ahead you'll probably build in even more as you get a better handle on the size of each box and bundle.

Organize your storage areas, whether the backroom or shelving underneath the front counters, so that similar items are stored together: all the cups in one location, with the lids next to them, and so on. Don't cram goods into every available space; you want to be able to reach everything in stock with minimum effort.

Clear the Air

When you expect an order, clear the backroom floor of broken-down cardboard boxes and anything else that might impede a delivery. Make room on shelves by consolidating items and restacking supplies on the floor; if you've labeled storage areas—which we suggested when discussing kitchen design—a quick look at the order sheet will let you know exactly where you need to make room. After you've received a few orders and are familiar with the box sizes, you'll know exactly how much room you need as well.

Make sure as you move boxes around that you place the oldest goods in front to be used first. Even with disposable goods such as plastic wrap that have a long shelf life, rotating goods will keep them from being dirty or damaged through repeated handling or getting lost behind other types of supplies.

Cold to Hot

After you receive the order, put away any frozen items first, then refrigerated goods (with the expiration date facing out so employees are sure to grab the oldest item first), and finally the dry goods that are okay spending time on the backroom floor.

If you have bug or rodent issues, or even a fear of attracting bugs or rodents, store tasty items like sugar in sealed containers. Label the containers clearly on the outside so that employees can find what they need quickly without having to open anything.

You can even go so far as to place plastic labels on the container and mark the expiration date on the label with an erasable pen.

Another safety issue is where to store cleaning supplies; they must be kept separate from food and anything used to serve food. They should also be stored as near the floor as possible to reduce the damage caused by any spills.

> **Beans of Wisdom**
>
> Don't forget about the customer during your time in the back room! Keep an eye on employees at the counter and assist them whenever they need a hand.

Up for the Count

At the beginning of every month, you should inventory every item you have for sale in the store. Create an inventory list of every single item you've ever ordered. Include space for six or twelve months of inventory as well as the cost of each item so that you can figure out the total cost of goods on-hand. Have employees participate in the count as well, both to educate them on where everything is and to provide variety in their workday.

Cash in Storage

Don't just think of taking inventory as counting cup lids and pounds of sugar, though. Think of taking inventory as counting money—your money. You spent money on all these items with the intention of selling them, either directly or indirectly, to make a profit. The only way to know whether you're achieving this goal is to track what's on hand, what's missing, and what's never moving.

Ideally, you'll have exactly the right amount of product on-hand to last from one delivery to the next. If you can manage this, you'll avoid having money tied up in excess product that never leaves the shelves. The longer goods stay in storage, the more likely they are to be damaged, which means you'll never get back the money you invested.

> **Beans of Wisdom**
>
> Don't forget to include waste items in the inventory. One or two cups isn't an issue, but if an employee accidentally dumps a 10-pound bag of sugar in a bucket of mop water, you should note that unexpected cost on the monthly summary. These notes might remove the need for detective work at the end of the month to find out why the numbers don't add up.

Know Thyself (and Thy Stockroom)

Inventory and ordering go hand-in-hand, with each constantly affecting the other. If you avoid taking inventory, you might constantly order twice as many small cups as large because you seem to recall selling twice as many small drinks. What a surprise you'll have months later when you have boxes and boxes of small cups with nary a space to put them.

By taking inventory, you don't let your memory play tricks on you, and you avoid ordering by intuition. You have the numbers on-hand to show exactly what's being used and what needs to be replaced.

Make sure to update your inventory sheets to reflect the current cost of replacing the goods. Prices fluctuate frequently due to market and weather conditions, and calculating the value of your inventory at the old rate doesn't yield valid information.

Turning Over a New Leaf

Beyond a mere inventory count is the idea of tracking your inventory turnover rate—that is, how quickly inventory moves through your coffee bar and is converted back into money. To determine your inventory turnover rate, use the following formula:

Inventory Turnover Rate

Step 1: Calculate the cost of goods used during a month

Inventory cost at the start of the month	3,500
Add: Purchases made during the month	11,400
Total cost of goods	14,900
Subtract: Inventory at end of month	3,800
Cost of goods consumed	11,100

Step 2: Calculate the average cost of goods on hand

Beginning inventory	3,500
Add: End inventory	3,800
Total amount	7,300
Average inventory (total amount divided by 2)	3,650

Step 3: Calculate the inventory turnover rate

$$\frac{\text{Cost of goods consumed}}{\text{Average inventory}} = \text{Inventory turnover rate}$$

$$\frac{11,100}{3,650} = 3.04 \text{ times}$$

In our example, inventory is turning over slightly more often than three times per month, roughly every nine to ten days. Ideally, you would like to have as high a turnover rate as possible. This would mean that goods are being instantly converted to cash with little money tied up in the stockroom.

This ideal is, alas, impossible to reach because if you cut inventory to the bare bones, you risk running out of drinks and supplies. Sure, the turnover rate will be in the double digits, but if you're sending away customers empty-handed, you're losing money and damaging the long-term health of your coffee shop.

Using your inventory sheets, you can break your inventory down into smaller categories (baked goods, hot drinks, disposable goods) and examine the inventory turnover rate for each category. Baked goods, for example, should have an incredibly high turnover since their shelf life is limited to a few days at most.

By examining the turnover rate on select goods, you might discover avenues for potential growth. If, say, you're using twice as much half-and-half as skim milk, that indicates a desire among your customers for richer, creamier drinks. What can you add to your menu to satisfy this desire?

Beyond the Beans: The Rest of Your Shopping List

While the equipment list in Chapter 9 warmed up your credit card, there are hundreds of other items that could come in handy for your business. Appendix B includes a thorough list of possible purchases—many of which might seem impractical, useless, or baffling at first glance—but before you go scooting off to the end of the book, let's look at a few items in more detail.

Hot Wraps

Your shop is all about delivering coffee, which means you need plenty of supplies that will make this happen. Typical coffee sizes are 8, 12, and 16 ounces, so when you're purchasing mugs and cups, search for these sizes. To cut down on inventory, search for a vendor who carries different sizes of paper cups that can be covered by the same size lid.

Beans of Wisdom

As with your tables and chairs, you want to purchase only those coffee cups, demitasse cups, and so on that can be easily replaced for years to come. You'll break more of these than you'll care to think about in the months ahead!

You can investigate the cost of imprinting your store's logo on these items, but you usually need to order massive quantities to make such a purchase cost effective. We recommend holding off on mugging yourself until the business has proved itself and won't leave you with a garage full of unused mugs.

In addition to standard coffee mugs, you need demitasse cups and saucers for espresso beverages. With all of these items, your best bet is to stick with plain white ceramic. Basic white is the cheapest option available, and any fancy designs on cups and saucers tend to give them legs—that is, they go walking out of the shop arm-in-arm with a customer.

Getting the Most for Your Money

While low-end coffee cups suit your wallet and the needs of your coffee bar, sometimes you'll be better off spending a little bit more.

Take a simple item like a hand tamper, which you use to tamp espresso grounds into a portafilter. Plastic tampers are cheap, but they tend to chip when dropped or mishandled, which means you have to buy another one—which makes them not so cheap after all. Spring for a hard wood or anodized aluminum tamper and you'll be set for a few decades.

A steaming pitcher is another purchase where you don't want to skimp since you'll use it dozens of times each day. Look for high-grade stainless steel with a welded-on handle since screws loosen over time. Pick one that holds at least 32 ounces, since milk doubles in size when you steam it. Search for one with a rolled pouring edge as that will allow you to develop your skill of pouring off foam, milk, or a mix of both.

Search for condiment shakers that balance the needs of function and form. You want ones that won't clog because the holes are too small, while still having holes small enough that customers don't shake out a pound of sugar or cinnamon with each tilt of the hand. You also want to make sure that the shakers are easy to clean and refill.

Buying with an Eye on the Law

Some purchases will be driven by style or cost, but others will come because the government tells you what to buy. Some health departments insist that napkins be available only in dispensers, for example, instead of loose in baskets or other holders. In your case this restriction is good: customers won't just grab a handful as they pass, then throw all but one away.

Another health issue concerns loose versus wrapped straws. Some communities insist upon individually wrapped straws, while others are fine with a dispenser that releases one loose straw at a time.

Cream and milk containers are another source of concern. Your health department might insist that milk be stored on ice or that you use a particular type of storage container at your coffee station. (Aside from health concerns, you want to select milk containers that reduce drips and are easy to use. Customers want to make their drinks and move on, not solve a Rubik's puzzle to access the milk.)

The health department might also have a few words to say about the type of soap and hand towels you place in washrooms. Bar soap is verboten in many areas due to fears that they spread germs through hand-to-hand contact. Soap spreads germs? Who knew?

The Least You Need to Know

- Suppliers are the source of your lifeblood, so cultivate relationships with them early and treat the salespeople well.

- While you can order most supplies on credit, the checks come due quickly, so don't let your eyes get bigger than your customers' stomachs.

- Arrange your stockroom so that you can find and store goods quickly.

- Calculate your inventory turnover rate to see which items you order too frequently and which are the real moneymakers.

- Make your list and check it twice to ensure everything you need is close at hand.

Chapter 17

Pricing to Sell—and Selling Those Prices

In This Chapter

- ◆ Why cost + cost + cost = price
- ◆ Using market research to fine-tune prices
- ◆ How low prices hurt your business
- ◆ Doubling every sale, just by asking
- ◆ Small goods lead to big profits

We're sure you hold your customers so dear that you would give them all the free drinks they want, but that's not really how business works. If you don't cover costs, not to mention make a bit extra to pay for your salary, the business will go bust and no one will get anything.

Setting prices is relatively straightforward. Making sure those prices will sustain the business is another matter. We'll take you through the pricing process, as well as point out what to do when the system falls out of balance.

Determining What You Should Charge

For most food establishments, the cost of the food they sell equals 30 to 35 percent of their total sales volume. Using this figure as a general target, you can determine the retail price of any food by tripling its cost. If, for example, a bakery charges your shop 40 cents for a bagel, you should charge your customer $1.25 or somewhere thereabouts.

By charging three times the cost of an item, you are working into the price all the intangibles that the customer purchases with that bagel, whether he's thought about them or not. This price includes, for instance, the cost of butter or cream cheese, the napkin that accompanies the plate, and the labor that delivers the goods.

Also included in the price is a small portion of the cost of the toaster, the knife that cut the bagel, the cutting board on which the bagel was cut, and the mortgage for the building that keeps everything dry and warm. This price also covers the cost of cleaning the knife and plate as well as the labor to wipe down the cutting board. Finally, we have the labor cost of wiping down the table after the customer leaves and the miniscule cost of garbage service to remove the butter wrapper and wadded-up napkin.

Whew! All that from 85 cents over the cost of the bagel? Yes, indeed, when you add up the sales of everything in the store. Every drink and every treat adds its share to the kitty to cover the costs of everything else.

What the Market Will Bear

We suggest using this pricing method almost across the board—and we say "almost" because in some cases you'd be wise to aim the figure a bit higher or lower.

> **Beans of Wisdom**
>
> Even though you own a competing store, feel free to visit the competition regularly to update your research on prices and goods on the menu. Don't just spy, though—be sure to buy something while you're there!

Back in Chapter 4, we sent you on a research mission to competing coffee shops to see what they offered and how much they charged. Now's the time to pull out that research once again and see if it says anything about your business.

Peaks and Valleys

When you examine a competitor's prices, you want to look for prices that are either much higher or much lower than yours. Multiple reasons exist for these differences, and since you don't have access to the competitor's frontal lobe to find out the exact reason why, we'll venture a few guesses.

First of all, the cost of a competitor's goods might differ from yours. If he pays a quarter more for an item than you do, that translates to a 75-cent difference on the retail price. A similarly low price probably means that his cost is lower than yours.

If you're contacting multiple suppliers to compare costs of goods before placing an order—a practice we recommended in Chapter 16—then you might be able to determine which supplier handles your competitor's account. By setting up an account with this supplier and cherry-picking the low-cost goods, you can lower your own costs, and therefore your retail prices.

Sometimes cost differences result from package deals offered by suppliers. If you take A, B, C, and D, they say, we'll knock 10 percent off the total. Don't rush into such deals unless you normally stock all of these items or feel that you can use them in your business. Otherwise, any cost savings you achieve will be eaten by unused goods that sit in your backroom forever.

Leading by Losing

Another explanation for why a competitor charges less than you is that he's using the item as a loss leader—that is, a ridiculously low-priced item that's meant to draw customers.

Supermarkets advertise loss leaders all the time: milk at half-price, cheap fruit in the winter at summer prices, free turkeys at Thanksgiving. Supermarkets don't push loss leaders because they're nice and want to give customers something for next-to-nothing. They push loss leaders because customers will use these sales as a reason to choose one store over another.

A supermarket gains nothing—heck, it might even lose money—on the sale of loss leaders, but shoppers rarely visit a store for just one item. They'll load up their carts with all sorts of other items, and in the end the supermarket will make a profit anyway.

Coffee bars use this practice of loss leaders, but on a smaller scale, perhaps along the lines of "buy two, get one free" or "a free biscotti

> **Beans of Wisdom**
>
> Discount coupons along the lines of "Save 20 percent when you spend $10 or more" work like generic loss leaders. By ensuring a certain dollar level of sales, you're guaranteed to break even on the purchase at a minimum.

with the purchase of any espresso." These items aren't really free, of course. You paid for them, and with a smart sales program, you'll make back the costs through sales of other items.

Practicing Premium Pricing

If a competitor charges significantly more for an item than you do, he may be doing so for a very simple reason: customers will pay the price.

When you sell dark chocolates or premium organic coffee beans, customers often expect to pay a premium. The rich taste of the good is worth paying more, and they don't think twice over whether the good actually costs more to make than milk chocolate or nonorganic coffee.

You can experiment with this type of pricing when you introduce new items on your menu, especially if no one else in your area sells a similar item. Price the item at 3.5 or even 4 times the cost and see whether customers are interested. If sales are slow, you can either drop the price or transform brownies into loss leaders and offer a free brownie with the purchase of said item. If customers learn to like the product, they might keep buying it once the promotion ends.

> **Beans of Wisdom**
>
> Don't apologize to customers whenever you raise the price of an item to account for higher costs. Let the prices stand on their own. Quick, quality service is the only support they need!

No Reason at All

A final possibility for widely diverging prices is that your competitor made a mistake—or you did. Examine your order receipts to make sure the problem isn't on your end. If you're not careful, you could miss a cost change and not realize it for months, therefore breaking even on an item that should carry a higher price.

How Not to Sell Yourself Short

Let's return for a moment to our $1.25 bagel that costs 40 cents from a local bakery. Now, a customer could visit that same bakery and purchase a bagel for far less than what you charge. That's understandable, since the bakery is selling directly to the customer and not through a middleman (you) who needs to cover costs and make a profit. The same situation likely applies to your coffee and soda. A customer could buy either at the supermarket for less, sometimes much less, than they can buy them from you.

Does this mean you're ripping off customers? Should you charge less for your bagels (and coffee and soda …)? No, for at least two reasons.

First, if you did lower prices to compete with those of the primary supplier (the bakery) or the discount seller (the supermarket), you would go out of business. No question about it. Your costs are not the same as their costs because they either make the goods themselves or order in volumes that dwarf yours. You can't compete against them in terms of price, and this brings us to the second reason.

Within your coffee bar, you offer customers an environment and a selection of goods they can't find anywhere else. Your coffee tastes better than any available on supermarket shelves, and you can offer a glass with ice to complement the already chilled soda. You provide comfortable seating and a desirable, social atmosphere so the bagel-eater can relax and enjoy his snack or meal. Creating an environment costs money, and that cost must be worked into the retail price. Customers know—or they should— that part of the price they pay is for the surroundings in which they sup.

In short, don't ever engage in a pricing war because even if you win, you'll still lose because you won't make any money on the now-discounted goods. Stick to providing quality and atmosphere, and your business will be far better off.

> **Contents May Be Hot**
>
> At some point, you will encounter a customer who demands to know why you're ripping off customers by charging such high prices. Don't let him bait you into an argument. Simply explain that based on your costs, you must charge the amounts you do to stay above water and leave it at that. You can't win this argument against cheap customers, so don't knock yourself out trying!

Boosting Your Bottom Line

Raising your prices is one way to boost sales volume, assuming customers aren't turned off by the higher prices. Another way to increase sales is to raise the average amount that customers spend at each sale.

Offering food is an obvious way to do this and one we've already discussed. When a customer picks up a croissant in the morning to accompany his café latté, he's doubled the amount of his check and added a couple of bucks to your bottom line. If you offer the right array of goods so that every customer does this, you'll double your gross income. Pretty sweet!

Would You Like Fries with That?

Unfortunately, not every customer will automatically reach for a sweet on the side. Many customers order on autopilot, after all, and don't even realize the true extent of your menu.

Your job—and you've already chosen to accept it—is to make them aware of other goods within your shop. Not the whole menu, mind you, since customers can only absorb so much at once, but mention one item on the menu that would nicely accompany his current order: a chocolate-covered cookie spoon for a young person ordering coffee, or a scone for a tea-drinker.

The practice of asking customers if they want to order something else is known as suggestive selling, and every successful restaurant uses it. Go into any fast food establishment to order a hamburger, and the cashier will automatically ask if you want fries as well. If you did order fries with the burger, the cashier will ask if you want a large fries; and if you ordered the large fries, she'll ask if you'd like an ice cream sundae to finish your meal.

Beans of Wisdom

Your suggestive selling can also be as simple as a sign near the register that features items new to your menu. Feature seasonal items, special offers, and other short-term promotions in this location so that customers always know where to look to see what's new in your shop.

Suggestive selling isn't badgering. You can't ask a customer more than once if he'd like something else because he will probably get annoyed and leave. The idea is always to mention a good that he might not see otherwise and leave it at that. If he doesn't order it now, perhaps he will next time. You lose nothing by asking and have the potential for huge financial gains if customers take you up on the offer.

Truffles Aren't Trifles

Suggestive selling works wonders in terms of boosting sales, but you have to use it on the right items. If you focus your energy on promoting the French presses you have for sale in the seating area, don't be surprised at the end of the day if they're all still on the shelf.

A better idea is to surround your register with low-cost items that require little from the customer in the way of investment. Individually wrapped truffles, for example, retail for somewhere between 25 and 50 cents, which is practically nothing compared to the prices of slices of cheesecake and large café mochaccinos.

That low price means you make only 10 to 30 cents for each one you sell, but that low price also inspires dozens upon dozens of customers to add one (or more) to their purchase. At the end of the day, those small gains add up to big bucks.

Feature the Future

In addition to using suggestive selling on the actual product, you can promote up-coming events at your coffee bar, such as an open-mic poetry night or a writers or readers group. If you encourage customers to return on a night when they would normally stay at home, that's just as good as having them spend more—maybe better if they bring a friend or two with them!

The Least You Need to Know

- Every item on your menu should sell for approximately three times its cost.
- Compare your prices with a competitor's to see where you might charge more and what you might be able to buy for less.
- Experiment with carrying premium-priced items to find out whether your market will support them.
- Practice suggestive selling to raise the average check total—and your profits.
- Surround your register with low-cost items that appeal to a wide variety of customers.

Part 5

Day-to-Day Operations

The money comes in, the money goes out, you put the money in and you shake it all about—as a business owner, turning a profit is what it's all about. That's why you need to learn how to count inventory, place and receive orders from suppliers, track sales, create business goals, and thwart thieves.

In addition to managing these money matters, you must keep customers happy: greeting them when they enter, presenting them with a clean environment, serving them the drink they ordered, and thanking them when they leave. It sounds easy, but there's many a slip twixt cup and lip, as Ben Franklin once wrote about the coffee industry. Don't worry, though—we'll explain how to recover from all types of mishaps, while also setting your sights on larger goals, such as expansion and franchises.

Chapter 18

Money Matters

In This Chapter

- ◆ Taming the cash flow
- ◆ Sales by the week, earnings by the month
- ◆ Taxman management
- ◆ How to beat the cheats

How can you tell if your coffee bar is a success? The number of customers served or the amount of goods sold per customer might sound like a good measuring bar, but to find out where you really stand financially, you need to look at far more concrete numbers: specifically, your net income, or the amount of money coming in minus the amount going out.

But nailing down your net income comes only after you've tracked a lot of other numbers as well, such as employee hours worked, utility expenses, and the cost of new goods and inventory on hand.

Tracking these numbers doesn't require a math degree—only an eye for detail and the patience to write down everything that enters and leaves your store. Sound tedious? In the long run, tracking sales figures becomes more like a game in which you do everything you can to push the numbers higher.

Naming Names, Taking Numbers

To keep your coffee bar's financial figure in fine shape, you want to track sales on a daily, weekly, monthly, and yearly basis. Don't think that you're making busy work for yourself or duplicating numbers for no reason. Each of these income and expense statements serves a different purpose.

At first the sales numbers will seem like random throws of the dice. They go up, they go down—they're out of your control! As the days and weeks pass, though, you'll start to see patterns in the numbers. Rain will drop (or raise) sales by this percent, snow will affect sales this much, three-day weekends push down Fridays and raise Saturdays, and so forth.

Over time, this knowledge will help you order goods and supplies more accurately and create less wasteful work schedules. Knowledge is power, as the saying goes— but more importantly for business, knowledge is money!

Your Daily Bread

At the end of each sales day, you need to reconcile what's in the cash drawer with the sales tracked by the cash register or computer. Use a daily cash sheet to note the amount of cash, checks, charge slips, coupons, and so forth in the register. (Sample income and expense statements of all types are included in Appendix B.)

You can count the drawer yourself or have the employee who manned the register do the count. Once you've finished the count, print out the daily record of sales from the register and note the number of sales (that is, customers) and the average check per sale. If the register doesn't give you this figure, divide the total net sales (gross sales minus sales tax) by the number of sales.

After you've summed the amount of cash, checks, and charges in the drawer, subtract the *float* from this total. This will give you a figure for *net cash*, also known as the deposit.

Java-nitions

The **float** is the amount of cash in the register drawer at the start of each day. The exact amount of the float is up to you, but make sure the drawer holds enough ones and fives that employees won't need to ask for change after only a few sales. **Net cash** is the actual amount of money that was added to the register over the day.

Subtract the total of gross sales on the sales tape from the net cash. If the sum is negative, the drawer is short (that is, has too little money); a positive sum means the drawer is over. If the figures match, the count in the drawer is exactly right and you should give your employee a high-five.

If you have multiple registers, have each employee complete a daily cash sheet for his or her own drawer. If different employees man the register throughout the day, you might consider using multiple tills, each with its own float, and have employees complete a daily cash sheet at the end of their shift.

Beans of Wisdom

Ideally, employees should complete the drawer count without seeing the register tape. You don't want to give them a target to shoot for; you just want to know how much is in the drawer, and then determine yourself whether that amount is correct or not. This practice avoids possible funny business by employees who will add (or remove!) funds to make the totals match.

Remove all the checks and charges and enough cash so that what remains is exactly equal to the float. At the beginning of the day, or any time any employee uses a fresh register till, he should count the cash first to make sure what's there matches the float.

Note the weather or any unusual happenings on the cash sheet so that you can use that information in your weekly summary. Speaking of which ...

Weekly Write-Ups

Every seven days you should carry over the daily sales totals onto a weekly summary sheet (also available in Appendix B). For this sheet to do its job, you must ignore dates and pay attention only to the days. Adopt a Monday to Sunday (or Sunday to Saturday) schedule and stick with it, even when the week crosses two months or two years.

We use this convention because sales on particular days of the week tend to be regular from week to week. Weekends will draw different crowds than weekdays and you'll miss this distinction if you compare June 6th with July 6th instead of the actual days of the week.

The purpose of a weekly summary sheet is to look for sales trends. Are certain days of the week bringing in more sales than usual? Are you using employees wisely, or having too many in the store during slow times?

In addition to sales figures, write down the total number of hours worked by all employees. Divide the day's sales figures by the number of labor hours to determine the sales per person hour (SPPH).

This measure is one way of looking at the value of each employee's labor. If SPPH varies widely over the course of a week, you might consider reworking your schedule to have employees start work an hour later or leave an hour earlier. In some cases, such as opening and closing the store, this might not be practical, but throwing money away on unused labor is hardly practical either.

Carry over the weather information from the daily cash sheets and note other relevant events, such as national holidays or local happenings.

A Monthly Subscription

While the weekly summary looks for sales trends, the monthly summary takes a snapshot of the financial health of your entire business, allowing you to compare income and expenses from month to month.

To start, add sales figures from a month's worth of daily cash sheets. (For the monthly summary, we do care about the dates.) Subtract from this total the cost of all goods sold. To determine this figure, start with the value of your inventory at the beginning of the month, add the cost of all purchases received during the month, then subtract the value of inventory on hand at month's end. This number is your gross income for the month. (We talk about taking inventory in more detail in Chapter 16.)

Next, list all expenses (except for loan payments) for the month in their appropriate places on the sheet, then sum these figures. Subtract total expenses from gross income to determine your monthly income prior to the cost of money borrowed. Subtract your loan payment from this number to determine your actual monthly income.

(Loan payments are different from other expenses in that they're eventually going to disappear. Raw materials, labor, insurance, and so on are all operating expenses that will be consistent every month as long as the business is open. If you ever try to sell the business—a topic we discuss in Chapter 21—you want to be able to show prospective buyers income prior to the cost of borrowed money since their borrowing costs will differ from yours.)

> **Beans of Wisdom**
>
> While you should keep records from the first day you open, don't rely too heavily on the results. During your first month, for instance, expenses will be much higher than in any other month since you must build up an inventory from nothing.

Divide each expense by the monthly sales figure at the top of the sheet to determine what percent of sales each expense represents. For example, if the cost of goods sold during a month is $8,500 while sales equal $28,000, then food costs equal 30 percent of your sales. (Keep in mind, of course, that the total for "food costs" includes expenses for napkins, cleaning fluids, and all other consumables.)

New Year, New Records

Each January 1 closes one financial year and opens another. Compile the monthly totals on one sheet and see what 365 days of labor have brought you.

This summary is similar to the monthly sheets in terms of creating a financial snapshot, but its primary purpose is to help you prepare for filing taxes. You need to know the numbers, both income and expenses, for the entire year so that your accountant can have everything he needs in one location.

While the sample sheets in the appendix are all you need, you might decide to spring for a computer-based accounting system such as QuickBooks or Quicken. As you plug in the daily numbers and pay your bills, you can create profit-and-loss statements as well as balance sheets at the push of a button. Your accountant will love you at year's end if you can hand over a digital file as well as paper printouts!

Making the Most of Your Money

We already explained how you can use the SPPH figure on the weekly summary sheets to adjust employee work schedules. The monthly summaries, with expenses listed as a percentage of sales, will point out where you should attempt similar cost-cutting measures.

Has electricity doubled from 1 to 2 percent of your monthly expenses? Contact the electric company and ask a representative to visit your business to point out what might cause such an increase. Have office expenses jumped unexpectedly? If so, what's the cause and what can you do to bring that expense back in line?

In general, you don't want to slash your marketing budget to save money. Advertising and promotions, topics we cover in Chapters 22 and 23, project your name into the world at large and bring new customers through the door. Cutting these costs is like cutting off the roots that make a tree grow stronger—it just doesn't work that way.

Aiming for the Goal

In addition to lowering costs, you can use the various sales records you compile to set sales goals for any time period of your choosing: daily, weekly, biennially, and so forth. At first glance, sales goals seem rather ridiculous. "If I'm going to set a goal," you think, "why not make it a million dollars a minute? It's not like I can control whether or not customers come in and spend money."

Au contraire! You have far more control over your sales volume than you might think. Don't clean the counters for a few days, and we're sure you'll come to agree with us!

As for *positively* influencing your sales, that's one reason we insisted in the previous section that you shouldn't reduce your marketing budget to cut costs. Every business loses customers over time: they move away due to marriage or work, their doctor tells them to cut down on sweets, they start new hobbies that take up all their time, and sometimes (gasp!) they migrate to the competition.

Customer attrition threatens the long-term survival of every business, large and small. The smart entrepreneur knows that marketing is an essential tool merely to keep the customer base from shrinking, never mind expanding it and boosting profits.

Sales goals help give direction to your marketing efforts. Instead of simply saying, "I'm going to make twice as much money next month," use the sales records to create specific sales targets: "I'm going to sell twice as many iced coffees this summer" or "This month, fifty percent more customers who buy cappuccino will buy a sweet to go with the drink."

With goals like these, you can narrow your marketing efforts down to make the goals a reality. You can hand out coupons that promise half-price sweets with the purchase of a hot drink; you can distribute fliers with a similar offer; you can teach employees to practice better suggestive selling; you can place signs and pictures near the register that make the cappuccino/sweet combination look so tasty that customers won't be able to resist!

Set sales goals so that they're challenging, yet still attainable. Trying to earn twice as much in a month is hopeless; trying to boost sales on a particular item or add-on isn't. Even if you don't achieve the goal, you're sure to see higher numbers than in the previous sales period, which means you just have to try a little harder next time. As coaches like to say, *making* the goal isn't what's important—trying is.

Crying Uncle

While you may have hired an accountant to double-check your sales figures and file tax returns, the bulk of the record-keeping load still falls on your shoulders. And if you want to keep Uncle Sam smiling and out of your hair, you'll take this responsibility seriously every business day.

In addition to tracking sales, you need to keep receipts and cancelled checks for every business expense you plan to deduct, no matter how small. Divide receipts into categories such as:

- Rent
- Utilities, with subdivisions for phone, gas, electricity, water, and Internet access
- Advertising
- Payroll costs
- Auto expenses
- Professional fees
- Travel and entertainment

It might go without saying, but we'll say it anyway: these expenses must be made with the intent of increasing your business income. Driving to the bank to discuss a business loan counts as a reasonable mileage deduction; driving to a restaurant to talk with your spouse about starting a business is borderline—especially if you order a whole lobster for your meal!

Beans of Wisdom

Tax-filing deadlines will depend on the type of legal structure you've set up for the coffee bar. Talk with your accountant to make sure you're not missing a date with that special someone!

If you do decide to classify questionable expenses as business-related, be ready to explain to the IRS why they were necessary and reasonable. Contrary to the American legal system, in the eyes of the IRS, you are guilty until you prove yourself innocent.

If you can't convince them that an expense was justified, you must recalculate your business income and pay any taxes owed. If the IRS feels that you deliberately tried to game the system, you could be charged an additional penalty.

As for sales taxes, these must be turned over to the state on a regular basis, with the exact time period (monthly, quarterly, or otherwise) determined by the state and your sales volume. Good record-keeping will help you avoid the stiff penalties that fall on those who pay less than what's due.

Managing Shrinkage

"Shrinkage" is business-speak for theft, whether it's a loss of inventory, a con man flimflamming the counterperson, or an employee dipping into the till. Opportunities for shrinkage abound in any business. We'll examine the most common ones below, along with how to rein in the robbery before it leads to ruin.

Quick-Change Artists

A quick-change artist works like a magician, misdirecting your attention so that you don't even realize that you're being tricked. One possibility is that someone shows you a large bill, but then hands over a bill of smaller denomination. If you didn't notice the switch, you'll hand over more change than you should and the drawer will come up short at the end of the day.

Another possibility is someone who purchases an inexpensive item but presents a large bill, say $100, for payment. But then, as you're handing over the change, he finds a $5 and offers to pay with that instead. You take the change back and return the hundred—just as he realizes that he *does* need to break the C-note to pay back $20 to his Uncle Joe. The money flies back and forth so quickly that you realize only later that you gave change for $100 but only got the $5!

Contents May Be Hot

Whenever you handle money, close the register as soon as possible and never step away while the till is open. While some thieves act sneaky, others will just reach over and grab what they can while you turn around to find a stirrer for them. Thievery takes less time than you think!

To prevent this type of con artist from pulling his trick, you should lay the bill you receive horizontally across the till. Pull out the proper amount of change and count out the transaction as you place the change, then the bills in his hand: "The total came to $3.28, and you paid $10, which means you receive 72 cents in change, and one and five to make $10."

If he protests that you're giving the wrong amount of change, you can point to the bill on the register to show what he paid. If he tries to pay with a different bill, stop him and make him accept the change, place the bill in the register and close it, and then ask him if he'd like you to make change separately.

In general, keep the bill the customer offers in view and finish the transaction before doing anything else. Con artists rely on confusion (and intimidation), so by sticking to one task at a time you can foil their plans.

Register Runarounds

While you'd like to think that register shortfalls are always the work of con artists, we unfortunately must inform you otherwise. Employees occasionally dip their hands in the till as well, and unless you know what to look for, you might not even realize that funds are missing. (In fact, the University of Florida's 2002 National Retail Security Survey found that employee theft was responsible for nearly half of the $32 billion in lost goods, while shoplifting and other outside theft accounted for less than a third of the total.)

Some problems that occur are undercharging (not entering a sale and pocketing the customer's money), overcharging (charging a customer a higher price and keeping the difference), and skimming (simply keeping money and having the drawer come up short).

To avoid these problems, start by having only one employee on a register at a time. If, for example, all three employees on a shift use a register and the drawer comes up $20 short, you have three people to question about what might have happened. When only one person is responsible for the cash drawer, the investigation is much quicker.

When you have a single person handling a register, you can also detect patterns over time. If the drawer is short each time Susie Q handles it, well, hmmm, you might need to have a talk with her. If John Smith has twice as many "no sales" as other employees, you need to find out why. (An employee who undercharges might hit "no sale" to open the drawer and give the customer change for his purchase without attracting suspicion.)

If an employee's drawer comes up short time and time again, despite her being warned about

Contents May Be Hot

Never accuse an employee of theft unless you are absolutely sure of the claim! Seeing him pocket money is proof. A register drawer that's constantly short is not; he might just be incompetent. If you accuse an employee of theft, that's sure to sour the relationship should he be exonerated later—not to mention the possibility of being sued for slander!

past errors, you might be better off letting her go. Don't imply that she's done anything illegal. Merely point out the section of the job description in the employee manual that says, "Must be able to make change correctly." No accusations—only a failure to perform a key job function.

Next, insist that every customer receive a receipt with his purchase. Forcing employees to issue receipts can lessen the temptation to under- or overcharge customers because the customers will have a printout of their order. (Customers can often be your best friend in revealing shady doings because they don't want to see your business wrecked by crooked employees.)

You can also do surprise register counts in the middle of an employee's shift. This might catch someone who undercharged a customer but didn't yet remove the booty (or vice versa). At a minimum, this practice will let potentially shady employees know that you're keeping a constant eye on the money.

Help Others Not To Help Themselves

Another way that employee wrongdoing can cost you money is through giveaways and a generous "self-serve" policy. Friends naturally like to treat friends, and a young employee might not feel like he's harming your business if he offers a free bagel or soda to a friend. Another employee might pay for a cookie when she leaves her shift, but actually take two since she worked extra hard that day.

A free cookie might seem like small potatoes, so to speak, but magnify this practice to 10 friends or 10 free cookies a week, and your profit margin will take a serious hit.

You can usually spot such giveaways through inventory records, but to pinpoint the real cause of the shortfall, you might need to take a daily inventory of certain items before and after an employee's shift. If the count comes up one cookie short each time Mary Lou works a shift, you need to have someone else pack Mary Lou's order before she leaves.

> **Beans of Wisdom**
>
> Make room behind the counter for a special trash container for waste products: cracked cookies, mashed muffins, and so forth. Track these items on the inventory so that employees can't take something for themselves, then claim it was waste.

In fact, this practice is a good idea for all employees, even you! Don't ring in your own orders, and don't serve your own drinks. Number one, by placing yourself in line with other employees, they'll never question this practice. Two, you'll share the retail experience that your customers do and know where it might need improvement.

Inventory records can also spot employees' gifts to friends, but this practice is harder to keep in line unless you want to watch employees every minute of the day. If you're sure that you've pinpointed the employee who's giving away certain items, you might convince him to mend his ways by casually mentioning the discrepancy in inventory. He'll pass the word along to his friends, and they'll stop looking for a handout.

Burglary Blunders

Most burglaries occur at night, so you need to insist that employees follow security procedures when closing the shop to protect both themselves and the business.

Once the doors are locked for the night, for example, you shouldn't open them for any reason. If a customer comes to the door and asks to use the phone, direct him to a payphone or offer to make the call for him. You should also:

- Keep the back doors locked at all times except during deliveries.

- Double-check the back door and office locks as well as the safe before you leave in the evening.

- Leave the register drawer open with an empty till inside so that thieves know there's nothing worth grabbing within easy reach.

- Never exit the shop by the back door in the evening; instead, leave by the front entrance.

Beans of Wisdom

Check windows and door locks periodically for signs of tampering. A burglar might need more than one try to break in, and a watchful eye on your part might notice foul play before any real harm is done.

If this entrance isn't lit by streetlights or other lighting, install timer lights yourself in the building's front (after asking the landlord, naturally) so that you and your employees can see the environment around you at night.

- Leave the store in pairs whenever possible so that no one is left on his or her own.

- Install a peephole in the back door so that you can verify that a delivery person is waiting, or insist that all drivers enter through the front of the store before you open the back door.

- Take all garbage out during daylight hours.

♦ If you encounter a burglar, or someone attempts to rob your store during the day, have employees hand over the money. Don't put anyone at risk by trying to be a hero.

Despite all these precautions, you might still be hit by burglars at some point. Insurance might cover lost product (depending on the size of your deductible), although the cash is gone for good. If this ever happens, learn what you can from the experience and change your security to prevent another hit in the future.

The Least You Need to Know

♦ Track sales on a daily, weekly, monthly, and yearly basis to balance the books, spot sales trends, keep expenses under control, and handle the demands of the taxman.

♦ Record all business expenses and file them in different categories so that you can ease the tax-filing process each year.

♦ Use sales records to set challenging, yet attainable sales goals for the future.

♦ Teach employees how to handle cash at the register so they avoid getting cheated by con artists.

♦ Take security precautions to prevent burglaries and employee theft.

Chapter 19

Customer Relations

In This Chapter

◆ Customers as guests

◆ How to encourage repeat sales

◆ Feedback without the shock

◆ When bad things happen to good customers

You might have the best-looking coffee bar in existence, with the freshest coffee, the finest selection of treats, and the most attractive environment of any this side of Alpha Centauri—but without customers you have nothing.

A business needs products and services to sell, but equally important are customers to purchase these items. When customers enter your store, you and your staff need to welcome them, find out what they want, and go the extra mile to satisfy their needs. They're in your store to satisfy their hunger, sure, but you can likely bring them satisfaction on a deeper level through close attention.

While some customer-winning tactics are easy—not insulting their looks, for example—you can go miles further in winning their loyalty and repeat business. In this chapter, we'll tell you how, as well as cover what to do in those rare situations when things go awry.

Keeping Customers Happy

Customers have many choices of where to shop for coffee. They can purchase drinks from a chain store or at a convenience store when they fill up with gas. They can order coffee at a restaurant after dining out. They can purchase grounds from the supermarket and make their own.

Or they can buy from you.

Which one they choose will depend on many factors—price, convenience, selection—but the important thing for you to remember is that they do have a choice. If you don't treat them well, they'll cast aside the reasons they initially chose you and go shop somewhere else.

This means you can never rely on any customer for sales over the long term. They're not tenants under contract; they're guests in your house. By treating them well, you encourage them to get into the habit of returning to the same place at the same time to order the same thing—and enjoy the same great service.

Smile and Say Hi

What's the first thing you do when a guest arrives at your home? You make eye contact, smile, and greet her, and the same principle applies for customers. By saying hello, you do many things:

- You acknowledge her presence, so she feels welcome.

- You let her know who to turn to if she has questions.

- You tell her that employees are paying attention, in case she intends any funny business. (Guests don't normally steal from your home, but you're inviting in lots of people you don't know.)

Beans of Wisdom

Employees follow where you lead, so if you're an enthusiastic greeter, they will be, too. Don't feel that you have to come up with lots of different ways to greet people either. A simple, sincere—that is, nonrobotic—smile and hello is all you need.

You and your employees need to warmly greet every single person who enters, whether they're daily drinkers or complete strangers. It doesn't matter what kind of mood you're in or how lousy sales have been that day; treat every encounter as if it might be the last and win over that customer. After all, if you greet some guests and not others, members of the latter group might feel slighted and take their business where they feel more welcome.

Take Them on a Tour

When a guest comes to your house for the first time, you show them around, pointing out the bathroom, the coat closet, and the location of the hors d'oeuvres so they can easily find what they need.

You should do the same in your coffee bar, providing an audio tour of the facilities so "guests" know what's interesting and special about your home away from home. This means you need to ask customers whether they've been in your shop before. If they haven't, offer a brief description of your business or mention something that might be new to them: "We're glad you could stop by. We offer six types of organically grown coffee, ground fresh every hour, along with a new line of flavorings in case you want a cup with a little something extra. Want to give one a try?"

You can also tailor your talk around the individual's order while he waits for it. If he ordered an espresso, whoever's minding the machine can talk about how you choose the beans. If he ordered an herbal tea, you can ask whether he'd like you to carry herbal iced teas in the summer.

Try to engage customers while simultaneously educating them about your shop. Keep it short and relevant since you don't want to risk taking up a customer's time if he's in a hurry. (If he sticks around to continue the conversation after receiving his drink, that's great—just be sure not to slight the next customer who's waiting in line.)

Above all, be sincere. If you feel like a recording machine spewing out the same thing over and over, customers will definitely hear it in your voice. Love your work, and let that love carry through your voice every time you talk about coffee!

Get on a First-Name Basis

When you're taking an order, do what you can to satisfy the guest's needs. Offer suggestions if he's staring at the menu without a clue. Find out whether he wants whipped cream or a dash of nutmeg in his drink.

Most importantly, ask for his name. Write it on the cup so that whoever makes his drink—whether you or another employee—can let him know when his order is ready. After all, if you yell out "Hot chocolate," you might have several

> **Beans of Wisdom**
>
> If you're not making a customer's drink yourself, don't yell the order down the length of the counter. Either write the order on a cup or walk over to the drink-maker and tell her in person. These approaches show more care for the order than the "loud" approach.

customers who are ready to claim it. Call out "Paul, I have your hot chocolate ready," and you'll avoid any confusion. Paul, along with everyone else, will appreciate this.

Before too long, you'll be able to place names, faces, and orders together and converse freely with customers when they approach you. You can offer suggestions based on previous orders or even start making their drink as soon as you see them.

Give Thanks

Don't forget about customers as soon as they've given you money and received their order. Walk around the seating area and see whether you can bring them anything else. Ask how they're enjoying a newly introduced flavored coffee or baked good. When they head for the door, thank them for stopping by and wish them well. You'd do the same with guests when they leave, right?

Keep 'Em Coming Back

Since you're unlikely to convince people from around the world to shop with you ("Inconveniently located on the other side of the Rockies!"), you need to build up a stable of repeat customers who will provide a steady stream of business.

Treating customers like guests is a good first step because everyone appreciates a good host or hostess. Beyond that, however, you need to recognize that customers are shoppers and will appreciate you giving them a financial incentive to return, such as:

- **A membership card** A frequent buyer card is one way to do this. Present these cards to each customer with the offer of a free drink once they purchase a set number of drinks. Ask each customer at the register whether he has a frequent buyer card. If he does, stamp it; if not, you get to tell him why he should have one.

- **Discount coupons** Another way to attract repeat business is to offer coupons that buyers can use during their next visit. Walk through the seating area and hand out coupons for, say, a free drink with the purchase of any bakery item or a free cookie with the purchase of any drink. These coupons make customers aware of aspects of your product line that they might

> **Beans of Wisdom**
> Be sure to include your store's address and phone number on everything that customers buy and you give away. Always include the area code in case the customer is visiting from out of town. Don't make them hunt you down in the phone book because they might find somebody else instead!

otherwise have ignored forever. More importantly, they may draw the customer back to the shop earlier than he otherwise would have visited.

◆ **A friendly mugging**   If you're more ambitious, you can have the store logo imprinted on plastic mugs and offer a discount to anyone who buys a mug and brings it in for a refill. Sure, you're making less per drink, but you're also lowering cleaning and labor costs—not to mention profiting from the sale price of the mug itself!

◆ **A volume discount**   Just as movie theaters sell a pass good for ten movies at the price of eight, you can offer a $20 card that is worth a certain number of drinks. By buying the card up front, the customer gives you money before you provide any service, which improves your cash flow. On future sales, you can serve the customer his drink faster because you don't have to exchange funds.

One final benefit of discount cards: customers tend to spend a bit more and buy more frequently when they're getting a discount. The coffee costs less, they figure, so why not add a cookie as well since the total order is only a few cents over the price of a nondiscounted coffee—not to mention that the money is already spent anyway.

◆ **Gift cards**   Of course you'd prefer to sell gift cards, but you can also give a gift (card) to current customers and ask them to pass it on to a friend or family member. By giving them something of value that they can pass on, you help them look good to others. The advantage to you, of course, is that the customer might bring new blood into your shop.

◆ **Free samples**   Cut a cookie or muffin into eight pieces, then walk around the seating area and offer samples to everyone. If one customer buys one item in response, you've broken even. What's more likely to happen, though, is that a customer (or two) will buy one or two items immediately, then continue to buy the item on future visits.

Samples give customers a taste—a tantalizing, tiny taste—of a treat they might have found visually appealing but not compelling enough to spend money on. Once the customer finally gets that taste, however, resistance is futile.

◆ **Receipt recommendations**   If your register or computer system allows you to add messages at the bottom of each receipt, include pitches for new products or a discount on a future sale to encourage customers to return in the future— or perhaps even make a second purchase right away!

Whenever you hand over coupons and other sales incentives to customers, express your appreciation for their support, but avoid communicating that gratitude in terms of dollars and cents. No customer wants to be thought of solely as a wallet that transfers money into your register.

Getting Stuffed on Feedback

Science has yet to prove the existence of telepathy and other mind-reading skills, so the only way to know whether customers are satisfied is to *ask them.*

You can pass through the seating area and ask for comments, but you're unlikely to get more than a "fine" or "great" from most customers. In most cases, they're talking with friends, reading, or doing something that requires more attention than the drink in front of them.

To get more detailed comments, you have to make it easy for customers to reply during their own time. Even more important, you have to let them do so anonymously, since many people will write what they'd never say in person.

In other words, you need comment cards. Make them available throughout the store by handing them out with to-go orders, leaving a supply near the restroom, and packing them in a display near the cream station. Place a locked box nearby so that customers can leave their feedback when they feel like doing so.

Beans of Wisdom

To encourage feedback, you can hold a monthly drawing for a complimentary cake or a free drink every month for a year. Post the winner's name to encourage further feedback.

Don't let this feedback disappear without comment. Let customers know that you're paying attention to them! Write to customers who leave their mailing address to answer their questions. For customers who don't ask questions, send a simple thank-you card and a coupon.

Even better, you can post the questions—and your answers—on a bulletin board near the bathroom or somewhere else in the store. A customer might ask, for example, why you don't carry a certain type of coffee, and by posting your answer you can explain the reasons why to him and to everyone else at the same time—or you can announce that you'll start carrying it next month.

Whole Foods Market, the rapidly growing supermarket chain that features many organic foods, uses feedback cards to communicate with customers, and the process often introduces new products to both the customer who asked the question and everyone else who reads the card.

Whatever the questions and answers are, you'll give customers a peek inside how you operate and make them feel like you appreciate their needs and concerns. You reduce the distance between customer and store owner, which creates a stronger connection between the two.

> **Beans of Wisdom**
>
> Don't treat feedback as a one-time communication. Assemble a mailing list of customers' addresses and send them thank-you cards once a year, perhaps right before Christmas or on your business's anniversary. Use a marketing newsletter—a topic we'll cover in Chapter 23—to stay in touch with past customers and introduce new products.

Emergency! What To Do When Bad Stuff Happens

Despite any precautions you might take, your coffee bar will be the stage for performances you wouldn't wish on your closest competitor. We'll run through common scenarios below so that you can learn how to play your role to perfection and win a standing ovation from the audience.

Spill in Aisle Two

A common statistic about automobile accidents is that 80 percent of them occur within five miles of the victim's home. This figure might make your home sound like a death trap—but once you realize that everyone spends roughly 80 percent of their driving time within five miles of their home, that figure is no longer quite so surprising.

The same holds true for spills at a coffee bar. You and your employees will handle hundreds of drinks in any given day, and you're bound to spill a few of them. If anyone is splashed with hot liquid, apply an ice pack to the affected part of the body to reduce the pain and swelling. If the burn is serious, drive the individual to the emergency room for treatment.

Customers spill things, too, so give them the same emergency treatment if necessary. If the spill is merely embarrassing, clean up the mess as quickly as possible and replace the customer's order without charge. By treating the customer as a guest and not as a nuisance, you'll leave a better impression and help her forget about the spill.

Customers from the Netherworld

No matter how friendly and speedy you are, some customers will never be satisfied. They'll complain about the length of the line, the size of their Danish, or the lack of a particular flavored syrup.

Don't become defensive or try to explain why they're mistaken. You cannot win this argument, and if you insist on trying to, you will only look worse in the eyes of other customers. Your goal with these customers, as with any customer, is to satisfy them the best you can, apologize for what you can't fix immediately, and promise to work on eliminating the problem in the future.

Contents May Be Hot

A sure way to kill repeat business is for employees to talk about one customer in front of another. Customers want to buy what they need without worrying that they're going to be criticized as soon as they leave the counter. Besides, what if the two customers know each other? Then you'll lose twice as much business!

Keep that promise, too, because in some cases difficult customers do have valid complaints. Perhaps you should hire another employee to keep lines moving faster or reassess your source for baked goods. If you dismiss the complaint solely due to the manner in which it was presented, you'll miss opportunities to improve your business.

A common belief about customers is that a happy customer might tell one person about his experience while an unhappy customer will spread the word to 10 people. If you do whatever you can to satisfy a customer before he storms out, not only do you save that customer, you also save 10 others who might have been turned away.

A Cry for Help

Part of your employee training should cover how to handle medical emergencies in the coffee bar, from customers who are choking to those suffering from cardiac arrest or seizure.

Before you open, for example, you might ask a medical intern to visit the store and speak to the entire staff about what they should do in an emergency. You can practice doing the Heimlich maneuver on one another and make sure everyone knows where all the telephones are in case they need to call 911. Place a medical kit behind the counter in case employees need to wrap a wound.

With each new hire, you or a senior employee can run through this safety training, both to teach it and to reinforce this material among everyone else.

"Hands Up!"

If you are ever confronted by a robber or group of robbers, your goal is simple: give them whatever they want, then urge them to leave.

Keeping everyone safe, both employees and customers, is far more important than whatever amount of money you'll lose. Respond to a robber's demands in a slow, nonthreatening manner, while at the same time mentally noting characteristics (height, hair color, facial hair, and so forth) that might help the police catch them later.

Contents May Be Hot

Media attention to a robbery might make it easier to find and arrest the perpetrators—but it might also draw attention to your business as a nice target for future thieves. To avoid this, don't quote an exact amount of money stolen when talking to the press.

Fire, Tornadoes, and Other Acts of God

Every airplane flight begins with a reminder of safety procedures, even though the number of air accidents is extremely small. Use the same amount of caution with your business and employees will be ready to tackle explosions, earthquakes, and any other natural disaster that might arise.

Make sure all employees know where to find the fire extinguishers, and keep them charged and up to date. Practice evacuating the shop through both the front and rear doors in case you need to leave in a hurry. In any emergency, you're automatically the one in charge since you own the business, but proper training will help every employee learn how to react automatically so that they can lead customers to safety.

With luck, you'll never have to use any of this knowledge and will experience nothing other than sunshine and friendly, nonspilling, nonrobbing customers. Don't keep your fingers crossed …

The Least You Need to Know

- In addition to wanting good food and drinks, customers want to be appreciated. Smile and welcome them as you would any friend or guest.

- Give customers a reason to return by offering frequent buyer cards and coupons.

- Ask for customer feedback, then put it to use. By showing that you care about their concerns, they'll develop a closer relationship with you and your store.

- Hope for the best, but prepare for the worst. Make sure that you and your employees are ready to handle calamities both big and small.

Chapter 20

Cleaning and Maintenance

In This Chapter

- Neat shops lead to neat profits
- What to clean hourly, daily, and weekly
- Employee hygiene
- Public vs. private cleaning

Every restaurant owner wishes that his or her shop worked like a self-cleaning oven. You'd lock the door, press a button, and whammo! All the dirt, dust, and grime that comes with food preparation would be incinerated and every surface sanitized, ready for the next day.

Alas, some wishes can never be fulfilled. The only way to clean your coffee bar is to use old-fashioned tools like clean water, linen cloths, and elbow grease.

Cleaning is essential both to creating a welcoming environment that customers want to come back to again and again and to maintaining good standing with the local health department. If you fall behind on cleaning, you'll face an uphill battle to whip the shop back into shape. You probably know this from experience in your house or apartment. If you let the cleaning go for a couple of days, when the weekend comes you have a huge mess to clean before your mother arrives!

Maintain a regular schedule, though—perhaps something along the lines of what we describe below—and cleaning will be relatively easy on a day-to-day basis.

A Schedule for Scrubbing (and Scouring and ...)

Creating an effective cleaning schedule takes only two steps. First, make a list of every single element within your shop: the utensils, the lights, the doormat, the inside of the portafilters on the espresso machine, and so on. If you don't list it on the schedule, it probably won't get cleaned—and even if it does, you won't clean it as often as you should.

Once you've listed everything, you need to decide how often each item needs to be cleaned: monthly, weekly, daily, hourly, or after each use.

Manufacturer guidelines will help you out in some cases; other times, you must rely on observation. If, for instance, you notice the shelf that displays French presses for sale is dusty each time you pass it, you need to move that area up a notch on the cleaning schedule. In general, your coffee bar can never be too clean. You're preparing items that people place inside their bodies, after all, and cleanliness is one way to avoid food contamination.

> **Beans of Wisdom**
>
> Ideally, the coffee bar will be so spic-and-span that each customer will feel that she is the first person to order from you, which means she will receive the most delectable drinks and the freshest food possible. Clean with this mindset and you can make it happen!

What's more, if your store gets a reputation as being unclean, you'll see customers trickle away as they decide to take their business elsewhere. Since you can hardly advertise that you're now cleaning on a regular basis ("Now featuring 75 percent less dirt and spider webs!"), once you lose dirt-phobic customers, they're unlikely to come back.

After Every Use

Of prime concern in this category is the espresso machine, which baristas should wipe down after each use. The steam wands must be cleared and the grounds from the previous shot dumped. Rinse the portafilters regularly as well. All of this activity ensures that each espresso product will be uncontaminated by the residue of drinks past.

Counters also fall under this category as employees should wipe them down immediately after finishing whatever task they're doing. The same directive applies for the front counters as well. If crumbs drop from a plate when you hand over a piece of cake or lint falls from a customer's hand when he hands you change, run a barely damp cloth over the counter once the customer moves on so that you can present the next customer with an unblemished surface.

If the cloth leaves the counter damp, be sure to follow up with a dry cloth to remove the water. Customers tend to get disturbed when they touch something wet that shouldn't be: Is that just water, or is it liquid sugar? Ammonia perhaps? Bleach?! If you keep the counter dry, they'll never have to guess.

At Least Once an Hour

When you consider what might need to be cleaned hourly, you'll find yourself returning again and again to the customers' point of view—what they expect to see when they visit your coffee bar.

Number one on the list, to the surprise of many, is clean bathrooms. The bathroom serves as shorthand for the entirety of your business. If the bathroom isn't clean, then (in the customer's mind) there's little hope for anything else.

> **Beans of Wisdom**
>
> Don't be content with doing hourly cleaning every 70 minutes or so. Stick to your schedule! If necessary, purchase an electronic timer that serves solely as a cleaning alarm. When the timer goes off, start making the rounds and leave no table leg unturned.

This means that employees must service the bathroom on at least an hourly basis, picking up paper towels, wiping fingerprints off mirrors and water off the sink, cleaning toilet bowls and urinals, and so forth. Back-up rolls of toilet paper must be available, and soap dispensers filled.

In addition to bathroom maintenance, survey the exterior of your shop every hour or so to make sure your doorway is unobstructed, the street or walkway free of debris, and your windows unblemished. Employees should use a broom and handled dustpan to clean up cigarette butts and food wrappers. (If customers do see debris outside your shop when they enter, with luck your staff will have it cleaned up before they leave, thus letting them know you're on the ball and concerned about how you look.) Another spot that needs attention at least once an hour is the sugar, cream, and milk station. Customers tend to make a mess when they prepare drinks, so you want to be there to clean up their spills and leave it fresh for the next person. Staying on top of this area will also help avoid the dreaded, "Do you have any more skim milk?" which interrupts service to that customer in addition to the one you're waiting on now.

Instant Facts

The Broken Windows theory, conceived by criminologists James Q. Wilson and George Kelling, states that crime inescapably results from disorder. If a window in a house breaks and isn't fixed, people assume that no one watches over the house. In short order, the house will be covered with graffiti and have more broken windows. In the same way, if your coffee bar has messy tables and a dirty milk station, customers won't feel guilty about adding to the mess. If you keep everything spotless, however, customers will tend to clean up after themselves. The moral? Cleanliness breeds cleanliness!

Employees should pass through the sitting area to clean off tables and remove trash that customers leave behind. Use a damp white cloth to wipe down tables, follow up with a dry cloth, then store these cloths out of the customer's sight. (White cloths don't stay white for long, after all.)

Your staff should also examine trash levels on these hourly rounds, replacing full bags with empties when appropriate. Hauling trash in front of customers is never pretty—but when the alternative is to risk trash falling out of the can and onto the floor, the choice is clear.

Several Times Each Day

Espresso machines are delicate beasts and need regular care to serve you well. In addition to cleaning steam wands and wiping down the machine, employees need to backflush the groups a few times each day to make sure old grounds are removed.

Contents May Be Hot

During the backflushing process, extremely hot water might be ejected from the group in unusual ways. Wear padding on your arms to protect yourself from being burned!

To backflush, the employee places a blind filter—that is, a filter without holes—into a portafilter, attaches it to a group, and runs the water for up to one minute. He then runs the water in short bursts while simultaneously loosening and tightening the portafilter in the group; doing this loosens residue in the group's sealing gasket. Replace the blind filter with a regular one, run the water a few seconds more, and you're good to go.

In slow moments after a rush period ends, employees should inspect counter displays and the pastry case for spills. Remove all uncovered foods before spraying any cleaner inside the case, and replace the serving utensils as often as needed. Make sure to inspect these cases from the customer's side of the counter so that you can see exactly what they see. In fact, it's a good idea to look at everything in the store from the customer's point of view!

Throughout the Day

Some simple cleaning chores are easy to overlook—until a customer points out you haven't done them, that is. Such tasks include refilling napkin holders and sugar dispensers, dusting displays of retail goods, and wiping down table and chair legs.

Restocking cups, lids, stirrers, receipt tape, and other consumables also falls in this category. Train employees to use free moments to refill supplies so that you'll always have everything you need during busy periods.

Another all-day job involves cleaning used dishes and putting them away. If you have a dishwasher, this means scraping off plates, scrubbing off lipstick marks (which persist far longer than you might imagine), and loading the machine. Once the load ends, inspect the dishes as you unload and store them in their proper locations, mugs near the coffee carafes, plates by the display case, and so on. Look for chips and cracks and, if you find any, discard that item immediately. It can't be cleaned properly and therefore poses a health risk to customers.

If you're washing items by hand, set up your triple sink so that you wash in one sink, rinse in the second, and sanitize in the third. Fill the wash compartment with a detergent solution, and wash lightly soiled items first to give other pieces time to soak. Use clean hot water in the rinse compartment, and drain and refill it whenever the water becomes dirty. Fill the sanitizer compartment with a warm sanitizing solution, and let items soak in the solution for at least two minutes. (Ask your health department for details on the proper triple-sink procedure in your area.)

After Closing

Since you use much of your equipment throughout the day to make food and drinks, you often have to wait until after hours to clean these items. Again, let's start with the espresso machine:

- Pour hot water down the drain box to unclog any residue.

- Take off all removable parts—ask the supplier for a list if you're unsure what qualifies—clean them, and set them aside to dry.

- Remove the filters from the portafilters, soak them in hot water for 15 minutes, then brush them free of any remaining grounds.

- Soak the steam wands overnight by placing each wand in a pitcher of hot water.

As for other equipment, brush the dosing chambers of the coffee and espresso grinders free of all grounds, then remove the hoppers, wash them in soapy water, and let them dry overnight. Scrub the insides of the coffee carafes and the pitchers in which you steam milk. Drain clean water through the spout of each carafe to ensure no soap remains behind.

Dump the cream and milk that remain in the containers at the serving station; then break down the containers and clean them thoroughly, taking special care with rubber parts that could trap milk inside. (Again, your local health department will have details on how you should handle dairy products in your state or county. Depending on their guidelines and your storage techniques, you might be able to store the cream and milk in separate containers and reuse them the next day. If so, label the dairy products so that the next morning's employees know which supplies to use first.)

Contents May Be Hot

If you're located in an old building or a city environment, bugs and rodents will be scampering around your café. Consider hiring a pest control service on a monthly basis. Better to be proactive than wait until a mouse scampers across a customer's feet!

Many baked goods are at their best for only one day. Wrap these items and place them in a half-price basket for sale the next day, or mark them as waste on your inventory sheets, play "Taps," and discard them.

Wipe out the bakery display case to help prevent pests such as ants and rodents from being wooed by crumbs. Clean food labels in the display case, and replace those that are dirty. A greasy croissant label doesn't say "Fresh! Clean!" to your customers.

Empty the garbage cans, then hose them out in the mop sink in the back room so that no odors linger the following day. Sweep and mop the floor, no matter how clean it might look. (If you do mop while the store is open, place a "wet floor" sign out so that customers know to watch their footing.)

Once a Week

Aside from daily cleaning, your shop has hard-to-reach spots that require the occasional wipe-down to keep them looking good. Light fixtures and air circulation vents are good examples of this type of cleaning. Customers are hardly likely to examine such items up close, but the last thing you want is dust bunnies falling from the sky into someone's drink. Other overlooked spots include the kick guards underneath the front counters, curtains/blinds, window ledges (especially if you have curtains or blinds), and foot mats (not to mention underneath said foot mats).

You can purchase a squeegee and a bucket to clean the windows yourself or hire someone to do this job for you. A once- or twice-a-week cleaning should be enough to keep the front of your shop looking good.

Hiring a linen service might also be appropriate since you'll use a heaping helping of white cloths each day to wipe down equipment. You can always choose to use disposable cloths, but be sure to weigh the environmental and replacement costs before deciding which type of cleaning material suits your shop better.

In addition to regular backflushing each day, your espresso machine requires a weekly backflushing with special cleaner that foams in hot water to reach spaces that would otherwise go untouched. Run through the final step of backflushing—in which you loosen and tighten the portafilter to clean the group's gasket—at least a dozen times to rinse all the cleaner from the machine.

> **Beans of Wisdom**
>
> Replace dirty cloths with clean ones at every opportunity. In general, if you look at a cloth and can't tell whether it's clean or dirty, replace it with one you know is clean.

Long-Term Maintenance

On top of the day-to-day chores, you'll need to track maintenance schedules for the larger pieces of equipment. Either ask the suppliers to contact you at the appropriate times, or mark a yearly calendar with service dates. Notes on this calendar might include:

◆ When to change the filter on the water treatment or water-softening device.

◆ A reminder to change the burr on the grinder after every 1,000 pounds of coffee processed.

◆ A replacement schedule for portafilter inserts since the holes grow larger over time, which affects the taste of the espresso.

- A monthly reminder to vacuum the refrigerator coils.

- A regular schedule for checking tables and chairs for wobbly legs, loose tops, and torn fabric.

Marking these oddball cleaning chores on a calendar will also help you properly schedule staffing for the day, even if all you need to do is add a couple of hours to one employee's shift so that he can handle these tasks.

Keep the Staff Sparkling

On top of all the cleaning that you expect your staff to handle, they must also—we have to say it—take care to clean *themselves*. Naturally they should arrive for work each day in clean clothes, having showered and groomed themselves so they present a fresh face to customers. You would be wise to ask them to avoid using perfumes and colognes as such odors can overpower the aroma of the drinks and foods on sale.

Beyond these expectations, you must train the staff in how to handle food safely. They must wash their hands before touching food or preparing drinks, whether they just returned from the bathroom, took out the trash, or merely rearranged their hair. Even time spent at the register handling bills that have passed through dozens of hands necessitates a wash. Employees should wear rubber gloves when they use cleaning fluids, both for their own protection and the well-being of customers.

Try not to be too hard-nosed in how you approach this topic with employees. Instead, stress the need for courtesy towards your guests and observance of the Golden Rule about doing unto others.

> **Beans of Wisdom**
>
> You might consider keeping a spare shirt and pair of pants in your office or a spare locker just in case an employee (or, dare we say it, you) experiences a major flavor-shot *faux pas* and looks unpresentable. Better to wear ill-fitting clothes for the remainder of a shift than ones covered in goo!

What Customers Should (and Shouldn't) See

Customers appreciate a clean business environment, and if they have a choice between neat and so-so shops, they'll gravitate towards the clean one every time.

This doesn't mean, however, that they necessarily want to *see* every cleaning effort you make. If you walk out of the restroom with a toilet brush held high and proudly exclaim, "A beautiful bowl awaits you all," they will not be impressed.

While some cleaning chores must obviously wait until after hours, you would be wise to push some tasks—such as cleaning the lights—to times when the shop is empty or nearly so, even when they could be done during normal working hours. No one wants to see dust falling from the ceiling and imagine that this is a common occurrence.

Along the same lines, employees should remove boxes and paperwork from public view so that customers aren't reminded of the less appealing aspects of running a coffee bar. If, for instance, you mop the floor while customers are still in the store, they might inadvertently associate your products with dirty water instead of the pure image you'd prefer they have.

Despite all these warnings, customers will be pleased to see some cleaning going on. By clearing and wiping down tables, you make the seating area more inviting. By picking up debris in front of the store, you're beautifying the community. By posting a cleaning schedule inside the bathroom and having employees mark it each hour, you demonstrate a commitment to cleanliness. Just don't do it in front of them!

The Least You Need to Know

- ◆ Cleaning your shop is as important as stocking it with raw materials. After all, customers won't return if you can't offer an inviting environment.

- ◆ Go through your entire shop from top to bottom and make sure that each piece of it fits somewhere on your maintenance and cleaning schedule.

- ◆ Safe food-handling techniques must become second nature for your employees. Take the time to train and reinforce these skills so that customers always see the best you have to offer.

- ◆ Train employees to think clean, both in their personal lives and in how they spend time at work.

- ◆ Learn to distinguish what can and should be cleaned in front of customers and what should wait until after hours.

Chapter 21

Operations in Future Days

In This Chapter

- ◆ Menu morphing
- ◆ Workers to wunderkind
- ◆ First thoughts on a second store
- ◆ Time to sell?

When you're focused on the everyday struggle of servicing lines of customers, cleaning the seating area, and ordering and unloading supplies, it's easy to forget that you started this business with larger goals in mind: being your own boss, for example, or providing food, drinks, and atmosphere that weren't available anywhere else.

Learn to take a break from the daily grind to reassess the future of your business, both the products you offer and the manner in which you manage. If sales are so-so, this self-examination can help you determine what to change or adjust to make the business more profitable.

If, however, sales are constantly rising, examining how you do business is even more important. You might be better off hiring managers to handle the hourly needs of the shop while you focus on what to do next, whether it's tweaking the menu or planning for store number two. Determining which skills bring in the most dollars—and hiring others to take over the other roles essential for business—will bring you the most success in the long run.

Adjusting the Menu

No matter how much research you put into your initial menu, you're still going to have a few clunkers. The "no carbs" craze might have bashed brownie sales to bits, for instance, or you discover that no one appreciates cinnamon-flavored coffee as much as you do.

Stick with your initial menu for at least a month to give newcomers—and they're all newcomers at this point—time to experiment and develop favorites. (If you change your hours of operation, either during the start-up period or at a later date, you'll want to keep your current menu locked in place since after-dinner diners will have different tastes than early morning munchers.)

After this trial period, you should review the sales record and re-examine the menu with an eye towards replacing duds with new dishes that might get customers' taste buds a bit more excited. You can:

- **Look at the calendar.** If you're headed into summer, think about adding iced coffees, granitas, or milkshakes. If winter approaches, consider a special hot chocolate blend that you've never tried before or new flavorings that tie in with the season.

- **Keep an eye on trends.** Stop in at restaurants and other competitors and see how they've adjusted their menus. You might discover new items that you can personalize to fit your establishment, or realize that everyone but you has moved away from an item you still have faith in. Have they spotted a trend away from this item, or are they trying to create a trend of their own?

- **Simplify your offerings.** Do you really need to offer an ultimate chocolate chunk brownie *and* a double chocolate fudge brownie? Customers who buy one would undoubtedly switch to the other—and eliminating one type of brownie would leave you room for a new product or merely simplify your ordering process and reduce waste.

- **Play with the pricing.** Don't feel that every drink has to cost no more than $X or every sweet between $Y and $Y.99. Experiment with your offerings and let customers tell you with their dollars whether you're out of line. You may discover, for instance, that the market will support $5 per slice of chocolate-turtle cheesecake even though you used to offer nothing more expensive than a $2 can-noli. You might also find that selling individually wrapped gourmet chocolates at 3/$1 nets you far more money than you ever imagined possible from such an inexpensive item.

Expect resistance from customers—and possibly even employees!—when you remove slow-selling items from the menu. As newspapers discover each time they rearrange the comics page, every offering is someone's favorite, no matter how much it's hated or ignored by the public at large. Consider whether you can special order items for regulars or whether it's better in the long run to try to turn them on to something else.

Contents May Be Hot

Don't change your entire menu in one go! Once customers are used to your offerings, they will expect certain items to be available each time they visit. Changing only one or two items gives you a talking point at the register, while still allowing (most) customers to find old favorites.

Managing Managers

When you first open for business, you're likely to work every hour of the day for weeks on end. From morning to night, you'll be on hand to receive goods, keep employees on the right track, and match receipts to the sales tape at the end of the day.

While being involved with your business is a good thing, clearly you can't maintain this schedule forever. At some point you'll burn out and harm both yourself and your business. (And if you're married or engaged—well, let's not go there ....) The only solution is to hire other managers or train employees to open and close the shop.

Spread the Knowledge

When searching for a supervisor to supplement your oversight, promoting an employee who's currently on staff is probably the best bet, since she will already have a handle on what it takes to run the shop. She'll have seen you in action as you place orders or take inventory. She'll know how to handle every station in your shop and can train new hires with ease.

Knowing this, keep your eyes open for an employee who has a self-starter mentality—completing tasks on her own as she discovers them, for example—to complement an ability to follow the rules you've laid down. (A self-starter who insists she knows how to do things better than you is not the way to go.)

The key to preparing an employee for a management position is to offer her more responsibility over time and see how she responds. Teach her how to take inventory, for instance, or explain how to read the register tape to track sales and balance the till. See whether she takes on these tasks herself in the future, whether she waits for you to tell her what to do—or whether she goes on to learn other duties on her own. Some employees thrive when asked to do more, while others prefer to stick with what they already know.

Hand Over the Keys

Once you find an employee who seems like a good candidate, take her aside and tell her that you'd like to offer her a managerial position. Go over the duties that such a position involves—many of which she'll already know, thanks to your training—and the hours she'll be required to work. Explain her new rate of pay and her responsibilities over those who used to be her co-workers.

Don't be surprised if an employee turns you down. Some are happy to stay where they are, close to the customers with little responsibility beyond serving and smiling. If she does accept your proposal, work out a start date for her position. Make the date far enough in the future that you have time to cover everything she'll need to know to run the shop on her own.

If she does accept the new role, make it clear that this position is only a trial run. Give her checks and balances so that both of you can assess whether she's living up to the standards you've set. If she can't cut it initially, you both have choices: you can offer more training if you think she still has potential, or she can decide to return to her old position, if she disagrees. If you had just given her the position in the first place, you'd both be stuck if she didn't work out.

Contents May Be Hot

Don't expect employees to automatically embrace your choice of manager. Jealousy might rear its head among those who feel they could do a better job. Employees who are really hurt might even leave. Don't second-guess yourself. Anyone who gets bent out of shape over your decision isn't ready to be manager anyway—and might not even be suitable for your staff in the long run.

Once you make the position permanent, you'll still need to monitor her performance in the first months. If you're double-checking inventory dollars spent or labor dollars used, she'll naturally push herself to do the best possible job to show that she can do everything she needs to.

Both you and your new manager should spend time evaluating other employees for future managerial positions. You don't want to place your replacement in the same position you were in, after all! Ideally, you'll always be cultivating a supervisor or two so that you'll have a replacement on hand should one of you take ill.

As you assume the job of overseer and then leave even that aside, you need to redefine your role as owner or company president. You'll still brew an espresso from time to time, but you want the manager to feel that she can do her job without you constantly watching over her shoulder.

Positioning yourself as the owner also lets the staff know they can't rely on you to fill in for them whenever they need a day off. Create a list of duties—accounting, payroll, hiring, marketing—and share this list with the staff so they understand your new role in the business. (Admittedly, you handled all these duties even when you were involved with the day-to-day operations. In your new role, though, you'll concentrate more on the big picture and less on the brushstrokes.)

Bigger, Faster, Stronger

One question that every successful business owner faces is a question they never dreamed would be asked of them: "So when are you going to open a second location?"

"A second location?" they ask. "I'm barely in control of the first, and I still have two years of loan payments, and, and ..." Yet the idea sticks with them, and late at night when they should be sleeping, they wonder whether expansion might indeed be possible some day.

You're still at the start of your business adventure, but we advise you to always keep expansion and growth opportunities in the back of your mind. Even franchising isn't too outrageous to think about if you have a winning business formula.

However, before launching into any of the expansion activities listed below, make sure that your current business is profitable and runs smoothly. Any problems that exist in your current location will become twice as bad if you spread them to a new shop rather than spend the time needed to solve them first.

Second Acts

If one business is successful, then two businesses should bring in twice as much money, right?

Well, yes and no. All the rules for opening and running a first location apply equally to a second, so if your new store is in a remote location and never advertises, then you have no chance of hitting the ball out of the park a second time.

Beans of Wisdom

Duplicate the style of your first location in any subsequent shops so that customers recognize them as being part of the same company. While each shop will succeed or fail on its own, having a uniform style will encourage customers of one location to stop at others if they're in another part of town.

If, however, you apply all the knowledge learned while opening your current business to researching and merchandising a new location, then you will likely achieve a better return on the new investment than you did on the first. After all, consider the following benefits:

- **Your food and supply costs will likely be lower.** When you buy in larger volumes, whether beans, bagels, or bags, suppliers tend to offer larger discounts. This means that you can either charge lower prices at one or both locations (in case you need to go up against competitors) or net a higher return per item.

- **You can advertise for two stores almost as cheaply as one.** When you first open a new location, your advertising costs will likely jump as you'll want to spread the word about the new place as quickly as possible. After the initial rush, though, you'll get twice the bang for your advertising buck since you can promote both locations for the same price as one.

- **You'll have a stronger presence in the market.** Customers who might have visited infrequently due to distance might be able to shop at your new location more often, perhaps even every day. Having two locations also indicates a general level of success. After all, you wouldn't have opened a second shop if the first wasn't doing well.

- **You'll have a stronger staff.** Employees at your current shop will likely be able to work a day or two at the new location to help you get started. These seasoned employees will be able to train the new hires quickly, which means fewer mistakes and a higher level of customer satisfaction.

- **You can avoid "learning mistakes."** Just as new hires can learn from the old pros, you will learn from the mistakes you made while opening your first store and be in better shape at the second location. This isn't to say you won't make mistakes; you probably will, but then you'll have an even longer list of mistakes to avoid when you open a third shop in the years ahead!

When you make the move towards building a business empire—that's right, an empire!—you have to readjust your approach to day-to-day operations. You can't be as hands-on as you might have been in the past. You just won't have the time anymore.

Sure, you'll serve customers from time to time, but in general, you'll delegate authority to others rather than do the job yourself. You can only be in one place at one time, which means you'll need competent, independent managers at each location who can handle daily operations while you focus on ordering, accounting, and thinking about the big picture.

Once you have two stores, that picture takes on a new look. You've diversified your investment so that you're no longer relying on the success of one store. Slow sales at one location might be balanced by steady or rising sales at the other. The customers at one store will favor literary events, while those at the other turn out in huge numbers for craft workshops. (We'll talk more about holding special events in Chapter 22.) You'll start examining surrounding markets to see where a third location might go. This might be hard to picture now, but someday it could happen to you!

New and Improved

Instead of opening a second location, you might consider expanding the current shop to add a stage, make more room for tables, or enlarge the kitchen so you can make treats in-house.

Think through these plans carefully before launching into them. You'll need to get approval from the town to run a larger business, which might require new permits from the health department and other governmental agencies. You need to work out details of the expansion with the building owner, such as who will bear which costs. (Expansion might leave the owner with a more valuable property in the long run, so don't assume that you should bear all the costs.)

During the actual construction, you might have to close the business or restrict yourself to delivery sales. Do you have the cash flow to survive this interruption, and can you survive higher loan payments if you're financing the expansion? Will customers find another place to shop during this time? Will you pay employees during this time, or ask them to go for a week or two without pay?

Call in your crew of professionals—your attorney, accountant, and mentor—and ask their opinion on whether this expansion is right for you or whether you should take another path. There are many positive reasons for expanding a business, but expanding too soon is one of the top reasons that small businesses fail.

> **Beans of Wisdom**
>
> Expansion and an identical second store aren't your only options for growth! You can start an espresso cart in a mall, a café in a museum, a juice bar in a gym, or a snack shop in the park. By finding—or making—opportunities like these (called "bumpouts" in the restaurant trade), your business can grow in all sorts of unexpected ways.

You also need to ask what you expect to get out of this expansion. Are you adding products and services that will bring in more income, or are you expanding nonproductive space like seating? Will the increased income from making your own baked goods compensate for the expense of the equipment and the downtime?

Compare the costs for expansion with the cost of opening a second location. Expansion will allow you to stay more hands-on, since you'll still have only one shop, but you might receive even more benefits for the same cost by opening a new store.

Expanding Without Getting Bigger

Aside from bumpouts, expansions, and multiple stores, you can find growth opportunities by reaching out to new customers. If you roast whole beans in-house, you can approach gas stations, convenience stores, offices, and other businesses about supplying them with fresh ground beans once or twice a week. (And if you *don't* roast beans, you can always consider adding this service to your shop.)

If you've developed unique blends and roasts, you can try to market them from coast to coast over the Internet or by mail order. Develop a website that focuses on mail-order sales (while still providing local store hours and addresses), and include the URL on everything you give to customers.

Promote mail order sales within the shop to encourage current customers to give coffee as gifts to faraway relatives. Experiment with mailing lists that you purchase from catalog companies or trade for with local businesses. (Mail order pitches typically have a low response rate—under two percent according to the Direct Marketing Association—but if you're selling pounds of coffee rather than individual cups, the funds you net might make it worthwhile.)

Consider adding services like delivery or catering to serve customers in specialized situations. As with wholesale roasting and mail order sales, these services require you to spend funds on labor and raw materials—expenses for which you are naturally reimbursed through sales—but you avoid the huge capital costs of a second building.

Carbon Copies

Aside from opening a second (or third) shop of your own, you can also think about franchising—that is, selling the concept of your business to other entrepreneurs.

You do have a concept, right? A unique approach to the coffee business that distinguishes you from the coffee chains, both local and national, that already exist? Sure you do—your concept encompasses the design, color, layout, and so forth of your existing shops.

Whether or not this concept has long-term potential is another question. Your best bet might be to contact a franchise expert to see whether your existing concept can be packaged in a way that will appeal to others across the country.

You might have the idea that franchising a business allows you to make money for doing practically nothing, but that's far from the truth. Once you franchise, your customers are no longer the ones buying the coffee; your customers are those who serve the coffee, the owners of the businesses that bear your name. You need to focus your energy on marketing strategies that will benefit the owners of these businesses because you will profit when they do better.

Instant Facts

Due to abuses in the sale of franchises in the 1950s and '60s, a number of government organizations adopted guidelines that franchisers must follow. These guidelines have been revised often over the decades, and the most widely used document currently is the Uniform Franchise Offering Circular (UFOC), available from the North American Securities Administrators Association (NASAA). Contact NASAA at 202-737-0900 or online at www.nasaa.org.

Franchising is a big step away from the day-to-day operations of a coffee bar. If interacting with customers and joking around with employees is what excites you the most about business, put aside thoughts of franchising and focus on the business at hand. If, however, you dream of larger things, plan for a franchise from your earliest days.

Getting Out While the Getting's Good

Although some business owners love the daily struggle to keep their head above water or the ongoing battle to raise current sales over those of the previous year, others learn that life as an entrepreneur really doesn't suit them. They might have enjoyed the challenge of opening a store, but the daily grind is reducing them to pulp.

If you're in this boat, don't feel that you have to stay in business forever. If your coffee bar is surviving and growing, you can likely find a buyer willing to take it off your hands.

Don't just throw an ad in the local papers, though! There's a lot more to selling a business than a simple financial transaction. To begin with, how much is your business even worth? A year's worth of sales? The value of your inventory? Business Brokerage Press publishes an annual reference guide for business valuations and estimates that a coffee shop should be valued at 40 to 45 percent of annual sales plus inventory.

> **Beans of Wisdom**
>
> When you're preparing to sell a business, keep costs as low as possible, both ongoing expenses and new charges. Don't introduce new products, for example, because sales of new items often take time to grow to acceptable levels.

This estimate is merely a starting point, however. You need to account for the location, your standing in the community, goodwill among customers (measured by the percentage of repeat customers), and many other factors that can boost or depress that price. Whatever number you arrive at, add at least 10 percent to the total to create negotiating space with potential buyers.

Aside from the base price, you have to worry about contracts, mortgages, and every other piece of paper that has your name on it. Once you sell the business, you want your name off everything so that you can't be held financially responsible for debts that develop after the new boss takes over.

Unless you've sold a business previously, you should probably hire a business broker to manage the sale. The broker will negotiate with potential buyers, explain how you can get more for your business, and handle all the legal nitty-gritty such as when exactly you'll hand the keys over.

Selling isn't forever, of course. If you enjoy the thrill of starting a coffee bar more than running one, you can always start another (noncompeting) one with the idea of selling that one as well. Starting a business takes a certain talent that not everyone shares. If you've got it, you can use it to finance many new opportunities.

The Least You Need to Know

◆ Examine your menu for slow sellers once a month and replace them with items that might excite customers more. Consider offering seasonal treats or other limited specials to encourage sales.

◆ Keep your eye out for employees who are smart and well-trained, and groom them for management positions. Offer supervisory roles on a trial basis so both you and the employee have the chance to decide whether you've found the right person.

◆ Plan for growth, whether expanding into a vacant store next door, opening a second location across town, adding new services, or franchising your business concept.

◆ Don't be afraid to get out. Some business owners like the thrill of opening a business more than the daily dullness of keeping the boat afloat. Consider selling the business and starting another if you find yourself in this position.

Part 6

Getting the Word Out

Having a well-run business is a good start, but you can't keep it a secret and hope to succeed in the long run. You need customers, which means you must spread the word about your shop—your delicious drinks, your scrumptious sweets, your comfortable seats—far and wide through continuous marketing efforts.

It takes money to make money, as the saying goes, and newsletters, flyers, coupons, and banners can all pay for themselves by bringing in new faces.

But you don't have to lay out cash to make a name for yourself in the coffee business. Through the power of publicity, you can be transformed into a coffee expert who's quoted in the media and praised in the community.

COME SEE THE WORLD'S *BIGGEST* CUP OF COFFEE!

Chapter **22**

The Power of Publicity

In This Chapter

- Press release pointers
- Creating the news
- Meet the press
- Turning customers into billboards
- You're the expert

Getting your name into the public eye doesn't have to cost an arm, two legs, and a spleen. By issuing press releases and positioning yourself as an expert, you can have reporters calling you for stories—and when an unbiased media source such as a reporter or TV news anchor puts you on stage, your credibility jumps a lot higher than it does from a paid advertisement that says, "Hey, I'm great!"

Want to get people talking about your coffee shop? Then prepare to become a publicity professional, pronto. We'll show you how to get your name in print, garner positive word-of-mouth, and turn your customers into walking billboards for your business.

Breaking the News

If you dream about seeing your name in print, realizing that dream is only a press release away. A press release—sometimes called a news release—is a one- to two-page description of what's going on at your business. You send press releases to media outlets like newspapers, magazines, and radio and TV stations in the hope that they'll find your happenings interesting enough to cover.

Don't worry if members of the media don't pick up your press release and run a breaking news story on the live music you offer or the new Himalayan coffee you sell. If your press release hits them right, they'll keep you on file as an expert to call for future stories, which can be just as good.

Contents May Be Hot

While publicity has a big benefit over advertising—its low, low cost of $0—the bad news is that you have no control over newspaper reviews, TV interviews, or a mention on the radio by the morning drive-time shock-jocks. Unlike in ads, you can't control what people write or say about you in the media.

Be Newsworthy

Press releases are not the same as advertising. If you want something in print that says you rock the house, buy an ad that says just that.

To be successful, a press release must present a reporter with information and news that will matter to his readers. A press release that's nothing more than a self-serving piece of fluff will be trashed quicker than a used coffee cup. Examples of real news are:

- A business opening—like yours!

- Health news such as a study linking caffeine to improved memory, with quotes from a coffee expert—namely, you!

- A special happening in your shop such as a networking event or a book signing (more on these topics later in this chapter).

- Community service, such as a donation of free coffee to a local sporting event or a percentage of a day's receipts to charity.

- A contest, such as an essay contest or a ticket drawing.

◆ A move to a new location.

◆ A new product or service—but *only* if it's truly new, such as, say, being the first to offer coffee catering to preschoolers or something of equal "Wow" value on the local news.

If you're not sure what qualifies as newsworthy, spend some time reading the publications in which you hope to appear. Not only will you discover which news is new—you'll also find charities you can sponsor, info about competing businesses, and much more. (If nothing else, you can respond to news stories with a letter to the editor, one that will naturally bear your business name should it appear in print.)

Shape Up Your News Release

When a member of the media opens up a press release, she expects to see certain things in certain places with a format that makes it easy for her to digest this information. If you design some wild-looking press release to stand out from the crowd, she will most likely toss your sheet without a second glance simply because she won't be able to quickly find the information she needs.

With that warning in mind, here's how to format your press release like a pro:

◆ If you have letterhead, print your news release on it.

◆ In the upper left-hand corner, write "For Immediate Release," or, if the release has limited time value, "Hold Until XX/XX/XX" or "For Release During the Christmas Season."

◆ Flush right on the same line, tell the editors who they can contact for further information: "Contact: Joe Java, 800-123-4567."

◆ Use an easy-to-read typeface such as Times or Courier in 12 points.

◆ Keep the news release to one page if possible. If it does go over one page, end each running page with "—more—."

◆ End with a short paragraph on your company and more detailed contact information. For example, you can write, "Coffee Express offers coffee, pastries, coffee-related gifts, and catering from its convenient location in downtown Boston. For more information, visit www.coffeeexpressshop.com or call 617-555-1212."

◆ End a news release with "###" centered at the bottom of the page.

Again, don't worry if your press release looks boring; it's supposed to look boring. Worry instead about making the information special, and not the style in which it's presented. Check out the press release below for an example of how it's done.

```
For Immediate Release          Contact: Bertha Bean, 212-555-1212
April XX, 2005                          Bertha's Bodacious Beans

Don't Roast Yourself! Learn How to Play with Fire
at Bertha's Bodacious Beans

Want to learn to play with fire? Come to Bertha's Bodacious Beans at
123 Main Street in Chance, Maryland, on April 1 for a free lesson in
juggling flaming batons from veteran circus performer Lotta Burns.

Burns ran away and joined the circus after her parents punished her
at age eight for playing with matches. She quickly became the favorite
student of the world-renowned fire juggler Smoky Tuckis, who taught
her all his secrets. After the circus burnt down in 1984, Burns took
her one-woman show on the road, giving fire juggling lessons to chil-
dren and adults across the country and even overseas in cities such
as Bern, Switzerland—and now, she's bringing her talents to Bertha's
Bodacious Beans!

"We're so excited to be able to bring Burns to our store," says store
owner Bertha Bean. "Learning to juggle fire can help our customers meet
new people, get into Harvard, win the Pulitzer Prize, and get rid of
unsightly warts."

Lotta Burns's workshop is just one in a whole lineup of exciting
classes offered at Bertha's Bodacious Beans, including sword swallow-
ing, monster truck driving, shark hunting, and knitting. "We always
take chances with our workshops," says Bean. "For example, knitting
can be very dangerous, what with those sharp needles and all. But we're
committed to bringing only the best and most interesting workshops to
our valued customers."

Bertha's Bodacious Beans sells organic, free-trade, free-range coffee
beans that are grown by elves in the Black Forest without the use of
herbicides, fungicides, pesticides, or fratricides. Bertha's Bodacious
Beans boasts the biggest disaster insurance policy on the East Coast.

For more information, call 212-555-1212, e-mail bertha@berthasboda-
ciousbeans.com, or surf over to the store's website at http://www.
berthasbodaciousbeans.com.
                             ###
```

Sample press release.

Make Them Look

Everyone and his brother sends news releases to poor, overworked editors and producers. Aside from writing it on scented paper in purple crayon, how can you make yours stand out? With a catchy headline that sounds exactly like a news headline!

Make your headline clear and interesting, such as **New Study Reports that Coffee Can Make You Live to 150**. That said, try to match the publication's style as much as possible. If every headline in a newspaper is at most four words long, chop the headline on the press release you send to that paper down to four words, say "Coffee Boosts Life Span." If you can't imagine the headline appearing in the paper, then neither will the editor.

Turn It Upside-Down

The body of your press release—that is, everything between the headline and the closing paragraph—should take the format of an inverted pyramid. Critical information (the who, what, where, why, when) goes in the first paragraph, information of next highest importance in the second paragraph, and so on.

Sometimes a harried editor prints press releases as is, and the inverted pyramid format allows her to slice off paragraphs from the bottom of the release as space requires, without sacrificing important information.

Send It Out

All right, you've honed your press release so well that editors and producers will knock each other over to run it first. That's great—but first you have to get it to them. Though press release distribution services do exist, you don't need to spend a fortune paying someone else to send out your press release. You can compile your own list for zilch.

Not sure where to send it? Flip through *Bacon's Magazine & Newspaper Directory* or *Bacon's Publicity Checker* at your local library. Or pick up a copy of a magazine directory

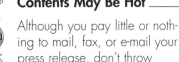

Contents May Be Hot

Although you pay little or nothing to mail, fax, or e-mail your press release, don't throw it at every editor from here to Timbuktu. Target your release at appropriate publications. If you want coverage for a new catering service, for example, you wouldn't send a release to *Wastewater Quarterly*. (You don't *want* your business associated with *Wastewater Quarterly*, do you?)

such as Writer's Market, which is available at most bookstores and online (www. writersmarket.com) for under $30. This directory includes local and trade publications that could be the perfect home for your release.

While *Bacon's* and *Writer's Market* have contact information for hundreds of publications, you won't find listings for every local gazette and ad weekly. To make contact with these titles, simply call the publisher's phone number and ask the news editor whether you should submit press releases by fax, mail, or e-mail.

Meet the Press

If you're persistent, the day will come when you send out a press release and a journalist or radio producer will call to schedule an interview. What a scary thought!

Have no fear, though—unless you've been scamming seniors or employing illegal immigrants, your media debut will be a piece of cake. The journalist won't (intentionally) try to trick you with tough questions. He merely wants information, and your press releases have demonstrated that you have all the answers.

You might still be nervous about appearing in print, but with the right preparation, you can transform yourself into a media personality to rival Oprah herself.

Prepare for a Grilling

Remember how you prepared for oral exams in high school and college? Well, get ready for a flashback—preparing for a media interview requires much the same work and dedication.

Brainstorm questions, with friends and family if you can, that the interviewer may ask you, and prepare interesting and concise answers to these questions. Hone your answers by having a friend grill you as if he were Chris Matthews on *Hardball*. If you're stumped for an answer, smile and say, "That's a very good question," to buy time.

Be prepared for some curveballs. For example, a reporter might ask, "What do you think about the way coffee growers are treated and paid?" Rack your brain for difficult questions you might be asked, and study hard to become a master of your domain. If you know your stuff and make their job easy, the reporter is sure to come back to you in the future.

Make Yourself at Home

Invite interviewers to visit you at your workplace to conduct the talk session. You'll be more comfortable in a familiar setting, plus you save travel time.

What's more, getting an interviewer into your store will allow her to get a better idea of what you do and dress up her article with details about your store. This means you should try to arrange for the journalist to arrive during a busy time of day. If she's going to describe your location, which would you rather see in print: "devoid of customers and smelling of failure" or "packed with happy faces enjoying drinks of all varieties"?

Admit Your Ignorance

Don't get us wrong—you don't need to confess to not knowing how to solve the Pythagorean Theorem or who the current ruler of Bangladesh is. No, we mean that sometimes an interviewer will ask a question you simply can't answer, and the best thing you can say is, "I'm sorry, I don't know the answer to that, but maybe I can suggest someone who does."

Don't *fake* an answer, because you can be sure that someone in the audience will know the real answer, and if your "creativity" is uncovered, you'll lose credibility as an expert. Simply apologize for not knowing, then offer to get back to the reporter later with the information.

Can the Sales Pitch

There's nothing interviewers hate more than an interviewee who turns every question into an opportunity to spout off about how gosh-darn great his business is. Answer the question that's asked to the best of your abilities, and your professionalism and expertise will be the best possible advertisement for your business. Answer the question with a lot of self-promotion, and the journalist might leave you out of the article altogether, replacing you with someone who will stick to the topic at hand.

Take Small Bites

If you take 20 minutes to get your point across, the interviewer—not to mention her viewers, listeners, and readers—may be fast asleep before you've finished. Distill your message into a *sound bite*, that is, just a few memorable words that stress your message.

Lots of people complain that politicians speak only in sound bites, but if you had to choose between a few words that people listen to and a long answer that puts people to sleep, wouldn't you choose the short answer?

Don't Dress for Success

You heard us right—don't dress for success. We don't mean that you should show up for an interview wearing cat-hair–covered sweats, but neither should you spring for an Armani suit if that's not what you usually wear. Dress the way you normally do for work so that you'll feel comfortable and give the interviewer an idea of who you really are.

For television, avoid pure white shirts or suits with stripes, checks, or small patterns that can "jump" off the screen.

Holding Special Events

One way to get publicity while also bringing customers through the door is to hold special events at your shop. Events attract the news media, the media publicize the event, and the publicity brings people into your business, where they buy coffee. Takes a few steps, but you're sure to be pleased with the result.

> **Coffee Quips**
>
> "Good communication is as stimulating as black coffee, and just as hard to sleep after."
> —Anne Morrow Lindbergh, *Gift from the Sea*

Here's a sampling of events you can hold that will pack the house and get the news media buzzing. You're sure to think of other events that fit your target market and retail space. Just remember that no matter what kind of event you hold, not every customer will be interested. Leave room away from the crowd for these folks to enjoy their treats. In your efforts to draw in new faces, you don't want to drive away familiar ones.

Reading, Writing, and Reading That Writing

Books and coffee go hand-in-hand. The good news about holding a book signing is that it's free, gratis, without charge—get the idea? Authors are happy to visit your store, read from their work, and sign books because they get publicity for their writing.

In all likelihood, your area is home to one or more authors. You probably won't be able to lasso Stephen King into your store, but many lesser-known authors are probably available to hold events. To find authors in your area, check out:

♦ **The local paper.**   Look at the Arts and Calendar section of your local newspaper to find out who in your area has just published a book and which nationally known authors are on book tours.

♦ **Author event websites.**   Surf to www.netread.com, which is a listing of author events searchable by area. Plug in your zip code and find out which authors are touring your area. Call the authors and offer to host an event at your store.

♦ **Online writers' directories.**   Many websites for writers offer a directory of members that you can search for authors in your area. For example, Freelance Success (www.freelancesuccess.com) has such a list, as does the Cat Writers Association (www.catwriters.org). Similar directories probably exist for writers of all genres. Search on Google (www.google.com) to find authors near you.

♦ **Self-publishing houses.**   Authors who self-publish their books are especially interested in holding book signings, as this type of writer has difficulty selling his work in bookstores and other traditional venues. Check out self-publishing houses online such as Xlibris (www.xlibris.com) and iUniverse, the latter of which has an event calendar at calendar.iuniverse.com that you can search by town or state.

Once you find an author, work out an agreement (verbal is fine) as to what both of you will provide. For your part, for example, you might promise to advertise the event in such-and-such newspapers, devote 15 tables for seating, and provide free drinks to the author and his family. The author should bring copies of books that he wants to sell and commit to speaking and answering questions for a certain length of time.

Carrying the Club

Author signings work even better at drawing crowds if you regularly host a book club at your store. On their own, monthly book clubs draw patrons to your store on a regular basis. Add an author signing into the mix and club participants spread word of the event to their literary pals.

Contents May Be Hot

If you do start one or more book clubs in your establishment, be sure to keep on top of the reading and participate. Nothing annoys book club members more than the hanger-on who has nothing to add to the conversation. Stay involved, and club members will think of you as a reader first and a store owner second.

Rather than wait for a book club to spontaneously erupt in your seating area, start one yourself by posting signs at the local library and bookstore. You might even consider holding a fiction book club the first Thursday of the month and a nonfiction club on the third Thursday. This set-up will likely attract different crowds and spread word of your business in diverse ways.

Book clubs tend to start small, but with enthusiastic promotion they can draw a steady crowd to your business every month. Even better, participants will likely stop in between club meetings to discuss plot twists, offer suggestions for the next selection—and buy drinks!

Work the Room: Networking Events

Bring people into your store to meet each other, and chances are the beverage of choice will be your delicious coffee. You can hold business networking events where people in a certain industry come to meet and greet. Depending on your area, you could invite media people, entrepreneurs/small business owners, local shop owners, or even local singles for a speed-dating experience.

One way to find out about groups that need networking space is to check out adult education catalogs such as The Learning Annex that are available online and in newspaper boxes on city street corners. These companies lack their own buildings and have to rent venues or find free space. Call adult education businesses and colleges near you to offer your coffee shop as a free venue for their events.

You can also call your local Chamber of Commerce, which holds networking and other events for its business-owner members, and offer up your coffee shop.

Turn Up the Volume: Music Events

Get people's toes a-tapping—and their wallets a-opening—by inviting bands to play in your shop. Music events are a great way to get your business's name in the local media.

Sidestep pricey booking agents by finding bands on your own. Check the calendar in your local newspaper to see who's playing where, and visit those venues to check out the bands. If you find one you like, approach the members and ask them if they'd like to play at your shop. Many local bands will play for free for the chance to publicize their music and sell CDs.

We probably don't need to tell you this, but heavy metal bands aren't the best choice for a coffee shop. (Naturally this statement doesn't apply to any store named "The Headbanger's Beanery.") To decide on the best type of music for your retail environment, think about the image you want to project. If you're homespun, for instance, you might want to host a bluegrass group; for contemporary tastes, a jazz band may work for you.

As with any event, you'll need a publicity plan for it to work. If a band schleps all the way to your shop to be greeted by a grand total of three customers, you may have trouble getting bands to play at your shop in the future. Send out news releases, hang signs, and hand out flyers about the event to generate interest.

Contents May Be Hot _____

One drawback to holding music events is that attendees may stake out a table in your shop, buy one cup of coffee (or none), and sit there all night watching the band, taking up space that could be used by paying customers. Decide whether the publicity you'll get from hosting music events is worth this inconvenience.

We'll warn you now that not everyone appreciates music events. Some patrons, upon entering a shop and seeing musicians setting up, will even turn around and leave. To minimize this type of response, you can stick with acoustic solo artists (since patrons can still talk to one another over the music) or split your seating area into music and nonmusic sections. Your ability to do this will obviously depend on the design of your shop, so it's something to keep in mind if you're still in the planning phase.

Those Who Can, Teach: Workshops

Everyone's an expert at something, and experts love to show off their stuff. The good news is that you can likely get them to show off in your store, especially as it would be great publicity for their own businesses. Even better, holding these workshops usually sets you back no more than a free drink or two.

The list of possible workshop topics is endless, but we'll suggest only five to keep this book down to a manageable length.

- ◆ Writing workshops, such as classes on how to write a memoir or how to break into freelance writing

- Classes on how to grind and brew a great pot of coffee—gee, who would be the expert speaker for that?

- Ethnic cooking demonstrations from a local chef

- Jewelry-making workshops, or any other craft such as knitting, quilt-making, or beadwork

- Business or financial seminars such as how to invest for retirement or how to start a business

To find experts in your area, check the business section of your local paper and ask around at shops in your neighborhood. Adult education catalogs are also good sources for experts. By asking these experts to hold a workshop at your shop, you get a free lesson in their field of expertise while allowing them to advertise their services.

Games People Play

Yet another way to attract people to your shop is to host a weekly game night. Board games have come a long way since your childhood, when Monopoly had you and your siblings throwing dice at one another across the room. Witness the success of Cranium, a party-style board game initially available only at Starbucks that has sold more than a million copies.

While we don't expect you to finance and produce a best-selling board game, you can take advantage of the appeal of games to draw players into your store or—as is more likely the case—keep them in the store longer.

Approach a local toy or game store and ask them to donate (or sell at cost) copies of games for your seating area. Offer to place stickers on the games so that customers know where to buy them. Set the games up so that customers can dive right in. Physical games like Jenga (in which players try to build a tall wooden tower) and Pounce (in which one player tries to catch the mice of other players) work well as the noise of game play will draw other customers to watch and participate.

Beans of Wisdom _____

Choose games that don't rely on specific pieces to work since customers will undoubtedly drop pieces through the heating grate or accidentally throw them out. You can write publishers for replacement parts, but it's better to avoid the problem in the first place by choosing the right games.

You Know Best: Positioning Yourself as an Expert

You want to be the person that the media come to when they have a question about coffee. This won't happen on its own, of course. Putting your name in the public spotlight and winning people over requires constant effort on your part. Writing press releases about coffee-related news and holding seminars on brewing are good steps that require little from you but time.

To take this promotion a step further, write articles about the history of coffee, how blends are created, how grinding methods differ, how to "cup" properly, or any of a hundred other facts you've learned and submit them to local daily and weekly newspapers. Such articles usually include a bio of the writer at the end that will mention your business.

These papers often rely on contributions by business owners, and your contributions can likely spur sales depending on your topic. If you describe how to roast your own beans, you can mention your store as a source of green beans. You can cover the different ways that coffee is brewed around the world and mention your stock of French presses in the closing bio.

Don't worry that self-roasting will steal business from you as customers create their own. Consider instead that you're promoting the growth of coffee consumption in your area—and with you as the expert on all things coffee, this will only increase your standing in the media.

Turning Buyers Into Sellers

No one can give your business more publicity and better word-of-mouth than a happy customer. Your role? *Make the customer happy.*

Beyond mere happiness, however, you should aim for bliss, nirvana, and satori rolled into one. You want to satisfy the customer's needs, while at the same time encouraging him to spread the word about your business.

The first step is the most important and obvious, yet one that can be missed in the day-to-day grind of business: give every customer 100 percent of your effort and make sure that your staff members do the same.

Ask customers what they need, and either fulfill their needs immediately or do what you have to do so that you can satisfy them the next time they come in. Don't do this quietly, either. Speak up and let them know what you've done to fulfill their needs.

They'll be impressed that you remember them, never mind that you are actually satisfying their demands.

Plant surveys on tables that customers can fill out to tell you where you can improve your products and services. If they provide contact information, write or call them with the answer; if not, post their question and your answer on a bulletin board in the store, perhaps one posted near the restrooms. Customers love to know that business owners listen to their requests!

> **Beans of Wisdom** _____
>
> You'll receive plenty of questions that have nothing to do with the coffee bar: Where's this restaurant? How do I get to that street? Where's the closest payphone? Make sure you know the area around your store so that you can answer questions like these even though doing so doesn't directly help your business. Good will and a helping hand always make people remember you fondly.

Make your business card and copies of your menu available at all times. Don't make customers ask for these items. Let them take cards and menus home and pass them on to others. Hand coupons to repeat customers to thank them for their continued business. Again, these coupons might end up in the hands of others, which is all to the good. (Just make sure the coupons bear the store name, address, and phone number, or else all this effort is for naught.)

Sell T-shirts and mugs that boast your business name and logo. They probably won't be quick sellers, but you could give them away as prizes during seminars and events to help spread the word. What's more, customers do like being able to take home a piece of a beloved environment. And if you've done everything else right, they'll be happy to call your shop home.

The Least You Need to Know

- ◆ Publicity starts with a well-written press release.
- ◆ To generate news about your shop, hold events such as band appearances, workshops, and book signings.
- ◆ Don't pay for expensive news release distribution services! You can build your own media list using local and online business directories and even your Yellow Pages.
- ◆ Position yourself as the preeminent local coffee expert to get quoted in the media.
- ◆ Make customers happy so they'll spread the good word about your services.

Chapter 23

Getting the Word Out: Marketing Your Coffee Business

In This Chapter

♦ Ready, aim … target!

♦ Advertise or no?

♦ Writing flyers, brochures, and newsletters

♦ Marketing on a shoestring

If you want to make any money in this coffee biz and not keep all those great beans to yourself, you need to tell potential customers that you exist. Marketing makes this happen.

"Marketing?" you say. "Sure, that sounds great … for a company like MacrogigantoglobaCorp. But what about poor little me?" Don't worry—most entrepreneurs do their own marketing, and they manage to do it even with a marketing budget that jingles when they shake it.

The key to marketing success for a coffee shop is to remember that you don't need to make a name for yourself across the nation. All you need to do is create a presence in your local community. With this aim in mind, we'll give you all the information you need to get the word out about your business without breaking the bank.

Targeting Your Market

Who do you want to tell about your fine establishment? Everyone in town? Only those who can afford to buy your limited edition diamond-laden bagels? The entire world?!

Telling six billion people that they can buy coffee at your store would take a long time, so you need to develop what marketers call a *target market*—that is, the group of people you want to *target* with your *marketing*.

Java-nitions

A **target market** is any group of people, numbering from one to one billion, that you feel would shop at your coffee bar if they knew that it existed. While you want your target market to be as large as possible—since only a small percent will actually become customers—keep your expectations reasonable.

Nailing down your target market before you blanket the universe with coupons will save you bundles of money. If, for example, you feel that office workers in the nearby corporate park make up your target market, placing ads in college newspapers would be a waste of money. If your target market consists of college students, don't drop a load of moolah handing out discount cards at the old folks' home.

Name Your Niche

Way back in Chapter 6, while developing your name and logo, you investigated how to position yourself in the market. Maybe you wanted to be known as the coffee shop that caters to refined tastes with gourmet beans and gifts, or the shop that packs in a hipper-than-thou crowd with live music, or the shop with quiet study areas that's a haven for local students.

If you've done your job well, your coffee shop's logo, name, décor, and product line all project this self-image to the world at large. Marketing provides yet another way to present this entire package to potential customers and make you stand out in their minds.

But to do so, you need to delve deep into the psyches of the people that comprise your target market and figure out what makes them tick and how you can interest them in your services. Ask yourself these questions about your ideal clients:

- ◆ **How old are they?** What age groups will feel most comfortable in the retail environment you've created: mid-career execs, students, young families, older adults, or a mix of these?

- ◆ **How much do they earn, and where do they live?** In what type of environment do the members of your target market spend most of their time? Do they live in the city, suburbs, or country? Do they live in houses, apartments, or dorms? Do they commute long distances, or work close to home? Does their style of living allow them to spend freely on gourmet items, or would coupons be more likely to catch their eye?

- ◆ **How do they spend their free time?** Do they focus on earning money and working, spending time at home, donating time and money to social issues like the environment? How can your business complement their causes and become an important part of their lives?

- ◆ **Why will they visit you?** Are your customers interested in grabbing a quick pick-me-up for work, visiting with friends, studying or reading in a quiet place, shopping for gifts, or stopping in for a quick bite while shopping?

This final question is the one you need to spend the most time answering. Unless you're located on a remote mountain peak, your customers will have multiple opportunities throughout the day to purchase coffee and other hot drinks. For your business to survive, they must choose *you*. What makes your shop so special? Once you know the answer, share it with the general public so that they'll come in and experience it themselves.

And if for some reason you decide that your shop really isn't that special, it's not too late to revisit earlier chapters for inspiration and an image overhaul.

The Target Comes Into View

Now that you have a clearer idea of your target market, break out that pencil and describe the kind of client you want to attract.

> **Beans of Wisdom**
>
> Don't feel that you have to limit your marketing efforts to only one target market. Your coffee shop might attract commuters in the morning, mothers at midday, teenagers in the after-school hours, and families at night. Each of these groups is a separate target market that you can try to appeal to in different ways.

A sample description might read, "I want to attract young families. They're concerned with balancing work and family life, and they'll stop in to have a nice bite together while shopping in the local stores." Another possibility: "My ideal customers are students from the local college, who will want to study during the day and hear live music at night. They're interested in inexpensive but tasty coffee and unusual coffee gifts."

This description will help you determine who your target market is and how you can best reach it. Refer back to your description as you read through this chapter and develop a marketing plan.

Should You Play the Advertising Game?

You may be tempted to shell out money to place ads in newspapers, on the radio, or even on TV. Despite the rise of satellite radio and personal recording devices like TiVo, these types of ads are still the most common ways to introduce your business to thousands of potential customers—and just think about how cool it would be for your mom and all your friends to see you on the small screen!

> **Beans of Wisdom**
>
> The sole exception to our "no ad" decree is Yellow Pages advertising since the phone books are distributed locally and referred to again and again throughout the year. You don't need a four-color quarter-page placement either; a bold-face listing or a tear-out coupon might be all you need.

We say no way. Placing ads like these are expensive—mortgage-your-house and sell-your-firstborn-child expensive—yet you can't accurately hit your target market in a meaningful way that will lead to a long-term boost in sales.

Let's say, for example, that you pay to run an ad on your favorite radio station. Most of the people who hear the ad won't even live in your area, so most of the money you spent to hit their ears is wasted.

In addition to this problem, what really works with paid advertising is repetition, running an ad over and over again until the radio or TV audience sings the jingle in their dreams. To make this happen, you'd have to lay out a huge pile of cash up front—then cross your fingers and hope. For the small business owner, Vegas casinos offer better odds for success than radio and television advertising.

Marketing on a Shoestring

If your marketing budget consists of pocket change and lint, don't let that bring you down! Lint has a really good exchange value on the open market.

Seriously, smart business owners know how to market without spending a mint. The publicity tips covered in Chapter 22 are a good start, but you have plenty more options for getting the word out on the cheap.

Mirror, Mirror ...

The cheapest marketing medium is by chance the one you have the most control over: you. Your dress, your voice, your manner behind the counter, everything you do can make a customer excited about buying from you now and returning another day—or running the other way.

Without coming across like a used-car salesman, you want to project confidence and enthusiasm about your business and the products it sells. Try everything on the menu and develop favorites: a favorite hot drink, a favorite snack to accompany that drink. When a customer asks for your opinion on an item, you can then ask questions about her tastes to guide her to the perfect treat.

Needless to say, you should look the part of a successful business owner and leave the sweats for your off-hours. While customers won't expect you to wear a suit or formal dress, they do appreciate a professional appearance.

Your employees are also walking billboards for your business, but you have much less dictatorial control over them than you might wish. Do your best to make sure they're presentable and happy, so that spirit carries over to their interactions with customers. (More on dealing with employees in Chapter 11).

Bartering and Reciprocal Arrangements

Long, long ago, before Visa and MasterCard, people traded for goods and services: chickens for baskets, a new axe in exchange for babysitting little Glog.

In these modern times, instead of trading chickens for baskets, you can exchange coffee products and services for marketing services, graphic design, copywriting, web design, and printing. In addition to saving money right away, the people who trade their products and services for coffee could end up becoming lifelong customers or referring their friends and business associates to you!

You can barter in two ways: by joining a retail barter exchange, or by creating a barter group of your own among local businesses.

◆ **Retail barter exchanges**   These let professionals in the same state or across the country trade with one another. You can find retail barter exchanges online or in the Yellow Pages Business-to-Business Directory under "Barter and Trade Exchanges."

   The downside to these barter exchanges is that they can be el-expensivo. National Trade Association, for example, charges $695 for a membership.

   Before committing yourself to a retail barter exchange, do a little research to ensure that you'll be able to recoup your investment through barter. Ask who the other members are and see whether you're interested in what they have to offer. Find out how transactions are conducted: can you "pay" for an expensive item over time, or are you expected to hand over a ton of coffee in one shot? Most importantly, make sure a dozen other coffee vendors haven't signed up ahead of you!

◆ **Solo Swapping**   Don't feel like signing on the dotted line at a retail barter exchange? Barter solo. Just approach a professional with whom you'd like to barter, and offer to trade X for Y. Explain how the trade will benefit him. If you trade coffee coupons for, say, the printing of 1,000 menus, the printer can pass the coupons on to his customers as a goodwill gesture.

Contents May Be Hot _____

Thought you could put one over on Uncle Sam by bartering instead of buying and selling goods and services? No dice. Products and services you obtain through bartering are considered income, so you must include their "fair market value" in your earnings at tax time.

Generally, you report income from bartered services on Schedule C, Profit or Loss From Business, or Schedule C-EZ, Net Profit From Business (Form 1040). Check with your accountant or take advantage of the IRS's Help page at www.irs.gov for more detailed information.

In a barter, you know the cost of what you're giving away (because you calculated all those costs back in Chapter 17). Ideally, you've researched the market enough to know the retail value of what you're asking for. You still need to trade items of roughly equal value to make each side feel comfortable with the deal, but bartering lets you lay out less cash for the same end product.

Donating Your Services

Want to do good for the community and generate positive word-of-mouth at the same time? Sure you do! Then donate your products and services to charity.

Many charities auction goods and shunt the proceeds toward their cause, and you can easily provide a set of products or a certificate for services for such an auction. Charities might approach you about participating in such auctions, but if you want to be proactive, research local charity organizations, contact them, and offer your coffee products and services for their next fundraiser. You can serve coffee to the auction volunteers, donate pounds of grounds for the auction itself, or both.

Auction organizers typically include your company's information in their catalog of goods being auctioned, so even if people don't win your wares, they'll see your name and know that you're involved!

Another idea: donate a percentage of a day's (or a week's, or whatever) take to a local charity, and send a press release about the offer to the local papers both before and after the event. (See Chapter 22 for more information on how to write a press release.)

The possibilities for community service are limited only to your imagination. You can donate coffee to organizers of a church fair, cold drinks to officials in a marathon, or day-old pastries to a homeless shelter.

Naturally, you'd like to pick up regular customers and positive press coverage as a result of your generosity, but if you push too hard, you might come off as an opportunist instead. Never insist on press coverage as payment for your good deeds. Be satisfied with what you've done and let karma pay you back in the long run.

Find a Partner

As we explained in Chapter 22, the best thing about publicity is when someone else says you're great while your hand is nowhere near their back. This praise is more believable because it comes from an unbiased source.

You can mimic this kind of endorsement in your marketing by teaming up with partners willing to spread the word about your business. The best way to do this is to give these partners free items that they can pass on to their customers. Coupons for, say, free hot drinks or a free muffin with any purchase are naturals for this type of promotion.

Shell gas stations ran a promotion like this in 2004 in which they gave away coupons for free McDonald's hamburgers with fill-ups. Hamburgers and gas don't normally go together—at least not in the minds of your humble narrators—but clearly both Shell and McDonald's found positive reasons to push this association.

To find a promotional partner, search for local shops that appeal to the same target market as you. Approach the owners of these shops and ask whether they'd be willing to hand out coupons to their customers. Bring samples of your wares so that they know your food and drinks are something their customers will enjoy. Acknowledge that you're asking the owner to commit his employees' time to an outside cause, but stress the benefits for him: a gift for each of his customers that costs him almost nothing.

Whichever shops you partner with, try to arrange the giveaway campaign so that it will reach each customer at least once. If customers at gas stations fill up roughly once a week, make the coupon giveaway last ten days; if you team up with a flower shop, time the giveaway to occur during a holiday like Valentine's Day or Mother's Day. Even better, tie the coupon to the needs of the customers or the time of year. Offer Valentine's Day shoppers a free heart-shaped cookie or gym-goers a free flavored water.

Ask the shop owner how many coupons he'll need, then print out that many and hand-deliver them along with instructions for handing them out. Good rules of thumb are that employees should hand a coupon directly to the customer, not set them in a stack on the counter, and each customer should receive only one coupon per visit.

Beans of Wisdom

If you run promotional offers with more than one local business—and there's no reason why you shouldn't—be sure to label each store's coupon in a different way so that you can judge which set of customers responds better to your offer. If you find, for example, that customers of dog grooming salons rarely cash in the coupon, spend your time cultivating other partners for your next promotion.

Drop by the store on the second or third day of the promotion to ensure that the coupons are being handed out and see whether the owner has any questions. Follow up regularly to make sure the store doesn't run out of coupons, and pass along any praise about the gift that customers might say to you.

Putting It in Print

Handing out product is all well and good, but sometimes you can achieve a much greater return with an investment of naught more than a bit of paper and an hour of labor. Printed newsletters, brochures, and flyers give customers-to-be something they can hold onto, something that expresses the pure wonderfulness of your shop, something that—most important of all—has your address and phone number on it.

Printing has changed a lot in the 500+ years since Gutenberg did his thing, but the permanence and impact of the written word remains the same.

Extra, Extra!

Newsletters are a great way to get the word out about your business, offerings, and events—but they won't do much good if customers toss them in the wastebasket.

To start with, you have to send newsletters to folks who might care to read it, namely those in your target market. Collect mailing addresses from customers who fill out survey cards and from anyone else who shows an interest in your business, and compile these into a mailing list. Compatible businesses such as gourmet food stores may exchange or rent lists of their own.

Decide how often you want to send out your newsletter, then stick with that schedule. A weekly newsletter might be tempting to begin with when you're trying to drum up business, but don't saddle yourself permanently with such burdens when sales will inevitably pick up in the months ahead and take up more of your time. Monthly, bimonthly, and quarterly are all better choices.

Don't automatically make your company's name the title of your newsletter as this does nothing to grab attention and make customers want to read on. Instead of the oh-so-drab "The Perfect Brew Newsletter," choose something more evocative like "Coffee Creations," which will inspire potential readers to look further.

Make your newsletter worth a reader's time by tossing out the hard sell and instead offering lots of take-home knowledge: the health benefits of caffeine, for instance, or advice on how to brew coffee in a stovetop pot. Include coupons and contests to keep your name in a reader's mind after he closes the newsletter and sets it down.

Beans of Wisdom _____

To find news bites that you can include in your newsletter, check out PR Newswire (www.prnewswire.com), a media site that posts press releases on all sorts of topics, from business to health. You can also scan magazine stands at the bookstore for food mags like *Bon Appétit*, *Gourmet*, and *Cooking Light*. These magazines can provide topics you'd like to include in your newsletter, but don't use the articles word-for-word without getting the writer's permission first.

Include contact information—mail, phone, e-mail, and website—so potential clients know where you're located and can call you ahead of time with questions or for directions.

To look professional, adopt a clean, attractive layout, and use a traditional serif typeface such as Times, Palatino, or Courier to improve readability. For headlines, make the type two to three times larger than the text, and use subheads to break up long articles and keep the reader moving through the newsletter.

Pull quotes—that is, quotes copied from the text and set in larger type elsewhere on the page—attract your reader's attention and break up large blocks of text. Use plenty of white space to set off graphics, headlines, and pull quotes. Too little white space will create a cluttered, confused look.

Signed, Sealed, (Hand) Delivered

Brochures are printed sales pieces that tell potential customers what you offer and how it will benefit them. They can include a menu of your products and prices as well as any information on catering or delivery.

Give away brochures like there's no tomorrow. Hand them out to customers, hang them on bulletin boards, leave stacks of them in office buildings and on college campuses. Don't just pass through an area once and consider it covered. If a brochure is effective, customers will take it home so that they don't forget your name and address. Revisit bulletin boards and other drop-off points on a regular basis so that you can restock them.

Don't think that to be effective, brochures must be full-color, glossy, fold-out pieces with perforated coupons ripe for the tearing. You can create brochures that do the job just fine with nothing but a word processing or desktop publishing program, paper, an inkjet or laser printer, and some time. Follow these steps to create a brochure that will entice customers into your shop—but not break the bank.

- ◆ **Size it up.** A brochure can be one piece of paper folded in thirds (which gives you six panels), two pieces of paper folded in half and stapled in the middle (which gives you eight pages), or any other size and shape you want. The less paper, the cheaper the brochure will be to produce, but don't cut important information (address, hours of operation, and so on) that will leave customers befuddled.

- ◆ **Choose your paper.** You can find all sorts of nice paper at your local copy shop or at an office supply store like Staples or Office Depot. Alternatively, head to a specialty paper company like Paper Direct (www.paperdirect.com), which offers papers with decorative and professional borders and other graphics that are perfect for creating your own brochures (not to mention business cards and letterhead) at home.

- ◆ **Push your benefits.** Brochures should stress benefits, not features. A feature is a new type of coffee; a benefit is the fact that your new coffee will be a hit at the buyer's next business meeting, ensuring that she gets a big promotion and a raise. You still get to mention your new coffee, but stressing benefits over features gives the reader a reason to care.

- ◆ **Don't date yourself.** Instead of writing "Doing business in the community for four years," write "Doing business in the community since 2001." That way, your brochure never goes out of date (and you won't have to reprint it every year).

- ◆ **Quote your clients.** Include a list of testimonials from happy customers, especially those that talk about results: "My party was a huge success thanks to The Perfect Brew's catering!" or "Everyone at the meeting loved The Perfect Brew's new chocolate raspberry coffee." Customers are usually happy to be quoted, and you can be sure they'll show off their starring role to others.

- ◆ **Be stylish.** Follow the style tips listed in the newsletters section earlier in this chapter.

One Sheet, No Waiting

A flyer is a single sheet of paper printed on one or both sides. It will naturally contain less information than a brochure, but it's also less pricey. The point of a flyer is to produce it as cheaply as possible and spread it far and wide.

Don't be shy about flinging your flyers—or hiring others to do the flinging—on car windshields, in office lobbies, in flyer racks in supermarkets, and on bulletin boards in libraries, supermarkets, and university buildings.

Make sure your flyer carries a catchy headline, the name of your business, a list of the benefits of visiting your shop, any special offers you want to make (such as half-price espresso), and your location and phone number. Much of this info and even the design work can often be lifted straight from your brochure.

Tell Customers to Cut It Out

Coupons have been a staple savings tool with supermarket shoppers for decades. Why do coupons work? For shoppers, it's the idea that they're getting a special deal available to a limited number of people. "Sure, others can buy the same thing that I am," they think, "but they have to pay much more."

For supermarkets, coupons either bring in customers who wouldn't have shopped at that store in the first place or pull in regular customers outside of their normal shopping patterns. Whichever category the shopper falls under, the supermarket wins because the shopper will spend money that she normally would have spent elsewhere. Even when coupons promote loss leaders (a practice we explained in Chapter 17), shoppers throw other items into their carts, and the supermarket ends up ahead of the game.

When used effectively, coupons will work just as well for your coffee shop as they do for gigantic chain stores. One option is to participate in a coupon deck—that is, a deck of coupons that local residents receive in the mail. The advantage of using a coupon deck is that you can choose which ZIP codes will receive your coupon, thus allowing you to blanket an entire area (and by default, your target market) with your sales pitch.

Beans of Wisdom

Again, label each type of coupon in a unique way so that you can track which promotional efforts bring the biggest results. Don't just focus on the number of coupons returned either; use special codes on your register to track every sale that involves a coupon. You may find that you merely broke even on one promotion, while another sale encouraged customers to add lots of other goodies. If you track the stats, you'll build more effective marketing campaigns in the future.

Coupon decks, however, do suffer from the same faults as other direct mail efforts: namely that a large percentage of those who receive the coupon will toss it without even looking at it. A study by the Direct Marketing Association in 2003, for example, found that just over 1.5 percent of direct mail advertisements received a response— and these ads were targeted at specific households. Blanket advertising like coupon decks are estimated to receive a response roughly 1 out of 1,000 times!

A more effective way to use coupons is to find a business partner (as described earlier in this chapter) or team up with other shops to create a coupon booklet particular to your geography. If you're located in a strip mall, talk with other businesses in the strip about creating a coupon booklet that every store will distribute to its customers. You might pick up customers from the dry cleaner, the dog grooming salon, the tailor, and other businesses that previously had no effect on your sales.

Wave the Flag High

Don't feel that you have to stick to paper to get your message across. You could also choose to print banners that advertise special offers and place them above the entrance to your shop. If you want to try this high-impact ad medium, keep the following in mind:

- ◆ **Keep it simple.** As we explained in Chapter 8, people will be passing by this sign with lots of other things on their minds: what time they're meeting a girl-friend, the cop that just pulled out in traffic behind them, and so on. If your banner is going to catch their eye, the message on it must be short and to the point.

- ◆ **Use bright colors.** The reasons for this are the same as in the previous bullet point, but if your store colors are brown and red, don't opt for a neon green banner. There's a difference between bright attractive and bright "Ow, my eyes!"

- ◆ **Keep it timeless.** Don't add dates or other restrictive limitations on the sign. If your banner touts sweets "two for the price of one," you can choose to use the banner anytime you'd like. Throw a time limit on the offer, however, and you've doomed yourself to using that banner only once a year.

- ◆ **Remember that timeless doesn't mean all the time.** Banners should be used sparingly. Their size and bright colors attract a lot of attention, but if you keep one on your store all year, potential customers will dismiss the promotion as a sham. We've seen mattress stores, for example, that have displayed "half-price sale" banners for six straight years; this phony promotion makes us wary of spending our money there. Have the same mattresses been in stock six years, too?

While you can let a banner stand on its own, you can also use it as the entry point for an entire in-store promotion. Carry the colors of the banner onto signs inside the store, and repeat the message on display cases and at the register.

Don't Forget to Have Fun

Many business owners feel that marketing and promotion are the most tedious, time-wasting parts of their business—and if you approach the topic with that attitude, they might well be.

If, however, you approach marketing from a different angle, you can really enjoy yourself. After all, you've created a great business that relies on the efforts of skilled, friendly employees to deliver tasty and appealing drinks and eats to everyone who lives in your community. If some of your neighbors haven't yet visited the store, you should feel sorry that they're missing out on a good thing and try to convince them to stop by and try your wares.

Running a business is indeed an awful lot of work—but when you believe in yourself and the company you've created, you should do all you can to share your creation with the world. We look forward to stopping in someday and saying hello!

The Least You Need to Know

- Before you can reach your market, you have to know who they are and what you're selling them.
- Paid advertising in newspapers, on TV, and on the radio is almost always a waste of money for a small coffee shop.
- You don't need to spend a lot of money to get the word out about your business. Try bartering coffee and catering for marketing services and materials.
- A good, inexpensive marketing plan can include newsletters, brochures, and flyers.
- Track the sales that result from your marketing campaigns so that you know which ones are the most effective.

Glossary

acidity   The usually pleasant bitterness of coffee that's characterized by a feeling of dryness at the back and edges of the mouth; one of the three characteristics used to describe a coffee's flavor.

adjusting collar   The part of the grinder that the operator rotates to increase or decrease the fineness of ground coffee.

aftertaste   The flavor, or bouquet, that remains in the mouth after swallowing coffee.

airpot   An insulated thermal coffee pot with a built-in pumping mechanism; also known as a "thermal carafe."

Arabica   One of the two major types of coffee; typically grown at high elevations and known for creating better-tasting coffee than Robusta coffee beans.

aroma   The smell of fresh brewed coffee; one of the three characteristics used to describe a coffee's flavor.

autofill   A feature on espresso machines that controls and maintains the water level within the machine's boiler.

barista   Italian for "bartender"; in English, a professional maker of espresso beverages.

bean hopper   The cone-shaped holder on the top of an espresso grinder that's filled with whole coffee beans.

blend   A batch of coffee beans from different crops, whether from one region or from different parts of the world.

body   The feel of the coffee in your mouth, how heavy or fluid it feels; one of the three characteristics used to describe a coffee's flavor.

boiler pressure gauge   The instrument inside an espresso machine that can determine the steam pressure within the machine's boiler.

breve   An adjective that describes a beverage made with steamed half-and-half instead of milk, e.g., breve cappuccino.

brew button pad   The switches on an espresso machine that correspond to a desired shot, e.g., double shot or single ristretto.

burr   The sharp plate or plates within a grinder that chop and mill coffee beans. Also known as a grinder burr.

cafés latté   One or more servings of espresso, with steamed milk filling the rest of the cup and a topping of foamed steamed milk.

café lungo   An espresso made with a bit more water than usual, resulting in a weaker drink.

café mocha   One or more servings of espresso mixed with chocolate syrup or powder, with steamed milk filling the rest of the cup and a whipped cream topping.

cappuccino   One or more servings of espresso that's topped with equal amounts of steamed milk and foam.

chai   A common word for tea in many countries; in the U.S., a milky spiced tea made with some combination of cardamom, cinnamon, cloves, ginger, pepper, fennel, and allspice, as well as a sweetener.

coarse picking   A harvest of tea leaves that grabs up to five leaves from the stem of the tea plant; these leaves produce a harsher-tasting tea than those gathered in a fine picking.

condiments   Anything added to hot or cold drinks, such as sugar, honey, nutmeg, cinnamon, cocoa, vanilla, milk, and half-and-half.

crema   The rich, golden-brown foam at the top of a good shot of espresso; the sugars of the coffee are concentrated in this foam; also known as "creama."

CTC   An acronym for "crush, tear, curl," which describes the manufacturing process for teas that end up in tea bags.

cup fault   A general term for any problem with the taste or odor of coffee; also known as cup taint.

demitasse   A small porcelain cup, holding only 1.5-3 ounces, used to serve a straight shot of espresso.

demitasse spoon   A small spoon offered with a demitasse cup.

diffusion disc   A component in the group of an espresso machine that diffuses hot water; also known as a "diffusion block."

dispenser   Resembles an old-time seltzer bottle; uses nitrous oxide charges to blast liquid cream into a whipped condition and dispense it through a nozzle.

dispersion screen   A mesh screen in the group of an espresso machine that diffuses hot water after it passes the diffusion disc and before it reaches the coffee grounds.

dome lid   A rounded coffee cup lid that leaves room for whipped cream and foam on specialty coffee drinks.

doser   The device attached to a grinder that measures and dispenses ground coffee into a portafilter.

double   Any beverage that contains two shots of espresso, e.g., double café mocha.

dry   An espresso beverage made with more foam than usual.

earthy   A term often used to describe the flavor of Indonesian coffees.

espresso   Very strong coffee brewed in one-and-a-half-ounce batches at an extremely high temperature and pressure.

espresso puller   An old term for a professional maker of espresso beverages that's outdated since most espresso machines are now automatic and don't require the user to pull down on a handle.

exotic   A term used to refer to coffees with unusual aroma or flavor; typically applied to coffees from East Asia and Indonesian.

extraction   The passing of hot water through ground coffee.

extraction time   The amount of time that the water stays in contact with the coffee grounds during extraction.

filter insert   The stainless steel basket that forms a cup inside a portafilter to hold coffee grounds during the brewing process; available in single-, double-, and triple-shot sizes.

fine picking   A harvest of tea leaves in which only the top two leaves and bud are plucked from the plant.

flavored syrup   A sweet syrup used to flavor coffee drinks and other beverages.

float   The amount of cash in a register drawer at the start of each day.

floral   A flavor characteristic that reminds one of flowers and their aroma.

foam   Steamed milk that has had air added to turn it into a light froth.

fruity   A term used to refer to coffees that carry overtones of fruit flavors in their aroma or taste.

granita   A flavored, slushy drink that originated in Italy and is often served by espresso operators.

grinder   A machine that mills coffee beans into a powdered or granulated form.

group   A brewing port on an espresso machine.

group casting   The part of the espresso machine where the portafiler is locked in for brewing.

group portafilter gasket   The bit of rubber that seals off air when the portafilter is placed in the group casting.

insert retaining spring   A wire clip that holds the filter insert in the portafilter.

knockbox   A container into which coffee grounds are disposed after completing an espresso shot.

latté   Italian for "milk"; shorthand for café latté.

macchiato   An espresso topped with only a bit of foam.

manual fill valve   A device used to manually add water to the boiler of an espresso machine.

milk thermometer   A thermometer, typically measuring from 0 to 220 degrees, used to measure the temperature of milk as it's being steamed.

portafilter   The filter handle of an espresso machine, which contains a filter insert and is attached to a group for brewing.

pump pressure gauge   The instrument on an espresso machine that measures the extraction pressure of the water used in brewing.

ristretto   A half-sized or restricted shot of espresso, typically only .75 ounces.

Robusta   One of the two major types of coffee; grown at low elevations and preferred by producers of canned coffee for its low cost and high yield.

shot   A single serving of brewed espresso, typically 1.5 ounces.

single   Any beverage that contains one shot of espresso, e.g., a single espresso macchiato.

skinny   Any beverage made with skim milk.

spicy   A term that describes coffees with the flavor or aroma of a particular spice or blend of spices.

steam valve   The part of an espresso machine that controls how much steam flows into milk during the steaming process.

steam wand   A pipelike extension from an espresso machine that emits steam; typically made from stainless steel with a nozzle on the tip.

tamp   The act of pressing ground coffee into the filter insert before brewing.

tamper   A device used for tamping.

thermal carafe   An insulated thermal coffee pot with a built-in pumping mechanism; also known as an "airpot."

varietal   The specific coffee grown in each region or country.

wet   An espresso beverage made with less foam than usual.

Business Forms

Daily Cash Sheet

Date: _____ Day of week: _____

Store Location: _____

Completed by: _____

Hours worked: _____

Comments and Weather: _____

_____

_____

Evening Count

Cash

Rolled coins:	_____	Cash:	_____
Quarters:	_____	Checks:	_____
Dimes:	_____	Credit cards:	_____
Nickels:	_____		
Pennies:	_____	Total receipts:	_____
$1:	_____	Minus float:	–_____
$5:	_____		
$10:	_____	Net cash:	_____
$20:	_____	Tape reading:	_____
$50 and up:	_____		
		Amount over/under:	_____

Cash total: _____

Sales reports

10:00 A.M.	Total sales: _____	Cust. Count: _____
1:00 P.M.	Total sales: _____	Cust. Count: _____
Close	Total sales: _____	Cust. Count: _____

Avg. check (sales/cust. count): _____

		Payouts	Cost
Amt. over/under:	_____		
Overrings:	–_____	_____	_____
Payouts:	–_____	_____	_____
Final over/under:	_____	_____	_____
		_____	_____
Total:		_____	_____

Weekly Summary

Date: _____ Week ending: _____

Completed by: _____ Store Location: _____

	Sales Forecast	Actual	Comments/Weather
Monday	_____	_____	_____
Tuesday	_____	_____	_____
Wednesday	_____	_____	_____
Thursday	_____	_____	_____
Friday	_____	_____	_____
Saturday	_____	_____	_____
Sunday	_____	_____	_____
Total	_____	_____	_____
Cust. count	_____	_____	_____

Average check (Sales/Customer count):

	Forecast	Actual	
	_____	_____	_____

Labor hours:	Forecast	Actual	
Monday	_____	_____	_____
Tuesday	_____	_____	_____
Wednesday	_____	_____	_____
Thursday	_____	_____	_____
Friday	_____	_____	_____
Saturday	_____	_____	_____
Sunday	_____	_____	_____
Total	_____	_____	_____

SPPH (Sales Per Person Hour)

	Forecast	Actual	
Monday	_____	_____	_____
Tuesday	_____	_____	_____
Wednesday	_____	_____	_____
Thursday	_____	_____	_____
Friday	_____	_____	_____
Saturday	_____	_____	_____
Sunday	_____	_____	_____
Total	_____	_____	_____

Monthly Income and Expense Summary

Month: _____ Year: _____

Income		Expense as a % of Income
Sales	_____	(a) _____
Cost of goods	–_____	(b) _____ (b/a)
Gross Income	_____	(c) _____

Expenses		
Labor	_____	_____
Rent	_____	_____
Phone	_____	_____
Electricity	_____	_____
Gas	_____	_____
Office expenses	_____	_____
Prof. fees	_____	_____
Insurance	_____	_____
Advertising	_____	_____
Promotion	_____	_____
Total expenses	_____ (d)	
Income prior to the cost of money	_____ (c – d) = (e)	
Loan payments	_____ (f)	
Total income	_____ (e – f) = (g)	
Total income as a % of sales	_____ (g/a)	

Inventory Sheet

Date: _____ Count taken by: _____

Item	Number On-Hand (a)	Unit Cost (b)	Extended Cost (a × b)
_____	_____	_____	_____
_____	_____	_____	_____
_____	_____	_____	_____
_____	_____	_____	_____
_____	_____	_____	_____
_____	_____	_____	_____
_____	_____	_____	_____
_____	_____	_____	_____
_____	_____	_____	_____
_____	_____	_____	_____
_____	_____	_____	_____
_____	_____	_____	_____
_____	_____	_____	_____
_____	_____	_____	_____
_____	_____	_____	_____
_____	_____	_____	_____
_____	_____	_____	_____
_____	_____	_____	_____
_____	_____	_____	_____
_____	_____	_____	_____
_____	_____	_____	_____
_____	_____	_____	_____
_____	_____	_____	_____
		Total cost	_____

Pre-Opening Shopping List

Office Supplies and Equipment
- ❏ computer
- ❏ printer
- ❏ answering machine
- ❏ fax machine
- ❏ printing calculator
- ❏ binders
- ❏ notepaper
- ❏ pens and pencils
- ❏ clipboards
- ❏ tape (Scotch, masking, duct)
- ❏ glue
- ❏ Velcro
- ❏ bulletin board & pushpins
- ❏ stapler
- ❏ calendar
- ❏ white board
- ❏ filing cabinet
- ❏ file folders

Cleaning Supplies
- ❏ short- & long-handled brooms
- ❏ dustpan
- ❏ mop
- ❏ buckets
- ❏ sponges
- ❏ toilet brush
- ❏ dusting brush
- ❏ garbage cans, large & small
- ❏ detergent
- ❏ squeegee

Dishes, Utensils, & Supplies
- ❏ 8-, 12-, & 16-oz. mugs
- ❏ 8-oz. demitasse cups
- ❏ demitasse saucers/spoons
- ❏ cold drink glasses
- ❏ tea pots/cups/saucers
- ❏ ceramic cake plates
- ❏ cake/pie servers
- ❏ bakery tongs/spatula
- ❏ knives/forks/spoons
- ❏ long-handled spoons
- ❏ milk thermometers
- ❏ grater
- ❏ ice cream scoop
- ❏ cutting boards
- ❏ display plates
- ❏ covers for plates
- ❏ trays for baked goods
- ❏ condiment dispensers
- ❏ napkin dispensers
- ❏ straws/straw holder
- ❏ measuring spoons
- ❏ hand towels
- ❏ soap
- ❏ towel & soap dispensers
- ❏ toilet paper
- ❏ garbage bags

Resource Guide

Coffee Roasters

California

Caribbean Coffee Company
Website: www.caribbeancoffee.com
Phone: 805-962-3201
E-mail: info@caribbeancoffee.com

Thanksgiving Coffee Company
Website: www.thanksgiving.com
Phone: 1-800-462-1999 or 707-964-0118
E-mail: pk@thanksgivingcoffee.com

Colorado

Allegro Coffee Company
Website: www.allegrocoffee.com
Phone: 1-800-666-4869 or 303-444-4844
E-mail: sales@allegrocoffee.com

Florida

Joffrey's Coffee & Tea Co.
Website: www.joffreys.com
Phone: 1-800-458-5282 or 813-250-0404

Maryland

Quartermaine Coffee Roasters
Website: www.quartermaine.com
Phone: 1-800-245-6563 or 301-230-4600
E-mail: info@quartermaine.com

Michigan

Leelanau Coffee Roasting Co.
Website: www.coffeeguys.com or www.leelanaucoffee.com
Phone: 1-800-424-5282
E-mail: info@coffeeguys.com

Minnesota

Midnight Coffee Roastery
Website: www.midnightroastery.com
Phone: 320-333-0168
E-mail: info@midnightroastery.com

New Hampshire

Prime Roast Coffee Co.
Website: www.demonroast.com
Phone: 1-888-374-6563
E-mail: info@demonroast.com

New York

Dallis Brothers
Website: www.dallisbros.com
Phone: 1-800-424-4252 or 718-845-3010
E-mail: info@dalliscoffee.com

North Carolina

Broad Street Coffee Roasters
Website: www.broadstreetcoffee.com
Phone: 919-688-5668
E-mail: info@broadstreetcoffee.com

Ohio

City Roast Coffee
Website: www.cityroastcoffee.com
Phone: 216-241-2479
E-mail: CityRoast@core.com

Rhode Island

Excellent Coffee Company
Website: www.excellentcoffee.com
Phone: 1-800-345-2007 or 401-724-6393
E-mail: inquiry@excellentcoffee.com

Vermont

Green Mountain Coffee
Website: www.GreenMountainCoffee.com
Phone: 1-888-879-4627

Washington

Batdorf & Bronson
Website: www.batdorf.com
Phone: 1-800-955-5282 or 360-754-5282
E-mail: javatalk@batdorf.com

Caffé D'Arte
Website: www.cafedarte.com
Phone: 1-800-999-5334 or 206-762-4381
E-mail: sales@caffedarte.com

Espresso Vivace
Website: www.espressovivace.com
Phone: 206-860-5869
E-mail: vivace@speakeasy.net

Kobos Coffee
Website: www.koboscoffee.com
Phone: 503-222-2302
E-mail: coffeeexperts@kobos.com

Seattle's Best Coffee
Website: www.seattlesbest.com
Phone: 1-800-611-7793

Tully's Coffee
Website: www.tullys.com
Phone: 206-233-2070
E-mail: customer.service@tullys.com

Wisconsin

Café Fair (Steep & Brew)
Website: www.steepnbrew.com
Phone: 1-608-223-0707

Green Bean Importers

Holland Coffee Group
Website: www.hollandcoffee.com
Phone: 415-893-1988
E-mail: beans@hollandcoffee.com

Organic Products Trading Company
Website: www.optco.com
Phone: 360-573-4433
E-mail: garth@optco.com

Royal Coffee
Website: www.royalcoffee.com
Phone: 1-800-843-0482 or 510-652-4256
E-mail: info@royalcoffee.com

Sustainable Harvest
Website: www.sustainableharvest.com
Phone: 503-235-1119
E-mail: info@sustainableharvest.com

Organic Coffee

Equal Exchange
Website: www.equalexchange.com
Phone: 774-776-7400
E-mail: info@equalexchange.com

Green Mountain Coffee
Website: www.greenmountaincoffee.com
Phone: 1-888-879-4627

Sustainable Harvest
Website: www.sustainableharvest.com
Phone: 503-235-1119
E-mail: info@sustainableharvest.com

Flavored Syrups

Kerry Food Service
Website: www.kerryfoodservice.com
Phone: 1-800-810-3752

Monin
Website: www.monin.com
Phone: 727-461-3033
E-mail: monin-usa@monin.com

Torani
Website: www.torani.com
Phone: 1-800-775-1925

Espresso Machines

Boyd Coffee Company
Website: www.boyds.com
Phone: 1-800-545-4077 or 503-666-4545
East of St. Louis: 1-800-223-8211
E-mail: info@boyds.com

Espresso Specialists, Inc.
Website: www.esiespresso.com
Phone: 206-784-9563
E-mail: info-esi@esiespresso.com

Espresso Zone
Website: www.espressozone.com
Phone: 1-800-345-8945 or 440-964-7400
E-mail: support@espressozone.com

Jason Enterprises
Website: www.faemasource.com
Phone: 1-877-335-2766
E-mail: bjason@faemasource.com

Rosito Bisani
Website: www.rosito-bisani.com
Phone: 1-800-848-4444 or 323-937-1888
E-mail: sales@rosito-bisani.com

Espresso Accessories

Espresso Specialists, Inc.
Website: www.esiespresso.com
Phone: 206-784-9563
E-mail: info-esi@esiespresso.com

Espresso Zone
Website: www.espressozone.com
Phone: 1-800-345-8945 or 440-964-7400
E-mail: support@espressozone.com

Coffee Retailer Associations

Coffee Association of Canada
Website: www.coffeeassoc.com
Phone: 416-510-8032
E-mail: info@coffeeassoc.com

International Coffee Organization
Website: www.ico.org
Phone: +44 (0)20 7580 8591
E-mail: info@ico.org

National Coffee Association of USA, Inc.
Website: www.ncausa.org
Phone: 212-766-4007
E-mail: smwolfe@ncausa.org

Organic Crop Improvement Association
Website: www.ocia.org
Phone: 402-477-2323
E-mail: info@ocia.org

Specialty Coffee Association of America
Website: www.scaa.org
Phone: 562-624-4100
E-mail: coffee@scaa.org

Coffee Industry Publications

CoffeeTalk Magazine
Website: www.coffeetalk.com
Phone: 1-877-426-6410 or 206-617-2189
E-mail: kerri@coffeetalk.com

Fresh Cup Magazine
Website: www.freshcup.com
Phone: 503-236-2587
To subscribe: 1-800-868-5866

Specialty Coffee Retailer Magazine
Website: Specialty-Coffee.com
Phone: 847-550-0207

Tea & Coffee Trade Journal
Website: www.teaandcoffee.net
Phone: 212-391-2060
E-mail: editor@teaandcoffee.net

Uker's International Tea and Coffee Directory
Website: www.teaandcoffee.net
Phone: 212-391-2060

Websites

Coffee Review
www.coffeereview.com

Coffee Universe
www.coffeeuniverse.com

CoffeeResearch.org
www.coffeeresearch.org

Coffee/Tea on About.com
coffeetea.about.com

Index

D

F

Q

T

U

V-W-X

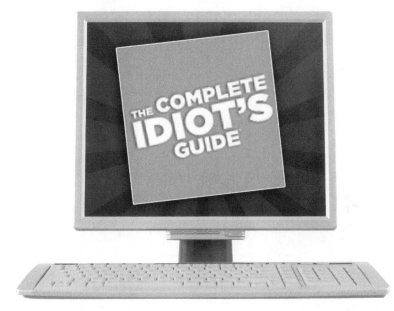

CHECK OUT THESE BEST-SELLERS

More than 450 titles available at booksellers and online retailers everywhere

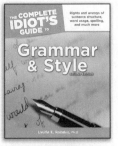

THE COMPLETE **IDIOT'S** GUIDE TO
Rights and wrongs of sentence structure, word usage, spelling, and much more

Grammar & Style
SECOND EDITION

Laurie E. Rozakis, Ph.D.

978-1-59257-115-4

THE COMPLETE **IDIOT'S** GUIDE TO
301 twisters and teasers for a stimulating mental workout

Word Search Puzzles

Matt Gaffney

978-1-59257-900-6

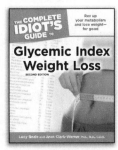

THE COMPLETE **IDIOT'S** GUIDE TO
Rev up your metabolism and lose weight—for good

Glycemic Index Weight Loss
SECOND EDITION

Lucy Beale and Joan Clark-Warner, M.S., R.D., C.D.E.

978-1-59257-855-9

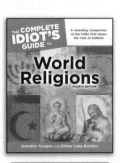

THE COMPLETE **IDIOT'S** GUIDE TO
A revealing comparison of the faiths that shape the lives of millions

World Religions
FOURTH EDITION

Brandon Toropov and Father Luke Buckles

978-1-61564-069-0

THE COMPLETE **IDIOT'S** GUIDE TO
Give your resume a professional makeover—and stand out from the pack

The Perfect Resume
FIFTH EDITION

Susan Ireland

978-1-59257-957-0

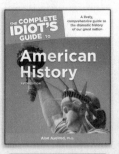

THE COMPLETE **IDIOT'S** GUIDE TO
A lively, comprehensive guide to the dramatic history of our great nation

American History
FIFTH EDITION

Alan Axelrod, Ph.D.

978-1-59257-869-6

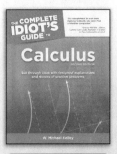

THE COMPLETE **IDIOT'S** GUIDE TO

Calculus
SECOND EDITION

Sail through class with foolproof explanations and dozens of practice problems

W. Michael Kelley

978-1-59257-471-1

THE COMPLETE **IDIOT'S** GUIDE TO
Easy, effective, and enjoyable methods for you and your dog

Positive Dog Training
THIRD EDITION

Pamela Dennison

978-1-61564-066-9

THE COMPLETE **IDIOT'S** GUIDE TO
Money-management tips and investment strategies to put your money in your pocket

Personal Finance in Your 20s & 30s
FOURTH EDITION

Sarah Young Fisher and Susan Shelly

978-1-59257-883-2

THE COMPLETE **IDIOT'S** GUIDE TO
Tips and tricks to getting your house in order—one room at a time

Organizing Your Life
FIFTH EDITION

Georgene Lockwood

978-1-59257-966-2

CD INCLUDED!

THE COMPLETE **IDIOT'S** GUIDE TO
Audio exercises let you listen, learn, and practice.

Learning Spanish
FIFTH EDITION

Step-by-step lessons help you speak Spanish like a native

Gail Stein

978-1-59257-908-2

THE COMPLETE **IDIOT'S** GUIDE TO
Refine your taste in the finest in vino

Wine Basics
SECOND EDITION

Tara Q. Thomas

978-1-59257-786-6

THE COMPLETE **IDIOT'S** GUIDE TO
Make friends with the social network

Facebook®
SECOND EDITION

Mikal E. Belicove and Joe Kraynak

978-1-61564-118-5

CD INCLUDED!

THE COMPLETE **IDIOT'S** GUIDE TO
Audio CD *The Complete Idiot's Guide® Ear Training Course*

Music Theory
SECOND EDITION

Michael Miller

978-1-59257-437-7

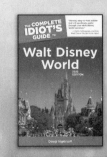

THE COMPLETE **IDIOT'S** GUIDE TO

Walt Disney World
2010 EDITION

Doug Ingersoll

978-1-61564-112-3

ALPHA

idiotsguides.com

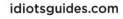